ROBERT CARRIER

Cooking for You

HAMLYN
LONDON · NEW YORK · SYDNEY · TORONTO

Published by
The Hamlyn Publishing Group Limited
London · New York · Sydney · Toronto
Astronaut House, Feltham, Middlesex, England
© Copyright The Hamlyn Publishing Group Limited 1973
First published 1973
Fifth impression 1977
ISBN 0 600 37541 2

Printed Offset Litho in England by
Cox & Wyman Ltd, London, Fakenham and Reading
Cover photograph by John Lee, by courtesy of Grants of St. James's
Photography by Roy Rich, Angel Studios
Photographs on pages 20, 62, 90 and 146 by Jack Nisberg
D. L. TF. 956-1974

Mozart & Dux

Contents

Useful facts and figures

Note on metrication

In this book quantities have been given in both metric and Imperial measures. Exact conversion from Imperial to metric measures does not usually give very convenient working quantities and so for greater convenience we have rounded off metric measures into units of 25 grammes. The table below shows recommended equivalents.

Ounces/fluid ounces	Approx. g. and ml. to nearest whole figure	Recommended conversion to nearest unit of 25
1	28	25
2	57	50
3	85	75
4	113	100
5 ($\frac{1}{4}$ pint)	142	150
6	170	175
7	198	200
8 ($\frac{1}{2}$ lb.)	226	225
9	255	250
10 ($\frac{1}{2}$ pint)	283	275
11	311	300
12	340	350
13	368	375
14	396	400
15 ($\frac{3}{4}$ pint)	428	425
16 (1 lb.)	456	450
17	484	475
18	512	500
19	541	550
20 (1 pint)	569	575

NOTE: When converting quantities over 20 oz. first add the appropriate figures in the centre column, *then* adjust to the nearest unit of 25. As a general guide, 1 kg. (1000 g.) equals 2·2 lb. or about 2 lb. 3 oz.; 1 litre (1000 ml.) equals 1·76 pints or almost exactly 1$\frac{3}{4}$ pints.

This method of conversion gives good results in nearly all recipes. However, where the proportion between liquids and solids is critical, for example in baking recipes, a more accurate conversion is necessary to preserve the exact proportions of the recipe. In these cases we have used a conversion to the nearest 5 grammes; for example, in the recipe for Victoria sandwich on page 105, 4 oz. has been converted to 110 g. instead of 100 g. to give a more exact quantity.

Can sizes Because at present cans are marked with the exact (usually to the nearest whole number) metric equivalent of the Imperial weight of the contents, we have followed this practice when giving can sizes. Thus the equivalent of a 14-oz. can of tomatoes would be a 396-g. can, and not 400 g. which is the usual recommended conversion when you are measuring your own ingredients.

Liquid measures The millilitre is a very small unit of measurement and we felt that to use decilitres (units of 100 ml.) would be less cumbersome. In most cases it is perfectly satisfactory to round off the exact millilitre conversion to the nearest decilitre, except for $\frac{1}{4}$ pint; thus $\frac{1}{4}$ pint (142 ml.) is 1$\frac{1}{2}$ dl., $\frac{1}{2}$ pint (283 ml.) is 3 dl., $\frac{3}{4}$ pint (428 ml.) is 4 dl., and 1 pint (569 ml.) is 6 dl. For quantities over 1 pint we have used litres and fractions of a litre, using the conversion rate of 1$\frac{3}{4}$ pints to 1 litre.

Tablespoons You will note that often measurements are given in tablespoons. The spoon used is the British Standard measuring spoon of 17·7 millilitres, and all spoon measures are *level*. A tablespoon of butter is a generous $\frac{1}{2}$ oz., 1 tablespoon flour just over $\frac{1}{4}$ oz. Australian users should note that their standard tablespoon holds 20 millilitres, and the table below gives a comparison.

British	Australian
1 teaspoon	1 teaspoon
1 tablespoon	1 tablespoon
2 tablespoons	2 tablespoons
3$\frac{1}{2}$ tablespoons	3 tablespoons
4 tablespoons	3$\frac{1}{2}$ tablespoons

Oven temperatures

The chart below gives recommended Celsius (Centigrade) equivalents.

Description	Fahrenheit	Celsius	Gas Mark
Very cool	225	110	$\frac{1}{4}$
	250	130	$\frac{1}{2}$
Cool	275	140	1
	300	150	2
Moderate	325	170	3
	350	180	4
Moderately hot	375	190	5
	400	200	6
Hot	425	220	7
	450	230	8
Very hot	475	240	9

Introduction

It has often been said that careless eating is as anti-social as careless cooking, and that a child should no more be encouraged to be indifferent to the flavour of food than to sing off tune. I must confess that I am sometimes surprised in France to see some tiny tot out with its family for a Sunday restaurant lunch tucking into a sophisticated artichoke à la vinaigrette or a lobster mousse without a qualm. But why should it be so surprising? The subtleties of taste should be called to our attention early on in life.

Cooking can be a game in which you and the whole family can participate. I remember my own childhood in America during the early thirties when the Depression suddenly took away those little luxuries which we once thought of as everyday necessities. My mother kept her family together with the wonderfully simple expedient of making her three sons as well as her husband join in to make the family meals both inexpensive and pleasurable.

We all had our duties to perform. I was about six years old, and as the youngest in the family had the simplest chores to do. I used to set the table for dinner – knives, forks, glasses, side plates, pepper and salt—and then wash and dry the lettuce, leaf by leaf. My brother Jack, eight years older, prepared all the salad dressings, sliced the bread and then cleared the table after the meal was over. And brother Budd, the eldest of the three boys, used to help my mother in the kitchen during the week, while Sunday dinner was his full responsibility. Even my father was called into service to make the breakfast coffee and beaten biscuits each morning. He was justifiably proud of his batches of home-baked bread and rolls, a regular weekly ritual.

Ours was a family that revered its food. And every member of it was only too glad to contribute some part to the effort and work involved to make such meals possible.

It was in those early days that I first discovered that cooking a new dish could be an exciting adventure, one where intelligence, subtlety, a sense of poetry and friendship could all play an important role. Few things in life give more real pleasure than sitting down with family and friends to a dish that one has cooked with care and attention. Such a dish demands to be tasted, talked about, compared with other dishes, other meals. It is in fact an experience to be shared. Just add a light first course before it, a subtle sweet after it and accompany it with a bottle of good wine and you have a party to remember.

This book grew gradually out of a series of such lunches and dinners that I have enjoyed over the past years. It ranges from sauces, stews and meats to appetizers, vegetables, sweets, cakes and puddings, and from the very simple to the fairly complicated.

And every recipe has been thoroughly tested with you in mind. With a full-colour photograph of each finished dish, each recipe is presented in a new easy-to-follow series of numbered steps guaranteed to make each recipe foolproof.

So browse through it, a few pages at a time; select a recipe, or perhaps two; make the dishes and test them out first on the immediate family or one or two close friends. Then, when you feel you have mastered them, invite a few guests in for a fabulous meal.

You will find that the repertoire of recipes in this book is more than ample for planning well-balanced and varied menus for every occasion. Concentrate first on learning the techniques these dishes require and master the basic principles. Learn to grill a steak to pink-centred perfection, become familiar with two or three easy vegetable dishes, and 'patent' your own household salad dressing. Try each new method of cooking several times. And above all, don't be disappointed if you are unsuccessful at the first or even second attempt, but try to find out the reason you failed and remedy it the next time you try the recipe.

And don't forget: when you have mastered cooking a steak, take these same principles on to grill a lamb chop, or a veal chop. Then learn a few casseroles and half a dozen sauces. Soon you will be well on the way to being a super cook. It's as simple as that.

No matter what you serve, whether it be a poached egg or salmon steaks, a slice of fresh mushroom quiche or a boeuf bourguignonne, there should always be present and apparent the characteristics of good cooking: high quality ingredients, careful preparation and pleasing presentation.

Happy cooking!

Robert Carrier

Appetizers and Simple First Courses

Most of us agree that our first impressions—whether it is of a new friend, a work of art or a holiday resort—tend to linger on in our memory, making us overlook and forgive some subsequently discovered short-coming.

In the ephemeral, magic world of cooking, the burden of responsibility for this all important 'first impression' lies with the appetizer. In making your choice, you are deliberately setting the scene, whetting the appetites of your guests, evoking in them a state of delicious anticipation for what is to follow.

In this first chapter, we run through the simplest appetizers of all. Most of our recipes are composed of easily obtainable and economical ingredients. And even though the majority require little more than basic cooking processes to put them together, they nevertheless exemplify one of the cardinal rules of good cooking: careful attention to detail. For there is a world of difference between clumsily hacked herbs and those that have been finely chopped; between vegetables sliced thinly and evenly with a sharp knife, and thick chunks mutilated by a blunt blade; between a simple salad dressing carefully prepared with good olive oil and wine-flavoured vinegar or fresh lemon juice and some highly seasoned witches' brew that smothers flavours when it was meant to enhance them.

Just open and serve

The simplest appetizers of all are those we can buy already sliced, smoked, canned or frozen.

Frankly expensive

Caviar Black caviar is the roe of the sturgeon and the finest (and most expensive) of all. Red caviar, which is delicious for all that it is considered socially inferior to the black, usually comes from salmon. Caviar quickly spoils at room temperature as it is only lightly preserved in salt, so it must be served in a glass or porcelain dish (*never* metal) embedded in a larger container of ice. Serve with lemon wedges, parsley sprigs and fingers of black bread or toast. To make a little go a long way, either fold into an equal volume of sour cream and serve on canapés, or serve with *bliny*. Champagne or well-chilled vodka is a must.

Oysters Oysters should be served alive and freshly opened on the deeper half-shell. Serve individual portions, the shells embedded in cracked ice, with lemon wedges. To open an oyster, push an oyster knife (one that has a short, strong blade) in through the hinged side and work your way in until you can cut through the hinge and break the tension. You can then draw the knife all around the shell and open it. Work over a dish to catch any liquor that may escape. Check that there are no bits of cracked shell present. The oyster should be creamy-coloured and its liquor should be clear and fresh-smelling.

Smoked salmon Buy in paper-thin slices professionally cut *across* the grain. Serve on lightly oiled plates, accompanied by thin slices of brown bread and butter, and wedges of lemon to squeeze over the top. Have a coarse-grinding mill of black pepper at hand.

Smoked trout Skin and fillet smoked trout. Serve fillets on an oiled platter with lemon wedges (or whipped cream flavoured with grated horseradish) and thin slices of brown bread and butter.

Reasonable

Canned sardines and anchovies Serve on buttered fingers of toast or black bread, garnished with sieved hard-boiled egg yolk and a squeeze of lemon.

Canned tuna and salmon Mix with a little finely chopped onion and freshly ground black pepper and dress with olive oil or lemon juice to taste.

Sausages Salami, Cervelat, Mortadella, etc., should be thinly sliced. If you are slicing them yourself, remove the outer skin *first*. You'll find it comes off much more neatly this way.

Slice liver sausage medium-thick.

When buying any type of sausage, be sure you get the real Continental import. Home-produced imitations don't compare, I'm afraid.

Green and black olives If the black olives you buy are rather dry and wrinkled, pack them into a glass jar; cover generously with olive oil and leave for several days, at the end of which the olives will have plumped up, and, as an added bonus, the remains of the oil will taste quite marvellous.

Radishes Choose firm, round radishes with good colour; wash well and trim both ends. Serve chilled, with salt.

Canned vegetables Tiny pickled beets, artichoke hearts and red pimento (cut into strips) can add colour and flavour to a mixed appetizer platter. But always taste first, and if the liquid in which they have been preserved tastes too sharp, rinse it off lightly.

Canned white haricot beans, lentils, chick peas, string beans and tiny carrots, drained of their liquids and then mixed with a well-flavoured salad dressing, make excellent first-course appetizer salads. They are especially good if seasoned with a little chopped onion or garlic and sprinkled with finely chopped fresh herbs.

Creamed Artichoke Soup

IMPERIAL	METRIC
3 lb. Jerusalem artichokes	1⅓ kg. Jerusalem artichokes
salt	salt
1½–2 pints chicken stock	¾–1¼ litres chicken stock
4–6 tablespoons lightly whipped cream	4–6 tablespoons lightly whipped cream
1 egg yolk, lightly beaten	1 egg yolk, lightly beaten
freshly ground black pepper	freshly ground black pepper
freshly grated nutmeg	freshly grated nutmeg
finely chopped parsley	finely chopped parsley

1. Scrub artichokes clean and drop them into a large pan of salted, boiling water. Bring back to the boil, lower heat and simmer for 15 to 20 minutes, or until artichokes are tender. Drain artichokes and peel as soon as they are cool enough to handle.

2. Rub artichokes through a sieve or put them through a vegetable mill and return to the rinsed-out pan.

3. Add chicken stock to artichoke purée gradually, stirring with a wooden spoon until desired consistency is reached, and reheat gently until soup comes to boiling point, stirring occasionally.

4. Remove pan from heat. Stir in lightly whipped cream and thicken with beaten egg yolk. Season to taste with salt, freshly ground black pepper and a pinch of freshly grated nutmeg, and serve immediately, scattered with finely chopped parsley.

Serves 6

Chef's tip:
Do not reboil this soup once the egg yolk has been added, or it will curdle and ruin the appearance of the soup. The safest way to reheat it to avoid curdling is to warm the soup in the top of a double saucepan over simmering water.

French Watercress Soup

IMPERIAL	METRIC
4 tablespoons butter	4 tablespoons butter
2 tablespoons olive oil	2 tablespoons olive oil
1 Spanish onion, finely chopped	1 Spanish onion, finely chopped
1 clove garlic, finely chopped	1 clove garlic, finely chopped
8 oz. potatoes, peeled and thinly sliced	225 g. potatoes, peeled and thinly sliced
salt and freshly ground black pepper	salt and freshly ground black pepper
1½ bunches watercress	1½ bunches watercress
½ pint milk	3 dl. milk
½ pint chicken stock	3 dl. chicken stock
¼ pint single cream	1½ dl. single cream
2 egg yolks	2 egg yolks

1. Heat butter and olive oil until melted in a large, heavy saucepan, and sauté finely chopped onion and garlic over a moderate heat until transparent but not coloured.

2. Add sliced potatoes; sprinkle with salt and freshly ground black pepper and cover with ½ pint (3 dl.) water. Bring to the boil; reduce heat and simmer until potatoes are almost tender, 5 to 7 minutes.

3. Wash watercress carefully. Separate stems from leaves. Put about a quarter of the best leaves aside for garnish. Chop stems coarsely and add them to the simmering pan, together with remaining leaves.

4. Stir in milk and chicken stock. Bring to the boil and simmer for 15 to 20 minutes, or until all the vegetables are very soft.

5. Rub soup through a fine wire sieve, or purée in an electric blender. Pour back into the rinsed-out saucepan; correct seasoning if necessary and reheat gently.

6. Blend cream with egg yolks. Pour into the heating soup and continue to cook, stirring constantly, until soup thickens slightly. Do not allow soup to boil once the egg yolks have been added, or they will scramble and ruin its appearance.

7. Shred reserved watercress leaves; sprinkle them over the soup and serve immediately.

Serves 6

Chef's tip:
To chop chef's style use a French or cook's knife. Hold point of blade down between thumb and fingers of one hand; with other hand grasping handle move blade vigorously up and down on food holding tip of knife stationary. Repeat several times, keeping chopped food confined to a small area.

Creamed Spinach Soup

IMPERIAL	METRIC
2 lb. fresh spinach or 1 lb. frozen chopped spinach	900 g. fresh spinach or 450 g. frozen chopped spinach
4 tablespoons butter	4 tablespoons butter
½ pint double cream	3 dl. double cream
½–¾ pint chicken stock	3–4 dl. chicken stock
juice of ½ lemon	juice of ½ lemon
salt and freshly ground black pepper	salt and freshly ground black pepper
finely chopped hard-boiled egg, to garnish	finely chopped hard-boiled egg, to garnish

1. If using fresh spinach, wash leaves in several changes of cold water, nipping off any tough stems and discarding yellowed leaves. Drain well in a colander, pressing out excess moisture, and chop roughly.

2. Melt butter in a heavy saucepan; add spinach, either fresh or still in a frozen block, and simmer gently, stirring occasionally, for 8 to 10 minutes, or until spinach is soft.

3. Purée spinach in an electric blender. Pour back into rinsed-out pan.

4. Stir in cream and dilute to taste with chicken stock, using ½ pint (3 dl.) if you want a very thick, rich soup, ¾ pint (4 dl.) for a lighter consistency. Heat through over a moderate heat, stirring.

5. Season to taste with a little lemon juice, salt and freshly ground black pepper, and serve hot, each portion garnished with a sprinkling of chopped hard-boiled egg.

Serves 6

Chef's tip:
Hard-boiled eggs make an attractive garnish when the whole egg is rubbed through a sieve; or, sieve the yolk and finely chop the white separately. Arrange the yolks and whites with finely chopped parsley in bands of white, yellow and green to give a colourful garnish to hors d'oeuvres.

Family Dried Pea Soup

IMPERIAL	METRIC
1 large Spanish onion, coarsely chopped	1 large Spanish onion, coarsely chopped
1 small clove garlic, crushed (optional)	1 small clove garlic, crushed (optional)
1–2 tablespoons bacon fat or lard	1–2 tablespoons bacon fat or lard
8 oz. split peas, soaked overnight	450 g. split peas, soaked overnight
8 oz. smoked bacon ends, or smoked ham bones	225 g. smoked bacon ends, or smoked ham bones
2 carrots, coarsely chopped	2 carrots, coarsely chopped
1 tablespoon wine vinegar	1 tablespoon wine vinegar
1 teaspoon sugar	1 teaspoon sugar
2 pints beef (cube) stock	generous litre beef (cube) stock
bouquet garni	bouquet garni
2–3 black peppercorns	2–3 black peppercorns
salt and freshly ground black pepper	salt and freshly ground black pepper
Cheese croûtons:	*Cheese croûtons:*
slices of white bread, toasted	slices of white bread, toasted
grated hard Cheddar	grated hard Cheddar

1. In the pan in which you intend to make soup, sauté chopped onion and garlic, if used, in bacon fat or lard until soft and golden.

2. Drain soaked split peas and add them and all the remaining ingredients except salt and freshly ground black pepper. Top up with 1½ pints (scant litre) water; bring to the boil and simmer gently with the lid half on for about 2 hours, or until vegetables are disintegrating.

3. To make cheese croûtons, stamp out small shapes of toast with a biscuit cutter, or trim the crusts from slices of toast and cut into squares or triangles. Lay them on a baking sheet; sprinkle with grated Cheddar and slip into a moderate oven (350°F., 180°C., Gas Mark 4) for 10 to 15 minutes to dry out croûtons and melt cheese.

4. Remove bacon ends, bouquet garni and peppercorns from soup pot. Rub soup through a fine sieve or purée in an electric blender.

5. Season soup to taste with salt and freshly ground black pepper; bring to the boil again and serve very hot, accompanied by cheese croûtons for each person to scatter over his portion.

Serves 6

Potted Shrimps or Prawns

IMPERIAL	METRIC
12 oz. cooked peeled shrimps or prawns	350 g. cooked peeled shrimps or prawns
juice of 1 lemon	juice of 1 lemon
generous pinch cayenne	generous pinch cayenne
salt and freshly ground black pepper	salt and freshly ground black pepper
butter	butter

1. Preheat oven to moderate (350°F., 180°C., Gas Mark 4).

2. Toss shrimps or prawns with lemon juice, cayenne, salt and freshly ground black pepper, to taste.

3. Pack them tightly into four individual ovenproof ramekins 2½ inches (6 cm.) in diameter, and dot each ramekin with 1 tablespoon butter.

4. Bake ramekins for 10 minutes.

5. Remove ramekins from the oven and pour in enough clarified butter to cover shrimps generously (about 2 tablespoons per ramekin). Cool and chill.

Serves 4

Grapefruit and Prawn Salad

IMPERIAL	METRIC
8 oz. shelled prawns, fresh if possible	225 g. shelled prawns, fresh if possible
2 tablespoons finely chopped onion	2 tablespoons finely chopped onion
4 tablespoons finely chopped parsley	4 tablespoons finely chopped parsley
2 teaspoons lemon juice	2 teaspoons lemon juice
2 teaspoons dry white wine	2 teaspoons dry white wine
4 tablespoons olive oil	4 tablespoons olive oil
salt and freshly ground black pepper	salt and freshly ground black pepper
4 grapefruit	4 grapefruit
½ pint thick mayonnaise	3 dl. thick mayonnaise
6–8 drops Tabasco	6–8 drops Tabasco
To serve:	*To serve:*
lettuce leaves	lettuce leaves
paprika	paprika
stoned black olives	stoned black olives
small tomatoes, quartered	small tomatoes, quartered

1. Put prawns in a pan with finely chopped onion, parsley, lemon juice, white wine, olive oil, and salt and freshly ground black pepper to taste. Heat until sizzling, then remove from heat and leave to become quite cold again.

2. Meanwhile, peel grapefruit and divide into segments. Drain segments of excess juice.

3. When prawns are cold, drain them thoroughly and combine with grapefruit segments. Fold into mayonnaise and season to taste with Tabasco and a little more salt and freshly ground black pepper if necessary.

4. Serve chilled in individual glass bowls lined with lettuce leaves, sprinkled with a pinch of paprika and garnished with stoned black olives and tomato wedges.

Serves 6

Chef's tip:
Classic potted shrimps or prawns should be made with the best butter you can buy. They will keep well in the refrigerator for up to a week. To clarify the butter, melt it in a saucepan without allowing it to sizzle, then strain through fine muslin.

Chef's tip:
When buying citrus fruits, bypass any that feel light or soft; they will be horrid and juiceless inside. Go for the grapefruit which have brown blemishes on the skin; they are usually the best, contrary to their appearance.

Raw Mushroom and Prawn Appetizer

IMPERIAL	METRIC
4 oz. tight white button mushrooms	100 g. tight white button mushrooms
6 tablespoons olive oil	6 tablespoons olive oil
2 tablespoons wine vinegar	2 tablespoons wine vinegar
$\frac{1}{4}$ teaspoon dry mustard	$\frac{1}{4}$ teaspoon dry mustard
salt and freshly ground black pepper	salt and freshly ground black pepper
pinch sugar	pinch sugar
2 oz. peeled prawns	50 g. peeled prawns
lettuce leaves and finely chopped parsley, to garnish	lettuce leaves and finely chopped parsley, to garnish

1. Wipe mushrooms clean and trim stems.

2. In a bowl, beat olive oil, wine vinegar and dry mustard with a fork until mixture emulsifies. Season to taste with salt, freshly ground black pepper and a pinch of sugar.

3. Slice mushrooms thinly into bowl. Toss until each slice is thoroughly coated. Cover bowl and leave to marinate for 1 hour.

4. Add peeled prawns; toss thoroughly and pile into a shallow dish lined with lettuce leaves. Serve immediately, sprinkled with finely chopped parsley.

Serve as part of a selection of appetizer salads

Herrings in Sour Cream

IMPERIAL	METRIC
1 lb. salted herrings	450 g. salted herrings
2 tablespoons finely chopped onion	2 tablespoons finely chopped onion
6 tablespoons coarsely chopped apple	6 tablespoons coarsely chopped apple
8 tablespoons sour cream	8 tablespoons sour cream
2 tablespoons lemon juice	2 tablespoons lemon juice
$\frac{1}{2}$ tablespoon sugar	$\frac{1}{2}$ tablespoon sugar
1 tablespoon finely chopped parsley, chives or spring onion tops	1 tablespoon finely chopped parsley, chives or spring onion tops

1. Desalt herrings thoroughly by soaking them in cold water for about 48 hours, changing water frequently. (It is advisable to leave herrings under cold running water for the first half-hour.)

2. Fillet herrings, discarding skin and bones, and cut fillets into bite-sized pieces. Place in a shallow dish.

3. Fold finely chopped onion and coarsely chopped apple into sour cream; flavour to taste with lemon juice and sugar and mix well.

4. Pour sour cream mixture over filleted herrings and sprinkle with finely chopped parsley, chives or spring onion tops. Leave for a couple of hours to allow flavours to develop before serving.

Serves 4

Chef's tip:
Prawns are available all year round, canned, bottled and frozen, but they are at their best fresh, from February to October. If you buy them unpeeled, reckon on about 60 to 65 per cent weight loss in discarded shells (minced, the shells can give a delicious flavour to a sauce for fish).

Chef's tip:
Salted herrings are sold from the barrel by delicatessen specialising in Eastern European food. Salted and spiced Norwegian herrings are also available in 1-lb. plastic packs; both of these are suitable. But herrings preserved in vinegar just will not do.

Tuna-stuffed Eggs

IMPERIAL	METRIC
6 eggs, hard-boiled	6 eggs, hard-boiled
1 7½-oz. can tuna fish	1 212-g. can tuna fish
2 tablespoons capers	2 tablespoons capers
2 teaspoons lemon juice	2 teaspoons lemon juice
salt and freshly ground	salt and freshly ground
black pepper	black pepper
½ pint thick mayonnaise	3 dl. thick mayonnaise
1 tablespoon Dijon mustard	1 tablespoon Dijon mustard
fresh lettuce leaves, to	fresh lettuce leaves, to
garnish	garnish

1. Cool hard-boiled eggs under cold running water. Remove shells; cut eggs in half lengthwise and scoop out yolks. Rub yolks through a fine sieve into a bowl.

2. Crush tuna fish as finely as possible with a fork. When smooth, stir in capers and lemon juice, and season to taste with salt and freshly ground black pepper.

3. Blend mayonnaise with Dijon mustard.

4. Fold 3 or 4 tablespoons mustard mayonnaise into tuna mixture, together with a quarter of the sieved egg yolks. Correct seasoning with more salt, freshly ground black pepper or lemon juice if necessary, and pile up neatly in empty egg whites.

5. Arrange stuffed eggs on a flat dish lined with lettuce leaves. Spoon a little mayonnaise over each egg and sprinkle with remaining sieved egg yolk.

Serves 4–6 as a light, summery appetizer

Cold Curried Eggs

IMPERIAL	METRIC
6 eggs, hard-boiled	6 eggs, hard-boiled
1 teaspoon grated onion	1 teaspoon grated onion
1 teaspoon curry paste	1 teaspoon curry paste
3 tablespoons very finely	3 tablespoons very finely
chopped ham	chopped ham
3–4 tablespoons thick	3–4 tablespoons thick
home-made mayonnaise	home-made mayonnaise
½ teaspoon mango chutney	½ teaspoon mango chutney
salt	salt
lettuce leaves and	lettuce leaves and
watercress, to garnish	watercress, to garnish

1. Cool hard-boiled eggs under cold running water. Then carefully peel off shells; cut eggs in half lengthwise and scoop out yolks.

2. Rub yolks through a fine sieve into a bowl. Add grated onion, curry paste, finely chopped ham, mayonnaise and chutney, and beat with a wooden spoon until smoothly blended. Season to taste with salt.

3. Pile mixture up in empty egg whites and arrange on a flat serving dish, lined with lettuce leaves and sprigs of watercress, if you like.

Serves 6

Chef's tip:
To prevent eggs from cracking when they are boiled, pierce them with a tiny hole in the broader end with a needle before cooking them. This releases the pressure caused by a sharp increase in temperature. Never use eggs straight from the fridge.

Chef's tip:
Curry paste, if you can get it, gives a simple curry a much richer and less harsh flavour than curry powder. Do not boil the eggs for any longer than 10 minutes, then plunge them immediately into cold water; this prevents the yolks discolouring.

Chopped Egg Appetizer

IMPERIAL	METRIC
2 oz. young spring onions	50 g. young spring onions
8 eggs, hard-boiled	8 eggs, hard-boiled
3 tablespoons rendered chicken fat	3 tablespoons rendered chicken fat
salt and freshly ground black pepper	salt and freshly ground black pepper
lettuce leaves, to garnish	lettuce leaves, to garnish

1. Clean spring onions; trim them and chop them finely, using all of the white part and about half of the green.

2. Shell and finely chop hard-boiled eggs and mix well with chopped onions and rendered chicken fat.

3. Season to taste with salt and freshly ground black pepper. Chill for 2 hours.

4. Serve chopped egg on a bed of lettuce, either in individual portions or mounded up on a serving dish.

Serves 4–6

Spanish Omelette (Tortilla)

IMPERIAL	METRIC
olive oil	olive oil
2 oz. Chorizo sausage, sliced, or cooked ham, diced	50 g. Chorizo sausage, sliced, or cooked ham, diced
4 oz. raw potato, cut into $\frac{1}{4}$-inch cubes	100 g. raw potato, cut into $\frac{1}{2}$-cm. cubes
2 oz. Spanish onion, coarsely chopped	50 g. Spanish onion, coarsely chopped
4 eggs	4 eggs
salt and freshly ground black pepper	salt and freshly ground black pepper

1. Heat 1 tablespoon olive oil in a 6-inch (15-cm.) omelette pan. Add sliced sausage (or diced ham), cubed potato and coarsely chopped onion, and sauté gently until potatoes and onion are cooked through, about 10 minutes.

2. In a bowl, mix eggs vigorously with a fork or a wire whisk until well blended. Season to taste with salt and freshly ground black pepper.

3. Pour a third of the egg mixture into the pan and cook over a moderate heat until set, lifting up sides of omelette with a spatula to allow liquid egg to run underneath. Add remaining egg in the same manner, cooking the omelette until a golden crust has formed underneath.

4. Place a large plate over the top of the pan and turn the omelette out onto it upside down.

5. Scrape off any bits adhering to the pan and add a little more olive oil (about $\frac{1}{2}$ teaspoon). Then carefully slide omelette back into the pan to brown the other side.

6. Slip out onto a hot plate and serve immediately, cut in wedges like a cake.

Serves 2

Chef's tip:
Rendered chicken fat is made from lumps of fat found near the cavity opening of an uncooked chicken. Fry fat gently in an ungreased pan, pressing it gently to extract as much fat as possible. Pour off fat and use it in cooking as you would butter or oil.

Chef's tip:
The ideal omelette pan is made of very thick sheet metal; it should be used *only* for omelettes or pancakes. Never wash an omelette pan; if it sticks, heat some salt in the pan then rub it over inside of pan using a wad of kitchen paper. Wipe clean with a dry cloth.

Avocado Mousse

IMPERIAL	METRIC
1 chicken stock cube	1 chicken stock cube
2 ripe avocado pears	2 ripe avocado pears
juice of 2 lemons	juice of 2 lemons
½–1 teaspoon finely chopped chives	½–1 teaspoon finely chopped chives
½–1 teaspoon dried tarragon	½–1 teaspoon dried tarragon
½–1 teaspoon onion juice	½–1 teaspoon onion juice
dash Tabasco	dash Tabasco
½ oz. powdered gelatine	15 g. powdered gelatine
½ pint double cream	3 dl. double cream
salt and freshly ground black pepper	salt and freshly ground black pepper
paper-thin slices of cucumber, tomato wedges and stoned black olives, to decorate	paper-thin slices of cucumber, tomato wedges and stoned black olives, to decorate

1. Dissolve stock cube in ½ pint (3 dl.) boiling water.

2. Peel and stone avocados and dice roughly.

3. Put diced avocados in an electric blender with dissolved stock cube, lemon juice, herbs, onion juice and Tabasco, and blend until smooth.

4. Sprinkle gelatine over 3 tablespoons cold water in a cup and leave for 5 minutes. When softened, place cup in hot water and stir until gelatine has completely dissolved and liquid is clear.

5. Scrape avocado mixture into a bowl. Beat in dissolved gelatine.

6. Whip cream lightly and fold into avocado mixture. Season to taste with salt and freshly ground black pepper. Mixture should be highly flavoured.

7. When mousse is cold but not set, pour into individual ramekins or one large mould. Chill until set.

8. To turn out mousse, dip mould(s) into very hot water for one or two seconds only; lay a dish on top and invert, shaking gently to dislodge mousse. Serve very cold, decorated with paper-thin slices of cucumber, tomato wedges and stoned black olives.

Serves 8

Chef's tip:
To obtain even, paper-thin slices of vegetables use a vegetable-slicing implement called a mandoline. The cutting blade is adjustable to give varying thicknesses. By passing the vegetables to and fro over the cutting edge you achieve even slices with the utmost speed.

Bagna Cauda

IMPERIAL	METRIC
8 oz. butter	225 g. butter
3–4 tablespoons olive oil	3–4 tablespoons olive oil
3–4 cloves garlic, crushed	3–4 cloves garlic, crushed
6 anchovy fillets, crushed	6 anchovy fillets, crushed
salt and freshly ground black pepper	salt and freshly ground black pepper

1. Prepare bagna cauda in a flameproof earthenware dish with a short handle, which can then be kept hot at the table over a small burner in the traditional style. Melt butter with olive oil to prevent butter burning. Add crushed garlic and sauté until lightly golden.

2. Remove dish from heat; add crushed anchovies and mix thoroughly. Then return to a low heat and simmer, stirring constantly, until anchovies have dissolved into a paste.

3. Season to taste with a pinch of salt if necessary (anchovies may already be salty enough), and a few turns of your peppermill. Serve immediately.

Serves 4

Chef's tip:
This dish is one of the specialities of Piedmont. Its name literally means 'hot bath', and you dip into it raw vegetables such as strips of carrot, celery, fennel, wedges of sweet peppers and tomatoes, thick slices of cucumber, spring onions, raw cauliflowerets, etc.

Prosciutto with Melon

IMPERIAL	METRIC
2–3 small Ogen melons, chilled	2–3 small Ogen melons, chilled
4–6 tablespoons white port	4–6 tablespoons white port
6–8 oz. Parma ham, sliced paper-thin	175–225 g. Parma ham, sliced paper-thin

1. Cut chilled melons in half horizontally. Carefully remove seeds and drain off excess moisture.

2. With a melon baller, scoop out flesh, taking care not to break through shells. (Use a round 1-teaspoon measure to make balls if you don't possess a special gadget.) Return melon balls to half-shells. Sprinkle each portion with 1 tablespoon white port.

3. Top each half-melon with some paper-thin slices of Parma ham, crumpling them up attractively.

4. Chill until ready to serve.

Serves 4–6

Grapefruit Mint Salad

IMPERIAL	METRIC
1 round lettuce	1 round lettuce
1 cos lettuce	1 cos lettuce
2 grapefruit	2 grapefruit
2 teaspoons lemon juice	2 teaspoons lemon juice
2 teaspoons dry white wine	2 teaspoons dry white wine
5 tablespoons olive oil	5 tablespoons olive oil
salt and freshly ground black pepper	salt and freshly ground black pepper
6 leaves fresh mint, finely chopped	6 leaves fresh mint, finely chopped

1. Wash lettuces carefully. Pat each leaf dry individually and store in the chilling compartment of the refrigerator, rolled up in a clean cloth, until needed.

2. Prepare grapefruit, working over a dish so that no juice is lost. Using a sharp knife, slice off top and bottom of each fruit, taking all the pith and outer membrane away with the peel. Stand fruit on one (cut) end and, with sharp, straight, downward strokes, whittle off slices of peel and membrane all around sides. Turn fruit on its other end and repeat process. Finally, slice off ring of peel left around centre. Now take fruit in one hand and slip your knife between each segment and the membrane holding it on either side. Cut segment out, keeping it whole if possible; remove any pips and drop segment into the juice below. Proceed in this manner until all you have left is the central core and empty membranes, fanned out like the leaves of a book.

3. Drain the grapefruit segments and set aside. Combine the juice with lemon juice and dry white wine; add olive oil and beat with a fork until mixture emulsifies. Season to taste with salt and freshly ground black pepper, and stir in finely chopped mint.

4. Just before serving, break lettuce leaves into a salad bowl. Pour over dressing and toss thoroughly. Finally, add grapefruit segments; toss again and serve immediately.

Serves 6–8

Chef's tip:
Chill melon for several hours before preparing. If Parma ham is unavailable, substitute with a good raw Westphalian ham which is more readily available and also cheaper. The ham is also magnificent served with fresh figs, sliced fresh pineapple or ripe pears.

Chef's tip:
An effective way to dry salad is to shake off surplus water from leaves, place them in a clean tea-towel and gather together towel so no leaves can escape. Find yourself a large space, and, holding towel tightly, whirl it round in a circular motion with one arm, flinging out remaining water.

Raw Mushrooms with Sour Cream Dressing

IMPERIAL	METRIC
4 oz. tight white button mushrooms	100 g. tight white button mushrooms
5 tablespoons sour cream	5 tablespoons sour cream
2 tablespoons milk	2 tablespoons milk
$\frac{1}{2}$ teaspoon lemon juice	$\frac{1}{2}$ teaspoon lemon juice
salt and freshly ground black pepper	salt and freshly ground black pepper
1 teaspoon finely chopped chives, to garnish	1 teaspoon finely chopped chives, to garnish

1. Wipe mushrooms clean and trim stems.

2. In a bowl, beat sour cream with milk, lemon juice, and salt and freshly ground black pepper to taste.

3. Slice mushrooms paper-thin into the sour cream dressing.

4. Toss well. Taste for seasoning, adding more salt or freshly ground black pepper, and toss again. Serve immediately, sprinkled with finely chopped chives.

Serve as part of a selection of appetizer salads

Chef's tip:
Peppercorns quickly loose their spicy aroma once ground, leaving only a crude hotness. There is all the difference in the world between dishes seasoned with freshly ground black pepper and bought ground pepper. If you do not have a peppermill, buy one and see.

Herb-stuffed Mushroom Appetizer

IMPERIAL	METRIC
1 lb. large white mushrooms	450 g. large white mushrooms
4 oz. pork sausage meat	100 g. pork sausage meat
1 shallot, finely chopped	1 shallot, finely chopped
$\frac{1}{2}$ fat clove garlic, finely chopped	$\frac{1}{2}$ fat clove garlic, finely chopped
4 tablespoons finely chopped parsley	4 tablespoons finely chopped parsley
$\frac{1}{2}$ teaspoon dried thyme	$\frac{1}{2}$ teaspoon dried thyme
1 bay leaf, finely crumbled	1 bay leaf, finely crumbled
generous pinch dried tarragon or 1 sprig fresh tarragon, finely chopped	generous pinch dried tarragon or 1 sprig fresh tarragon, finely chopped
salt and freshly ground black pepper	salt and freshly ground black pepper
4 tablespoons olive oil	4 tablespoons olive oil
Topping:	*Topping:*
4 tablespoons fine dry breadcrumbs	4 tablespoons fine dry breadcrumbs
4 teaspoons finely chopped parsley	4 teaspoons finely chopped parsley
4–6 large croûtons, to serve	4–6 large croûtons, to serve

1. Preheat oven to moderate (375°F., 190°C., Gas Mark 5).

2. Wipe mushrooms clean. Trim stem ends and pull stems out carefully to avoid damaging caps.

3. Chop stems finely and combine with sausage meat, finely chopped shallot and garlic, and herbs. Mix well and season to taste with salt and freshly ground black pepper.

4. Heat 1 tablespoon olive oil in a heavy pan; add sausage meat mixture and cook over a moderate heat for about 5 minutes, crumbling and blending with a fork until lightly browned. Cool.

5. Divide stuffing between mushroom caps, smoothing it over neatly. Sprinkle with a mixture of breadcrumbs and parsley.

6. Heat remaining oil in a wide, flameproof baking dish; arrange stuffed mushrooms in it in one layer, and fry over a moderate heat for 2 minutes until bottoms are lightly coloured, shaking dish gently. Transfer to the oven and bake for 15 minutes, or until mushrooms are tender. (If tops have not browned by the time mushrooms are cooked, slip dish under a hot grill for a minute or two to finish cooking.)

7. Arrange three or four baked mushroom caps on each croûton and serve immediately.

Serves 4–6

Pepper Pissaladière

IMPERIAL	METRIC
olive oil	olive oil
1 lb. ripe tomatoes, peeled and chopped, or 1 14-oz. can peeled tomatoes, chopped	450 g. ripe tomatoes, peeled and chopped, or 1 396-g. can peeled tomatoes, chopped
½ teaspoon dried oregano	½ teaspoon dried oregano
½ teaspoon sugar	½ teaspoon sugar
salt and freshly ground black pepper	salt and freshly ground black pepper
3 Spanish onions, peeled and thinly sliced	3 Spanish onions, peeled and thinly sliced
2 tablespoons butter	2 tablespoons butter
2 large green sweet peppers	2 large green sweet peppers
1 9-inch shortcrust pastry case, prebaked	1 23-cm. shortcrust pastry case, prebaked
2 tablespoons finely grated Parmesan	2 tablespoons finely grated Parmesan

1. Heat 2 tablespoons olive oil in a heavy pan; add chopped tomatoes; sprinkle with oregano and sugar, and season to taste with salt and freshly ground black pepper. Cook over a low heat for 15 minutes, or until excess moisture has evaporated, stirring and mashing tomatoes with a wooden spoon to reduce them to a thick purée. Cool.

2. Sauté sliced onions in butter until soft and transparent. Let them cool as well.

3. Meanwhile, preheat oven to moderate (350°F., 180°C., Gas Mark 4) and light the grill, turned to its maximum setting.

4. When grill is hot, lay peppers in the grill pan and grill as close to the heat as possible, turning frequently, until their skins are charred and blistered all over. Rub skins off under cold water. Halve peppers; remove cores, wash out seeds and pat peppers dry with absorbent paper. Cut each half in three across the width.

5. Sprinkle bottom of pastry case with freshly grated Parmesan. Cover with sautéed onions and spread tomato purée over top. Dot with pepper chunks.

6. Brush top of tart and pepper chunks with olive oil, and bake for 30 minutes. Serve hot or warm.

Serves 6

Chef's tip:
My recipes all call for freshly grated Parmesan because there seems to be a world of difference in flavour between the tubs of grated Parmesan you can buy and grating a lump of Parmesan for yourself, as and when you need it. If you do not believe me, try for yourself and see.

Roquefort Cream Quiche

IMPERIAL	METRIC
1 10-inch pastry case, prebaked	1 25-cm. pastry case, prebaked
Roquefort cream filling:	*Roquefort cream filling:*
2 3-oz. packets Philadelphia cream cheese	2 85-g. packets Philadelphia cream cheese
3 oz. Roquefort cheese	85 g. Roquefort cheese
2 tablespoons softened butter	2 tablespoons softened butter
3 eggs, well beaten	3 eggs, well beaten
½ pint single cream	3 dl. single cream
1 tablespoon melted butter	1 tablespoon melted butter
1 tablespoon finely chopped parsley	1 tablespoon finely chopped parsley
2 teaspoons finely chopped chives	2 teaspoons finely chopped chives
freshly ground black pepper	freshly ground black pepper
salt	salt

1. Leave the pastry case in its tin if it is a loose-bottomed one, and lay on a baking sheet. Otherwise, unmould case and lay on the baking sheet. You could also use an oval ovenproof dish to make the pastry case in if you prefer.

2. Preheat oven to moderate (375°F., 190°C., Gas Mark 5).

3. In a bowl, work cream cheese with Roquefort and softened butter until smooth. Add well-beaten eggs, cream and melted butter, and blend thoroughly.

4. Stir in finely chopped herbs. Season to taste with freshly ground black pepper and a little salt if necessary.

5. Fill pastry case evenly with cheese mixture and bake for 25 to 30 minutes, or until filling is puffed and a light golden colour.

6. Serve hot, lukewarm or cold, cut in wedges.

Serves 6

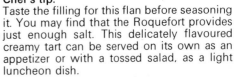

Chef's tip:
Taste the filling for this flan before seasoning it. You may find that the Roquefort provides just enough salt. This delicately flavoured creamy tart can be served on its own as an appetizer or with a tossed salad, as a light luncheon dish.

Bacon and Tomato Flan

IMPERIAL	METRIC
4 oz. streaky bacon	100 g. streaky bacon
3 tablespoons butter	3 tablespoons butter
2 medium-sized onions, finely chopped	2 medium-sized onions, finely chopped
2 lb. tomatoes, peeled, seeded and chopped	900 g. tomatoes, peeled, seeded and chopped
pinch each thyme and oregano	pinch each thyme and oregano
1 bay leaf	1 bay leaf
salt and freshly ground black pepper	salt and freshly ground black pepper
6 eggs	6 eggs
1 9-inch shortcrust pastry case, prebaked	1 23-cm. shortcrust pastry case, prebaked

1. Preheat oven to moderate (350°F., 180°C., Gas Mark 4).

2. Chop bacon into small pieces.

3. Melt butter in a large, heavy saucepan; add chopped bacon and onions and sauté over a moderate heat until a rich golden colour.

4. Stir in peeled, seeded and chopped tomatoes and the thyme, oregano and bay leaf, and season generously with salt and freshly ground black pepper. Cover pan and simmer gently for 20 minutes.

5. Break eggs into a bowl and whisk lightly until well mixed.

6. Remove bay leaf from tomato mixture and discard it. Cool mixture slightly and combine with the beaten eggs. Correct seasoning, adding more salt or freshly ground black pepper if necessary.

7. Pour mixture into prebaked pastry case and bake for 25 to 30 minutes until filling is set and golden. Serve hot or cold.

Serves 6–8

Chef's tip:
Peel tomatoes by placing them in a basin and pouring over boiling water to cover. Leave for one minute; drain and peel. Or, pierce tomato with a fork and rotate slowly over a flame until skin splits, then peel. The latter method seems the more satisfactory of the two.

Mushroom Quiche

IMPERIAL	METRIC
1 8-inch shortcrust pastry case, prebaked	1 20-cm. shortcrust pastry case, prebaked
2 shallots, finely chopped	2 shallots, finely chopped
1 tablespoon butter	1 tablespoon butter
4 oz. white button mushrooms	100 g. white button mushrooms
lemon juice	lemon juice
1 tablespoon finely chopped parsley	1 tablespoon finely chopped parsley
salt and freshly ground black pepper	salt and freshly ground black pepper
1 egg	1 egg
1 egg yolk	1 egg yolk
$\frac{1}{4}$ pint plus 2 tablespoons single cream	$1\frac{3}{4}$ dl. single cream
3 tablespoons freshly grated Parmesan	3 tablespoons freshly grated Parmesan

1. Leave prebaked pastry case in its tin.

2. Preheat oven to moderate (350°F., 180°C., Gas Mark 4).

3. In a frying pan, simmer finely chopped shallots in butter until soft but not coloured, 3 to 5 minutes.

4. Meanwhile, wipe button mushrooms clean; trim ends and slice mushrooms thinly.

5. Add to frying pan with a squeeze of lemon juice and toss over a moderate heat for a further 3 minutes until slightly softened. Remove from heat and stir in finely chopped parsley, and salt and freshly ground black pepper to taste.

6. Combine whole egg and egg yolk with cream and freshly grated Parmesan. Beat with a fork until thoroughly blended, adding salt and freshly ground black pepper.

7. Spread base of pastry case with mushroom mixture. Three-quarters fill it with cream mixture, pouring it in gently over the back of a tablespoon to avoid disturbing mushrooms.

8. Transfer pastry case on a baking sheet to the oven and carefully pour in remaining cream mixture.

9. Bake quiche for 25 to 30 minutes until filling is well puffed and set, and a rich golden colour on top. Serve immediately.

Serves 4

Chef's tip:
Mushrooms are often sautéed in a little butter with lemon juice; the lemon juice prevents the discolouration of the mushrooms to a large extent. Brushing the cut surfaces of fruits such as apples, pears and bananas with lemon juice also prevents browning.

Asparagus and Ham Crêpes

Brioches Stuffed with Mushrooms

IMPERIAL	METRIC
1 12-oz. can asparagus tips	1 340-g. can asparagus tips
8 slices lean ham	8 slices lean ham
½–¾ pint chicken stock	3–4 dl. chicken stock
8 crêpes, 6 inches in diameter	8 crêpes, 15 cm. in diameter
1–2 oz. Gruyère, freshly grated	25–50 g. Gruyère, freshly grated
Sauce:	*Sauce:*
1 oz. butter	25 g. butter
1 oz. flour	25 g. flour
¾ pint milk	4 dl. milk
3 tablespoons single cream	3 tablespoons single cream
1 oz. Parmesan, freshly grated	25 g. Parmesan, freshly grated
salt and freshly ground black pepper	salt and freshly ground black pepper

1. Drain asparagus tips. Lay ham slices out on a board and divide asparagus tips between them. Roll up tightly lengthwise and arrange side by side in a deep, flameproof dish, seam side down.

2. Pour boiling chicken stock over ham rolls and simmer over a low heat for a few minutes until they are thoroughly hot. Remove from heat and leave rolls in hot stock until required.

3. To make sauce, melt butter in a heavy pan. Add flour and stir over a low heat for about 1 minute to make a pale roux.

4. Gradually add milk, stirring vigorously to prevent lumps forming. Then bring to the boil and simmer gently, stirring occasionally, until sauce is smooth and thick, and reduced to about ½ pint (3 dl.).

5. Stir cream and freshly grated Parmesan into sauce. Season with salt and freshly ground black pepper, and continue to stir over a low heat until cheese has melted and sauce is smooth again. Strain through a fine sieve into a clean pan.

6. Drain ham rolls. Roll each one up in a crêpe and arrange side by side in a shallow, heatproof serving dish.

7. Just before serving, spoon sauce over rolls and sprinkle with freshly grated Gruyère.

8. Place dish under a hot grill until crêpes are golden and bubbling on top. Serve immediately.

Serves 4

Chef's tip:
This dish makes a delicate first course for a dinner party. The crêpes can be prepared in advance if you wish; stack them with a sheet of greaseproof paper between each crêpe. They can be stored in the refrigerator in a plastic bag for up to four days.

IMPERIAL	METRIC
1 oz. butter	25 g. butter
½ oz. plain flour	15 g. plain flour
¼ pint milk	1½ dl. milk
2 oz. Gruyère, freshly grated	50 g. Gruyère, freshly grated
salt and freshly ground black pepper	salt and freshly ground black pepper
4 oz. button mushrooms	100 g. button mushrooms
2–3 teaspoons lemon juice	2–3 teaspoons lemon juice
½ teaspoon oregano	½ teaspoon oregano
4 small brioches	4 small brioches
melted butter	melted butter

1. Make a thick white sauce with half the butter, the flour and the milk. Beat in cheese smoothly over a low heat and season to taste with salt and freshly ground black pepper.

2. Trim mushroom stems but leave them intact. Wash and wipe mushrooms clean and slice them very thinly lengthwise. Brush a few of the most attractive mushroom slices with a little lemon juice to prevent discolouration and put them aside for garnish.

3. Sauté remaining sliced mushrooms gently in remaining butter for 3 to 4 minutes, sprinkling them with remaining lemon juice. Add to sauce, together with oregano, and season to taste.

4. Preheat oven to moderate (350°F., 180°C., Gas Mark 4).

5. Remove tops from brioches and scoop out centres to leave firm cases about ¼ inch (½ cm.) thick.

6. Fill brioches with mushroom sauce and arrange them in an ovenproof dish. Trim tops neatly if they are thick and set them back on the brioches. Garnish each brioche with reserved mushroom slices and brush with a little melted butter.

7. Heat through in the oven for 10 to 15 minutes, or until very hot. Serve immediately.

Serves 4

Chef's tip:
When substituting dried herbs for fresh ones, use half the quantity called for in a recipe. Dried herbs are much more concentrated than fresh. Check that dried herbs do not get too old; if you sniff a herb and it doesn't reply with any conviction throw it away and buy some more.

Fish and Shellfish

Many cooks today neglect fish because they don't quite understand what to do with it. Too often they egg and breadcrumb it and fry it until it is hard, dry and tasteless; or they boil it until it disintegrates into a soft, flavourless mush.

Fresh fish

With modern methods of fishing, processing and transportation, many varieties of fresh fish are available all the year round no matter where you live. Learn how to buy it and cook it properly and you'll discover a whole new world of delightful and flavourful eating.

Half the battle, of course, is to go to a good fishmonger—one that you can rely on to give you good advice and the freshest fish available. But you can easily learn to pick out good fresh fish for yourself if you follow a few basic rules:

* Always buy fish on the day you intend to use it.

* A whole fish when it is really fresh has bright, bulging eyes (never sunken or opaque) and reddish pink gills.

* All fish should have firm elastic flesh that springs back when pressed and a pleasant, fresh aroma.

* If the fish has been cut into steaks or fillets, the flesh should be firm and resilient to the touch.

Ask your fishmonger to clean, skin and fillet the fish for you. And once you've got the fish home, unwrap it immediately and place it on a clean plate in the refrigerator, covered loosely with a clean cloth, paper or foil until required. But you'll find that you need to keep fish away from butter or sweets or puddings to prevent the fish affecting these delicately flavoured foods.

Fresh fish is sold in various forms. These are the ones you will find most often:

Whole Fish just as it comes from the water.

Drawn Whole fish from which the insides have been removed.

Dressed Fish that is ready to cook when you buy it because the scales and insides have been removed. The head, tail and fins are sometimes removed as well.

Steaks Pieces or slices, usually $\frac{1}{2}$ to 1 inch thick, that have been cut crosswise from a large fish.

Fillets Sides of the fish that have been cut lengthwise away from the backbone.

Frozen fish

Frozen fish can be purchased today whole, in steaks or fillets, or in prepared portions. They may be used just as fresh fish after thawing. You will also find frozen fish that have been partially prepared or are ready to heat and serve.

Buying and cooking fish

How much fish to buy? Appetites vary but a good rule is to allow 6 oz. to 1 lb. edible fish per serving. When in doubt, use this guide:

Whole fish 1 lb. for 1 serving
Dressed fish or steaks 1 lb. for 2 servings
Fish fillets or sticks 1 lb. for 3 servings.

Fish is delicate. For the best results treat it with care. Never overcook it and never let it get dry. I like to cook fish in a lightly flavoured *court-bouillon*, adding flavour to the fish in cooking instead of taking flavour away.

You will find that whole fish (or thick pieces of fish such as salmon, halibut, cod, ling, hake or turbot) are best for cooking in this way. Always put all fish—except salt fish—into liquid that is very hot, but not bubbling too hard, with salt to taste, and 1–2 tablespoons vinegar or lemon juice, or a cup or two of dry white wine, to 2 quarts ($2\frac{1}{4}$ litres) water. For extra flavour, add a bouquet garni (1 bay leaf, 1 sprig thyme, 1 stalk celery, 2 sprigs parsley) and sliced carrots and onion, and if fish is dry 1–2 tablespoons olive oil. Use only enough liquid for cooking to cover fish by 2 inches (5 cm.). Bring to the boil after fish is put in, then reduce to a bare simmer.

When cooked, the flesh should be creamy white and opaque, and should flake away from the bone at the touch of a fork.

Fish steaks or fillets—salmon, cod, sole, turbot— or whole small fish can be cooked to perfection by steaming. For a small quantity, you can use two plates: butter one generously, put fish on it with a little finely chopped mushroom and onion, and season with salt, pepper and lemon juice, to taste; cover with well-buttered paper or foil and invert second plate on top. Place plates on top of a pan of boiling water and steam for 20 to 30 minutes, or until fish flakes easily with a fork. The liquids in the lower plate should be served with the fish. For larger quantities of fish a steamer is necessary.

One of the most delicate ways of cooking fish fillets and small steaks or cutlets is to poach them in equal quantities of well-flavoured fish stock (or canned clam juice) and dry white wine. Just butter a heatproof gratin dish and put fish in it; season with salt, pepper and lemon juice and barely cover with fish stock and wine. Put well-buttered paper or foil over fish and cook in a slow oven (325°F., 170°C., Gas Mark 3) or on top of the stove until fish is tender and opaque. For sauce, reserve pan liquids and thicken slightly with a *beurre manié* (equal parts butter and flour mashed to a paste) or an egg yolk mixed with double cream and lemon juice.

Boiled new potatoes drenched in lemon juice and melted butter make a splendid accompaniment to these simple fish recipes. And a dry white wine, served slightly chilled, makes any fish dish taste better. Try Muscadet, Meursault or Sancerre, a good Rhine wine, or a Pouilly Fumé or Fuissé.

Baked Fish Spanish Style

IMPERIAL	METRIC
2½–3 lb. cod	1–1⅓ kg. cod
butter or oil, for baking dish	butter or oil, for baking dish
Tomato sauce:	*Tomato sauce:*
1 Spanish onion, chopped	1 Spanish onion, chopped
2 tablespoons olive oil	2 tablespoons olive oil
1 14-oz. can peeled Italian tomatoes	1 396-g. can peeled Italian tomatoes
¼ pint dry white wine	1½ dl. dry white wine
2 cloves	2 cloves
½ teaspoon sugar	½ teaspoon sugar
salt and freshly ground black pepper	salt and freshly ground black pepper
1 tablespoon cornflour	1 tablespoon cornflour
12 green olives, stoned and cut into pieces	12 green olives, stoned and cut into pieces
1 tablespoon chopped parsley	1 tablespoon chopped parsley
2 tablespoons capers	2 tablespoons capers

1. To make tomato sauce, sauté chopped onion in olive oil until soft, about 10 minutes.

2. Add peeled tomatoes, dry white wine, cloves, sugar, and salt and freshly ground black pepper, to taste; cover pan and simmer for 20 minutes.

3. Preheat oven to moderate (375°F., 190°C., Gas Mark 5).

4. Blend cornflour to a smooth paste with 1 tablespoon cold water. Stir into tomato mixture and simmer for 5 minutes longer.

5. Add olives, chopped parsley and capers.

6. Grease a baking dish with butter or oil.

7. Wash and dry fish and place in the buttered baking dish. Pour the tomato sauce over it.

8. Bake fish for 35 to 40 minutes, or until it flakes easily with a fork, basting occasionally with its own sauce. Serve hot with sauce.

Serves 4–6

Chef's tip:
You can substitute for the cod in this recipe hake or halibut, whichever you prefer. Buy olives loose in a delicatessen; they work out cheaper this way. This dish can be served hot, but it is also delicious chilled.

Baked Stuffed Haddock Fillets

IMPERIAL	METRIC
6 haddock fillets	6 haddock fillets
salt and freshly ground black pepper	salt and freshly ground black pepper
juice of 1 lemon	juice of 1 lemon
2 tablespoons olive oil	2 tablespoons olive oil
2 tablespoons finely chopped onion	2 tablespoons finely chopped onion
1 bay leaf, crumbled	1 bay leaf, crumbled
butter	butter
lemon slices, tomatoes and parsley, to garnish	lemon slices, tomatoes and parsley, to garnish
Stuffing:	*Stuffing:*
6 tablespoons soft white breadcrumbs	6 tablespoons soft white breadcrumbs
1 tablespoon grated onion	1 tablespoon grated onion
2 tablespoons finely chopped parsley	2 tablespoons finely chopped parsley
4 tablespoons milk	4 tablespoons milk
1–2 tablespoons softened butter	1–2 tablespoons softened butter
salt and freshly ground black pepper	salt and freshly ground black pepper

1. Wipe haddock fillets dry with paper towels, and season generously with salt and freshly ground black pepper. Arrange them in a shallow dish. Sprinkle with lemon juice, olive oil, finely chopped onion and crumbled bay leaf, and leave to marinate for at least 2 hours.

2. Meanwhile, prepare stuffing. Blend first four ingredients with 1–2 tablespoons softened butter, and season to taste with salt and freshly ground black pepper.

3. Preheat oven to fairly hot (425°F., 220°C., Gas Mark 7).

4. Drain fish fillets from marinade. Spread them with stuffing. Roll up tightly, starting from the tail end, and secure with toothpicks.

5. Arrange rolled fillets in a well-buttered baking dish; dot with 1 tablespoon butter.

6. Bake for 25 minutes, or until fish is cooked through, basting occasionally with pan juices. Serve immediately, garnished with lemon slices, tomatoes, and parsley.

Serves 4–6

Chef's tip:
Place the stuffing on the skinned side of the haddock fillets and roll up. It is better to do it this way because the skin side of the fish contracts during cooking. So, if the skin side was outside the rolls would start to unwind themselves during cooking.

Marinated Kippers

Smoked Fish Appetizer with Horseradish Chantilly

IMPERIAL	METRIC
2 large, plump kippers	2 large, plump kippers
1 Spanish onion, coarsely chopped	1 Spanish onion, coarsely chopped
about ½ pint olive oil	about 3 dl. olive oil

1. Fillet kippers carefully.

2. Select a small, deep china dish with a tight-fitting lid.

3. Lay two fillets side by side at the bottom of the dish. Cover with coarsely chopped Spanish onion and top with remaining fillets.

4. Pour in enough olive oil to cover kippers completely. Put on the lid.

5. Leave dish at the bottom of the refrigerator to marinate for a minimum of 2 weeks, preferably longer.

6. To serve, drain fillets and serve one per person with thinly sliced brown bread and butter.

Serves 4

IMPERIAL	METRIC
Per portion:	*Per portion:*
1 oz. thinly sliced smoked salmon	25 g. thinly sliced smoked salmon
½ smoked trout, skinned and boned	½ smoked trout, skinned and boned
freshly ground black pepper	freshly ground black pepper
1 sprig watercress	1 sprig watercress
2 lemon wedges	2 lemon wedges
Horseradish chantilly:	*Horseradish chantilly:*
(enough for 6 portions)	(enough for 6 portions)
6 tablespoons double cream	6 tablespoons double cream
1–2 tablespoons freshly grated raw horseradish	1–2 tablespoons freshly grated raw horseradish
pinch salt	pinch salt

1. Assemble each portion by arranging slices of smoked salmon neatly on a plate with ½ smoked trout, skinned and boned, beside it. Cover plates with lightly oiled greaseproof paper and chill in the refrigerator until ready to serve.

2. To make horseradish chantilly, whip double cream until it holds its shape in soft peaks. Add 1–2 tablespoons iced water and whisk until thick and light again.

3. Fold in freshly grated horseradish to taste, and season with a tiny pinch of salt.

4. Season each portion of fish with a turn or two of the peppermill. Garnish with watercress, lemon wedges and a good dollop of horseradish chantilly, and serve immediately, with thinly sliced brown bread and butter.

Chef's tip:
It is no exaggeration to say that treated in this fashion, a humble kipper enters the smoked trout and salmon league. You can serve the kippers after a fortnight's marination, but they continue to improve and are at their best after 6 to 8 weeks.

Chef's tip:
If you are grating raw horseradish for the first time, be prepared for a few tears. The operation can be rendered less unpleasant if you feed the horseradish root through the finest blade of your mincer, but the result is not as fine.

Poached Salmon or Turbot Kedgeree

IMPERIAL	METRIC
1½ lb. poached salmon or turbot	675 g. poached salmon or turbot
3 hard-boiled eggs	3 hard-boiled eggs
6 tablespoons butter	6 tablespoons butter
1½ teaspoons curry powder or paste	1½ teaspoons curry powder or paste
6 oz. long-grain rice, cooked and kept warm	175 g. long-grain rice, cooked and kept warm
salt	salt
freshly ground black pepper	freshly ground black pepper
¾ pint hot, well-flavoured white sauce	4 dl. hot, well-flavoured white sauce
6–8 tablespoons double cream	6–8 tablespoons double cream
2 tablespoons lemon juice	2 tablespoons lemon juice
3 tablespoons finely chopped parsley	3 tablespoons finely chopped parsley

1. Dice or flake fish very carefully, picking out any stray bones or pieces of skin.

2. Shell hard-boiled eggs; separate yolks from whites, and chop the latter finely.

3. Melt butter in a wide, heavy pan; blend in curry powder or paste; add fish and toss over a gentle heat until thoroughly hot and golden.

4. Add rice and finely chopped egg whites, and toss lightly until well mixed, taking care not to crumble fish.

5. Season to taste with salt and freshly ground black pepper; remove from heat and keep hot.

6. Combine hot white sauce with double cream and sharpen flavour with lemon juice, to taste.

7. Fold sauce into rice mixture, together with finely chopped parsley.

8. When well mixed, turn kedgeree into a heated serving dish. Sieve hard-boiled egg yolks over the top and serve very hot.

Serves 6

Chef's tip:
For a quick, well-flavoured white sauce, gently fry some chopped onion and celery in butter before stirring in flour and milk. Add a pinch of thyme, half a bay leaf and some peppercorns and simmer the sauce. Strain before using.

Grilled Salmon Steaks with Snail Butter

IMPERIAL	METRIC
6 salmon steaks, about 1 inch thick	6 salmon steaks, about 2½ cm. thick
2–3 tablespoons olive oil	2–3 tablespoons olive oil
salt and freshly ground black pepper	salt and freshly ground black pepper
lemon juice	lemon juice
Snail butter:	*Snail butter:*
3 oz. butter	75 g. butter
1–2 plump cloves garlic, crushed	1–2 plump cloves garlic, crushed
½ tablespoon very finely chopped shallot	½ tablespoon very finely chopped shallot
½ tablespoon very finely chopped parsley	½ tablespoon very finely chopped parsley
salt and freshly ground black pepper	salt and freshly ground black pepper

1. Prepare snail butter in advance and leave it to chill in the refrigerator until required. Work butter in a bowl with a wooden spoon until slightly softened. Add crushed garlic to taste, and continue to beat until thoroughly blended; then beat in very finely chopped shallot and parsley, and season to taste with salt and freshly ground black pepper. Shape butter into six neat pats or balls and chill until firm again.

2. Turn on the grill set at maximum heat about 20 minutes before cooking salmon. Line grill pan with a large sheet of aluminium foil.

3. Brush both sides of each salmon steak with olive oil and sprinkle with salt and freshly ground black pepper; arrange steaks side by side on the foil in grill pan; squeeze a little lemon juice over steaks.

4. When ready to cook steaks, turn grill down to moderate and grill steaks for about 15 to 20 minutes, depending on their thickness, turning them once and squeezing a little more lemon juice over. They are ready when the fish can be prised away easily from the bone with a fork.

5. Transfer salmon steaks to a heated dish and top each one with a pat of chilled snail butter. Serve immediately.

Serves 6

Chef's tip:
After preparing snail butter in advance beware of storing it in the refrigerator uncovered. The garlic odour will permeate the other dishes in the refrigerator if the butter is not firmly wrapped in foil or self-clinging plastic film.

Skate with Black Butter

IMPERIAL	METRIC
3 tablespoons wine vinegar	3 tablespoons wine vinegar
salt	salt
bouquet garni	bouquet garni
1 lb. skate wings	450 g. skate wings
4 oz. clarified butter	100 g. clarified butter
2 tablespoons finely chopped parsley	2 tablespoons finely chopped parsley
1 tablespoon capers	1 tablespoon capers
freshly ground black pepper	freshly ground black pepper
1 lemon, thinly sliced	1 lemon, thinly sliced

1. Select a saucepan large enough to accommodate skate wings flat. Half-fill with cold water and add 2 tablespoons wine vinegar, salt and the bouquet garni.

2. Add skate wings; bring to the boil over a low heat and simmer very gently for 10 minutes, or until fish is tender but not disintegrating.

3. Meanwhile, melt clarified butter in a frying pan. Continue to heat it, swirling pan, until butter turns a rich, warm brown colour. Remove from heat.

4. Stir in remaining vinegar, finely chopped parsley, the capers, and salt and freshly ground black pepper to taste.

5. Drain fish thoroughly and transfer to a well-heated serving dish. Pour over butter sauce and garnish with lemon slices. Serve immediately.

Serves 4

Chef's tip:
Watch the butter like a hawk during this operation. There is only a split second's difference between black butter and burnt butter. It is sometimes handy to have a bowl full of cold water nearby in which to cool the saucepan immediately to arrest the cooking process.

Deep-fried Sole Amandine

IMPERIAL	METRIC
1¼ lb. sole, filleted	550 g. sole, filleted
fat for deep-frying	fat for deep-frying
Marinade:	*Marinade:*
4 tablespoons olive oil	4 tablespoons olive oil
4 tablespoons dry white wine	4 tablespoons dry white wine
1 small onion, finely chopped	1 small onion, finely chopped
1 bay leaf, crumbled	1 bay leaf, crumbled
salt and freshly ground black pepper	salt and freshly ground black pepper
Fritter batter:	*Fritter batter:*
4 oz. plain flour	100 g. plain flour
pinch salt	pinch salt
2 tablespoons olive oil	2 tablespoons olive oil
2 egg whites	2 egg whites
4 oz. nibbed almonds	100 g. nibbed almonds

1. Cut each sole fillet in three with two diagonal slices.

2. Combine marinade ingredients in a shallow dish, adding a generous seasoning of salt and freshly ground black pepper. Lay sole in marinade, making sure strips are thoroughly coated, and leave for at least an hour.

3. Prepare fritter batter. Sift flour and salt into a bowl and make a well in the centre.

4. Pour in olive oil and 8 tablespoons tepid water, and stir with a wooden spoon, gradually incorporating flour from sides of well until blended to a smooth batter. Leave to rest for 30 minutes.

5. When ready to cook sole, heat a pan of fat for deep-frying to 375°F. (190°C.).

6. Whisk egg whites until stiff but not dry and fold into batter, together with nibbed almonds.

7. Drain strips of sole thoroughly. Coat a few strips at a time in batter, allowing excess to drain back into bowl, and deep-fry until crisp and golden brown, about 2 minutes. Drain thoroughly on absorbent paper.

8. Repeat coating and deep-frying with remaining strips, and serve immediately.

Serves 4

Chef's tip:
If you fillet your own fish, do not discard all the fish trimmings; cut them into reasonable sized pieces with a strong pair of kitchen scissors, gather them up and place in a suitable well-sealed container and freeze them— they will come in very useful later for a fish stock.

Trout with Shrimp and Mushroom Sauce

IMPERIAL	METRIC
4 large fresh trout	4 large fresh trout
salt and freshly ground black pepper	salt and freshly ground black pepper
2 oz. butter	50 g. butter
8 oz. small button mushrooms	225 g. small button mushrooms
juice of ½–1 lemon	juice of ½–1 lemon
4 oz. shelled shrimps	100 g. shelled shrimps
4–6 tablespoons double cream	4–6 tablespoons double cream
Garnish:	*Garnish:*
4 thin slices lemon	4 thin slices lemon
2 tablespoons finely chopped parsley	2 tablespoons finely chopped parsley

1. Clean trout if this has not already been done by the fishmonger. Wash them carefully and pat dry with paper towels. Season both inside and out with salt and freshly ground black pepper.

2. Melt butter in a frying pan large enough to take all the trout side by side. When it is hot, lay trout in pan and fry gently for 4 to 5 minutes on each side, or until they flake easily with a fork. Take care not to let butter burn.

3. Meanwhile, trim mushrooms; wipe them clean and slice them thinly. Sprinkle with lemon juice.

4. When trout are cooked, transfer them to a large, heated serving dish and keep hot in a slow oven.

5. Add sliced mushrooms to butter remaining in frying pan and sauté gently for 3 minutes.

6. Add shrimps to pan and continue to sauté until heated through, about 3 minutes longer.

7. Stir in cream; bring almost to the boil and simmer until slightly thickened. Taste for seasoning, adding more salt, freshly ground black pepper or lemon juice if necessary.

8. Spoon sauce over trout. Garnish each fish with a slice of lemon and sprinkle with finely chopped parsley.

Serves 4

Chef's tip:
To clean the trout, rinse each one then slit open the belly and pull out all the entrails; wipe with kitchen paper; rinse thoroughly with cold running water; dry with paper. The sauce can be thickened with a little cornflour paste if necessary.

Fried Fresh Trout with New Potatoes

IMPERIAL	METRIC
4 trout weighing 8 oz. each, gutted	4 trout weighing 225 g. each, gutted
milk	milk
seasoned flour	seasoned flour
2–3 tablespoons olive oil	2–3 tablespoons olive oil
4–6 tablespoons butter	4–6 tablespoons butter
6 slices lemon	6 slices lemon
small bunch parsley	small bunch parsley
1 lb. small new potatoes, cooked	450 g. small new potatoes, cooked

1. Wash and dry trout thoroughly both inside and out. Dip trout in milk, shake off excess. Coat with seasoned flour, patting it gently so that it sticks to the skin.

2. Melt half the oil and butter in each of two large frying pans. When it is hot and sizzling, lay two trout in each pan. Fry over a moderate heat for 8 to 10 minutes, turning trout carefully with a spatula halfway through.

3. Transfer trout to a large, heated serving dish. Garnish with lemon slices and tiny sprigs of parsley, and serve accompanied by boiled new potatoes.

Serves 4

Chef's tip:
The potatoes can be tossed in parsley butter for this recipe. To make parsley butter, beat 4 tablespoons butter with 2–3 tablespoons finely chopped parsley. Season with salt and lemon juice and freshly ground black pepper; refrigerate until firm again.

Turbot en Brochette

IMPERIAL	METRIC
$\frac{1}{4}$ pint olive oil	1$\frac{1}{2}$ dl. olive oil
1 tablespoon Robert Carrier's Provençal Blend	1 tablespoon Robert Carrier's Provençal Blend
4 small firm tomatoes	4 small firm tomatoes
1 large green sweet pepper	1 large green sweet pepper
1$\frac{1}{2}$–2 lb. turbot steaks, 1 inch thick	675–900 g. turbot steaks, 2$\frac{1}{2}$ cm. thick
salt and freshly ground black pepper	salt and freshly ground black pepper
4 oz. butter	100 g. butter
juice of 1 lemon	juice of 1 lemon
generous pinch cayenne	generous pinch cayenne

1. Combine olive oil and Provençal Blend in a shallow dish.

2. Quarter tomatoes and discard seeds. Cut pepper in half; remove core and seeds, and cut each half into eight pieces.

3. Cut fish into 1-inch (2$\frac{1}{2}$-cm.) cubes, discarding bones, etc. (You should have about sixteen cubes.)

4. Coat tomato, pepper and fish pieces with the aromatic oil; then thread them onto four skewers, starting with a piece of tomato, followed by a piece of turbot and ending with a piece of pepper. Continue in this manner until ingredients are used up, distributing them evenly among the skewers. Season lightly with salt and freshly ground black pepper.

5. Preheat grill until very hot.

6. Grill brochettes for about 10 minutes, or until the turbot can be flaked by a fork, but is still very firm. Turn brochettes occasionally while they are grilling, and take great care not to overcook the turbot.

7. In the meantime, put butter in a bowl and set it in a pan of hot water. When butter is very soft, remove bowl from hot water and with a wooden spoon beat in lemon juice a drop at a time as if making mayonnaise. Season sauce generously with salt and cayenne, and turn into a sauceboat.

8. Remove brochettes from grill and serve very hot, accompanied by butter sauce.

Serves 4

Chef's tip:
My Provençal Blend is a mixture of wild thyme, sarriette, rosemary and fennel. It is ideal for fish dishes, such as the one above, as well as pork, poultry, game and beef or lamb casseroles. It is important to preheat the grill to very hot 20 minutes before grilling the brochettes.

French Turbot Salad

IMPERIAL	METRIC
1 lb. turbot	450 g. turbot
salt	salt
4 tablespoons milk	4 tablespoons milk
8 oz. new potatoes	225 g. new potatoes
3–4 large fresh button mushrooms	3–4 large fresh button mushrooms
6–8 tablespoons olive oil	6–8 tablespoons olive oil
3 tablespoons lemon juice	3 tablespoons lemon juice
2 tablespoons finely chopped parsley	2 tablespoons finely chopped parsley
2 tablespoons chopped spring onion	2 tablespoons chopped spring onion
freshly ground black pepper	freshly ground black pepper

1. Cut turbot into slices about $\frac{1}{2}$ inch (1 cm.) thick.

2. Bring a pint of salted water to the boil in a saucepan. Add milk (to keep turbot white) and the slices of turbot. Reduce heat so that water barely bubbles and simmer turbot until it is cooked but still very firm, 12 to 15 minutes.

3. Scrub potatoes clean but do not peel them; boil them in salted water, then drain; plunge into cold water and peel off skins as soon as potatoes can be handled.

4. When turbot is cooked, drain it, and while still warm, remove skin and bones. Cut turbot into 1-inch (2$\frac{1}{2}$-cm.) cubes. Cut potatoes into $\frac{1}{4}$-inch ($\frac{1}{2}$-cm.) cubes.

5. Trim mushroom stems and wipe clean with a damp cloth. Peel mushrooms only if necessary and slice them thinly.

6. Combine warm turbot and potatoes with thinly sliced mushrooms in a large bowl. Toss with olive oil, lemon juice, finely chopped parsley and chopped spring onion, taking care not to break pieces of fish. Season to taste with salt and freshly ground black pepper, and allow to cool.

7. Just before serving, correct seasoning and add more olive oil and lemon juice if necessary. Serve cold.

Serves 3–4

Chef's tip:
It is important to cook turbot very slowly so that its juices do not escape into the stock. However, this is true with all fish; the greatest care should be taken not to overcook it, as is unfortunately so often the case.

Poached Turbot with Avocado (Guacamole) Sauce

IMPERIAL	METRIC
2 avocado pears	2 avocado pears
juice of ½ lemon	juice of ½ lemon
1 medium-sized onion, grated	1 medium-sized onion, grated
salt and cayenne pepper	salt and cayenne pepper
pinch ground ginger	pinch ground ginger
4 tablespoons olive oil	4 tablespoons olive oil
4 slices cold poached turbot	4 slices cold poached turbot

1. Cut avocado pears in half and remove stones. Scoop out flesh with a sharp spoon; sprinkle with lemon juice and purée through a fine sieve.

2. Rub grated onion into avocado purée through the same sieve; season to taste with salt, cayenne and a pinch of ground ginger, and gradually beat in oil until mixture has consistency of mayonnaise. Chill.

3. Place turbot slices on a serving dish. Top each slice with a little chilled avocado sauce. Serve remaining sauce separately.

Serves 4

Chef's tip:
If the avocado sauce is kept waiting for any length of time, it will discolour on the surface. If this happens, beat the sauce adding one or two drops of green food colouring to give it a more appetizing appearance. Serve immediately.

Turbot en Papillote

IMPERIAL	METRIC
1 2-lb. slice turbot	1 900-g. slice turbot
1 Spanish onion, finely chopped	1 Spanish onion, finely chopped
1 tiny clove garlic, finely chopped	1 tiny clove garlic, finely chopped
1 tablespoon finely chopped parsley	1 tablespoon finely chopped parsley
½ teaspoon dried tarragon	½ teaspoon dried tarragon
4 tablespoons dry white wine	4 tablespoons dry white wine
1 teaspoon Pernod	1 teaspoon Pernod
squeeze lemon juice	squeeze lemon juice
salt and freshly ground black pepper	salt and freshly ground black pepper
olive oil	olive oil
1 tablespoon butter	1 tablespoon butter

1. Preheat oven to hot (450°F., 230°C., Gas Mark 8).

2. Wipe turbot dry with absorbent paper.

3. Combine the next seven ingredients in a small bowl. Season with salt and freshly ground black pepper.

4. Cut a sheet of foil large enough to envelop turbot completely. Brush all over with olive oil.

5. Spread half of the onion mixture in centre of foil, roughly to shape of turbot. Lay turbot on top and spread with remaining onion mixture. Dot surface with small flakes of butter.

6. Bring up sides of foil to enclose fish completely and seal into a neat, watertight parcel. Place on a baking sheet.

7. Bake parcel for 30 minutes, by which time fish should come away easily from bones running through centre.

8. To serve, transfer parcel to a heated serving dish. Fold back foil to make a shallow container so that juices do not run all over dish, and serve immediately.

Serves 4

Chef's tip:
Make as neat a job as possible when wrapping the fish up in its foil packet—much as you would when wrapping an ordinary parcel. This lessens the chance of losing the valuable cooking juices onto the baking sheet.

Quick Fish Dish

IMPERIAL	METRIC
2 tablespoons butter	2 tablespoons butter
2 tablespoons flour	2 tablespoons flour
¼ pint milk	1½ dl. milk
¼ pint single cream	1½ dl. single cream
12 oz. cooked, flaked fish	350 g. cooked, flaked fish
4 oz. button mushrooms, thinly sliced	100 g. button mushrooms, thinly sliced
4 spring onions, finely chopped	4 spring onions, finely chopped
salt and freshly ground black pepper	salt and freshly ground black pepper
3 tablespoons grated sharp Cheddar cheese	3 tablespoons grated sharp Cheddar cheese
3 tablespoons dry breadcrumbs	3 tablespoons dry breadcrumbs
lemon juice	lemon juice
spring onion tops, to garnish	spring onion tops, to garnish

1. Preheat oven to hot (400°F., 200°C., Gas Mark 6).

2. Melt butter in a medium-sized saucepan; add flour, stir and cook for 2 to 3 minutes over a moderate heat.

3. Gradually pour in milk, stirring vigorously, followed by cream. Bring sauce to the boil and simmer for 2 minutes, stirring constantly.

4. Add flaked fish, sliced mushrooms and chopped spring onions to sauce, mixing gently, and season to taste with salt and freshly ground black pepper.

5. Divide equally between four individual ramekins or scallop shells.

6. Toss grated Cheddar and breadcrumbs in a small bowl and sprinkle over each portion.

7. Bake in the oven for 15 to 20 minutes or until golden brown on top and bubbling. Serve immediately with a sprinkling of lemon juice and chopped spring onion tops.

Serves 4

Chef's tip:
This dish can be made with fresh fish, and, if you do this, poach the fish in milk, to cover, with a blade of mace and a bay leaf, until fish is just cooked, then skin and bone if necessary. Strain poaching liquor and use in place of milk to make sauce.

Devilled Crab

IMPERIAL	METRIC
6 tablespoons butter	6 tablespoons butter
8 tablespoons fine white breadcrumbs	8 tablespoons fine white breadcrumbs
2 eggs	2 eggs
10–12 oz. white crabmeat	275–350 g. white crabmeat
4 tablespoons medium-dry' sherry	4 tablespoons medium-dry sherry
1 teaspoon Worcestershire sauce	1 teaspoon Worcestershire sauce
2 tablespoons flour	2 tablespoons flour
½ pint milk	3 dl. milk
1 tablespoon finely chopped parsley	1 tablespoon finely chopped parsley
2 teaspoons French mustard	2 teaspoons French mustard
½–1 teaspoon grated horseradish	½–1 teaspoon grated horseradish
salt and freshly ground black pepper	salt and freshly ground black pepper

1. In a wide-based pan, heat 4 tablespoons butter until frothy. Add breadcrumbs and sauté gently, stirring, until crisp and golden but not brown. Remove from heat and allow to cool.

2. In a medium-sized bowl, beat eggs until well mixed. Add crabmeat, sherry and Worcestershire sauce, and mix well.

3. Melt remaining butter in a medium-sized pan. Stir in flour and cook over a low heat for 2 to 3 minutes, stirring to make a pale roux.

4. Gradually add milk, stirring vigorously with a wooden spoon to prevent lumps forming; bring to the boil and simmer for 3 to 4 minutes. Remove from heat.

5. Stir in crabmeat mixture, parsley, mustard and horseradish. Season to taste with salt and freshly ground black pepper.

6. Divide mixture evenly among six scallop shells or small, heatproof ramekins. Sprinkle with buttered breadcrumbs.

7. Slip under a moderate grill until mixture is thoroughly hot again and bubbling on top, 3 to 4 minutes. Serve immediately.

Serves 6

Chef's tip:
If you cannot obtain fresh horseradish there are various brands of grated horseradish on the market but they are not nearly so strong as the fresh. If you use the bought variety you will have to go on adding a little at a time until you get the desired flavour.

Creamed Crab

IMPERIAL	METRIC
6 tablespoons butter	6 tablespoons butter
2 oz. flaked almonds	50 g. flaked almonds
1 lb. white crabmeat	450 g. white crabmeat
about $\frac{1}{4}$ pint double cream	about $1\frac{1}{2}$ dl. double cream
2 tablespoons finely chopped watercress	2 tablespoons finely chopped watercress
salt and freshly ground black pepper	salt and freshly ground black pepper
generous pinch cayenne or paprika	generous pinch cayenne or paprika
lemon juice	lemon juice
fried croûtons, to garnish	fried croûtons, to garnish

1. Melt 2 tablespoons butter in a large, deep frying pan. When hot but not coloured, add flaked almonds and sauté gently, stirring constantly, until golden. Take care not to let almonds colour too deeply. Drain on absorbent paper.

2. Melt remaining butter gently in the same frying pan and sauté crabmeat lightly for 3 to 4 minutes, tossing with a fork.

3. Mix in sautéed almonds, cream and chopped watercress. If mixture is too dry, add a little more cream (or top of milk). Season to taste with salt, freshly ground black pepper, a generous pinch of cayenne and a squeeze of lemon juice. Simmer very gently for 2 to 3 minutes, stirring frequently, until thoroughly hot.

4. Serve immediately, garnished with crisp fried croûtons.

Serves 4

Chef's tip:
Croûtons can be either shallow fried in a mixture of oil and butter or deep fried in oil. They can be varied in size and shape by using assorted pastry or biscuit cutters. This dish is also delicious if the creamed crab is served piled on top of crisp fried bread.

Mussels with Buttered Breadcrumbs

IMPERIAL	METRIC
2 quarts mussels	$2\frac{1}{2}$ litres mussels
6–8 tablespoons dry white wine	6–8 tablespoons dry white wine
1 shallot, finely chopped	1 shallot, finely chopped
2 sprigs parsley	2 sprigs parsley
1 sprig thyme	1 sprig thyme
$\frac{1}{2}$ bay leaf	$\frac{1}{2}$ bay leaf
6 black peppercorns, coarsely crushed	6 black peppercorns, coarsely crushed
3–4 tablespoons butter	3–4 tablespoons butter
4 cloves garlic, finely chopped	4 cloves garlic, finely chopped
4 tablespoons finely chopped parsley	4 tablespoons finely chopped parsley
6 oz. stale white breadcrumbs	175 g. stale white breadcrumbs

1. Scrub mussels thoroughly under cold running water and remove 'beards'. Discard any that have not closed up tightly by the end of this operation.

2. Put mussels in a heavy pan with a tight-fitting lid. Add dry white wine, finely chopped shallot, parsley, thyme, bay leaf and coarsely crushed peppercorns. Cover tightly and cook over a high heat, shaking pan frequently, for about 5 to 7 minutes, or until mussels have all opened. Any that are still closed should be discarded.

3. Drain mussels thoroughly, reserving liquor. Remove their top shells over the pan to catch any remaining liquor as it escapes.

4. Strain mussel liquor through a muslin-lined sieve; return to the pan and simmer over a low heat until reduced by half.

5. Melt butter in a wide frying pan large enough to hold mussels in one layer. When butter is hot but not coloured, add finely chopped garlic and parsley; lower heat and simmer for 3 minutes, stirring. Take care not to let garlic burn, or it will taste bitter.

6. Add breadcrumbs and stir over a low heat until they have soaked up butter and are tinged green with parsley. Sprinkle with reduced mussel liquor and continue to stir over a low heat until liquid has evaporated.

7. Add mussels to the pan and mix lightly until they are heated through and filled with breadcrumbs. Serve immediately.

Serves 4

Chef's tip:
Mussels should be alive when bought, i.e., with their shells fairly well closed. If any mussels remain open by the end of the cleaning operation it is a sure bet that the creature inside is dead; throw it away.

Mussels in Cream

IMPERIAL	METRIC
2 quarts mussels	2½ litres mussels
2 tablespoons butter	2 tablespoons butter
2 shallots, peeled and grated	2 shallots, peeled and grated
¼ pint dry white wine	1½ dl. dry white wine
¼ pint single cream	1½ dl. single cream
salt and freshly ground black pepper	salt and freshly ground black pepper
finely chopped parsley, to garnish	finely chopped parsley, to garnish

1. Scrub mussels clean with a stiff brush under the cold tap and remove 'beards'. Do this particularly carefully, as their cooking liquor will not be strained, and any sand overlooked at this stage will be present in the finished dish. Discard any mussels that have not closed up tightly by the end of this operation.

2. Select a wide, heavy pan or casserole with a tight-fitting lid. Melt butter in it and simmer shallots gently for 5 minutes until soft but not coloured.

3. Stir in wine and cream, and season lightly with salt and freshly ground black pepper. Add mussels.

4. Cover pan tightly. Place over maximum heat and cook for 5 to 7 minutes, or until mussels are all open—any stray ones that remain shut should be discarded for safety's sake.

5. Lift out mussels with a slotted spoon and distribute them evenly between four deep, heated bowls. Taste liquor and correct seasoning with more salt and freshly ground black pepper if necessary. Pour over mussels. Dust with finely chopped parsley and serve immediately.

Serves 4

Chef's tip:
To prepare mussels, place them, scrubbed, in a bowl; cover with water and salt to taste of the sea. Throw in half a cup of flour and stir. Leave bowl in the refrigerator overnight whilst mussels gorge themselves on flour. Next day mussels will be plump and clean; rinse again before cooking. The season for mussels is from September to March.

Blender Prawn Bisque

IMPERIAL	METRIC
8 oz. cooked peeled prawns	225 g. cooked peeled prawns
6 tablespoons tomato paste	6 tablespoons tomato paste
1 pint chicken stock	6 dl. chicken stock
½ Spanish onion, finely chopped	½ Spanish onion, finely chopped
4 tablespoons single cream	4 tablespoons single cream
¼ teaspoon paprika	¼ teaspoon paprika
salt and freshly ground black pepper	salt and freshly ground black pepper
1–2 tablespoons dry sherry (optional)	1–2 tablespoons dry sherry (optional)
1 tablespoon each finely chopped parsley and chives	1 tablespoon each finely chopped parsley and chives

1. Set aside half a dozen of the best prawns for garnish and put remainder in an electric blender with tomato paste, chicken stock and finely chopped onion. Blend at a high speed for 1 minute or until reduced to a smooth purée.

2. Pour prawn purée into a pan and stir over a low heat until just below boiling point.

3. Add cream and paprika, and season to taste with salt and freshly ground black pepper. Continue to cook over a low heat for 2 to 3 minutes longer, stirring constantly.

4. Add a little more stock if soup seems too thick, and flavour with sherry if liked.

5. Serve in bowls, garnished with reserved prawns and a sprinkling of finely chopped parsley and chives.

Serves 4–6

Chef's tip:
This is a very attractive rose-pink cream. It is also delicious made with clam juice, which is occasionally available in good food stores. If you are lucky enough to find it, use only ¼ pint (1½ dl.) clam juice (it has a very strong flavour) and make up volume of liquid with cream, or cream and milk.

Shrimp Potato Balls

IMPERIAL	METRIC
1 lb. well-dried hot mashed potatoes	450 g. well-dried hot mashed potatoes
2 teaspoons butter	2 teaspoons butter
4 tablespoons freshly grated Parmesan	4 tablespoons freshly grated Parmesan
1 tablespoon lemon juice	1 tablespoon lemon juice
1 tablespoon finely chopped parsley	1 tablespoon finely chopped parsley
4 oz. peeled shrimps	100 g. peeled shrimps
1–2 eggs, beaten	1–2 eggs, beaten
salt and freshly ground black pepper	salt and freshly ground black pepper
about 3 oz. fresh white breadcrumbs	about 75 g. fresh white breadcrumbs
oil for deep-frying	oil for deep-frying

1. Blend hot mashed potatoes smoothly with butter, freshly grated Parmesan, lemon juice and finely chopped parsley. Mix with shrimps, halved if large, and add enough beaten egg (1–2 tablespoons) to give the mixture a soft but manageable consistency. Season to taste with salt and freshly ground black pepper.

2. Form 1 tablespoon of the mixture at a time into a round ball. Coat with remaining beaten egg and roll in breadcrumbs.

3. Heat a pan of oil for deep-frying to 375 °F. (190 °C.).

4. Deep-fry potato balls, a portion at a time to prevent overcrowding, for 3½ to 4 minutes until crisp and golden brown. Drain on absorbent paper and serve immediately.

Makes 2 dozen

Chef's tip:
If you inadvertently make the potato mixture too wet, try refrigerating it, uncovered, for an hour before forming it into balls. Serve them accompanied by a simple tomato sauce, as an appetizer or light luncheon dish.

Mexican Scallop Ceviche

IMPERIAL	METRIC
8 large fresh scallops	8 large fresh scallops
juice of 2 lemons or fresh limes	juice of 2 lemons or fresh limes
8 oz. firm tomatoes	225 g. firm tomatoes
1 small green sweet pepper	1 small green sweet pepper
4 tablespoons olive oil	4 tablespoons olive oil
2 tablespoons wine vinegar	2 tablespoons wine vinegar
4 tablespoons coarsely chopped parsley	4 tablespoons coarsely chopped parsley
½ teaspoon oregano or marjoram	½ teaspoon oregano or marjoram
salt and freshly ground black pepper	salt and freshly ground black pepper
dash Tabasco	dash Tabasco
1 ripe avocado pear	1 ripe avocado pear
6 stuffed green olives	6 stuffed green olives

1. Clean scallops very carefully. Cut white lobes into two or three thick slices; leave red corals whole.

2. Place scallops and corals in a bowl. Pour over lemon or lime juice and leave to marinate for 3 hours, turning scallops gently from time to time.

3. Peel and seed tomatoes and cut them into ¼-inch (½-cm.) dice.

4. Cut green pepper in half; remove seeds and white pith, and cut flesh into ¼-inch dice.

5. Add diced tomatoes and pepper to scallops, together with olive oil, wine vinegar, parsley and oregano or marjoram. Mix gently but thoroughly, and season to taste with salt, freshly ground black pepper and a dash of Tabasco. Chill until just before serving.

6. When ready to serve, peel avocado, remove stone and cut flesh into small dice. Add to bowl, making sure the pieces are completely coated with dressing, otherwise they will quickly discolour.

7. Slice stuffed olives. Add to the bowl and mix lightly.

8. Transfer to a serving dish and serve immediately, while still very cold.

Serves 4

Chef's tip:
The prospect of eating raw scallops in a salad might seem slightly daunting, but you will find that the acidity of the lemon or lime juice virtually 'cooks' the scallops and transforms their texture. So do not be tempted to cut short the marination time.

Blanquette of Scallops

Scallops with Avocado Cream Dressing

IMPERIAL	METRIC
3 oz. butter	75 g. butter
12–16 large scallops with corals	12–16 large scallops with corals
2 tablespoons brandy	2 tablespoons brandy
3 medium-sized onions, finely chopped	3 medium-sized onions, finely chopped
1 tablespoon flour	1 tablespoon flour
$\frac{1}{4}$ pint fish stock	$1\frac{1}{2}$ dl. fish stock
$\frac{1}{4}$ pint dry white wine	$1\frac{1}{2}$ dl. dry white wine
1 small clove garlic, crushed	1 small clove garlic, crushed
pinch allspice	pinch allspice
salt and freshly ground black pepper	salt and freshly ground black pepper
8 oz. button mushrooms, thinly sliced	225 g. button mushrooms, thinly sliced
2 egg yolks	2 egg yolks
4 tablespoons double cream	4 tablespoons double cream
chopped parsley, to garnish	chopped parsley, to garnish

1. Melt 2 oz. (50 g.) butter in a sauté pan or deep frying pan and sauté scallops over a fairly high heat for just 1 minute, or until they stiffen without colouring. Flame with brandy.

2. When flames die down, add finely chopped onions; cover and simmer until softened, about 5 minutes. Remove scallops and keep hot.

3. Sprinkle flour over onions and stir over a moderate heat to make a pale roux. Add fish stock and dry white wine gradually, stirring constantly, then add garlic and season with a pinch of allspice and salt and freshly ground black pepper to taste. Stir for 2 to 3 minutes; or until sauce thickens, and continue to cook for 15 minutes over a very low heat, stirring occasionally.

4. Meanwhile, melt remaining butter in another pan and sauté thinly sliced mushrooms for 4 or 5 minutes until soft and golden. Add to simmering sauce and mix well.

5. Beat egg yolks with cream; add to sauce and continue to stir over a low heat until sauce has thickened, taking great care not to let it boil, or egg yolks will curdle.

6. Return scallops to sauce; heat through gently and serve immediately, garnished with chopped parsley.

Serves 4

Chef's tip:
Frozen scallops can be used for this dish but whether you use fresh or frozen be sure not to overcook them. It only requires a minute's overcooking for scallops to become tough and stringy. Serve this dish accompanied by a dish of plain boiled or steamed rice.

IMPERIAL	METRIC
12 large scallops	12 large scallops
finely chopped parsley to garnish	finely chopped parsley to garnish
Marinade:	*Marinade:*
4 shallots, finely chopped	4 shallots, finely chopped
$\frac{1}{2}$ pint dry white wine	3 dl. dry white wine
2 tablespoons lemon juice	2 tablespoons lemon juice
4–6 tablespoons finely chopped parsley	4–6 tablespoons finely chopped parsley
4–6 tablespoons olive oil	4–6 tablespoons olive oil
1 small bay leaf	1 small bay leaf
salt and freshly ground black pepper	salt and freshly ground black pepper
Avocado cream dressing:	*Avocado cream dressing:*
2 medium-sized ripe avocado pears	2 medium-sized ripe avocado pears
$\frac{1}{4}$ pint thick sour cream	$1\frac{1}{2}$ dl. thick sour cream
$\frac{1}{4}$–$\frac{1}{2}$ teaspoon finely chopped fresh tarragon	$\frac{1}{4}$–$\frac{1}{2}$ teaspoon finely chopped fresh tarragon
salt and freshly ground black pepper	salt and freshly ground black pepper
2 teaspoons lemon juice	2 teaspoons lemon juice
6–8 drops Tabasco	6–8 drops Tabasco
few drops onion juice	few drops onion juice

1. Combine marinade ingredients in a pan. Add scallops; bring to the boil and simmer gently for 4 to 5 minutes, or until scallops are just cooked.

2. Lift scallops out with a slotted spoon. Slice them into thick rounds and put in a bowl. Pour over hot marinade; leave to cool; chill slightly.

3. Meanwhile, prepare avocado cream dressing. Peel and stone avocados and press through a sieve into a bowl (or purée in an electric blender). Beat in sour cream and finely chopped tarragon. Season to taste; add lemon juice, Tabasco and a few drops of onion juice. If dressing is very thick, beat in a little more sour cream. Chill.

4. To serve, arrange scallops in a white porcelain dish and moisten with a little of the marinade. Garnish with a little chopped fresh parsley and serve, with dressing in a separate bowl for each guest to help himself.

Serves 6

Chef's tip:
If you buy scallops on the shell (they are at their best in January and February), the roe should be bright orange in colour and the flesh very white. Remove scallops from shells, wash and remove beard and black part; drain on kitchen paper. Keep shells for when you serve the quick fish dish (see page 29).

Beef and Veal

Beef

Gone forever are the days when massive joints of meat impaled on spits suspended from hooks in the chimney revolved slowly before open fires in vast country house kitchens. Nowadays, with the embers of the fires long cold, the great kitchen echoing to the footsteps of indifferent tourists, and the boys who strained at the spits as likely as not tossing prepacked hamburgers in high street cafés, only a small minority —the lucky possessors of electric rôtisseries or barbecues with revolving spits—can claim to *roast* their meat. For in the true sense of the word, roasting means cooking by direct, dry heat.

The rest of us must rely on our ovens. *Oven-roasting*—or even *baking*—would be a more accurate description of what we do, for it is impossible to cook meat in an enclosed space without some vapour accumulating around it.

To choose meat for roasting

Only prime cuts of beef or veal make successful roasts. If you are ever in any doubt about a piece of meat, pot-roast or casserole it instead.

A small joint—anything under 2 lb. (900 g.) doesn't make a successful roast either, however good its quality. By the time the inevitable shrinkage has occurred, there will be little of it left. Again, settle for pot-roasting or casseroling instead.

Sealing the roast

One of the aims of a high initial temperature is to seal the roast. Otherwise, as the fibres of the meat expand, the juices tend to seep out into the roasting tin—which will give you fabulous gravy to accompany dry, tasteless meat. As an added precaution, it is sometimes advisable to reinforce this seal by browning the surface of the meat in the frying pan before putting it into the oven.

Some cuts of beef

Sirloin This is the best cut for roasting, but it is somewhat expensive. The chump end (adjoining the rump) is considered the best, as it has the largest amount of undercut (see jacket photograph). The wing rib makes an excellent smaller joint for roasting.

Fillet The undercut of the sirloin; the tenderest part for entrées or fillet of beef.

Tournedos A 1-inch (2½-cm.) thick slice from the fillet, usually encircled by a thin strip of fat.

Ribs The cuts from the ribs are also good for roasting, those nearest the sirloin being the best. These better cuts are slightly less expensive than sirloin. Various sizes of joint can be cut according to special requirements. It is more economical to have the bone removed and the meat itself rolled. The bone can be used for soup. Two to three ribs make a good roast for a small family. When roasting a large cut whole, it is better to have the thin end cut off and used for a separate dish, otherwise it will overcook before the thicker part is ready. Back and top ribs are not so tender. They are better stewed or braised than roasted.

Rump This is an excellent piece of flesh meat. Some of the best steaks are cut from this part. It is a first-rate cut, if expensive, for pies, rolled beef, or a tender *carbonnade* or stew.

Topside, buttock or round This is another very fleshy piece of meat with little bone. It is one of the best pieces for braising or boiling, and is often salted. It can also be roasted, but, though economical, it is not as fine in flavour as the ribs or sirloin. The topside and the silverside are both cut from the buttocks.

Flank The thick flank (or top rump) is one of the most economical cuts to buy, as it contains no bone and very little fat. Suitable for slow roasting, braising, stewing and boiling, for pies and puddings. The thin flank contains much more fat, and is best salted and boiled, and eaten cold, or used for a moist, well-flavoured *pot-au-feu*.

Shin This is coarse-grained and very gelatinous. It is excellent for stocks and soups. When simmered slowly, the top part makes a rich, flavoursome stew.

Veal

A large joint of veal is a tricky piece to cook, whether you roast it, or indeed grill or sauté it. Cooking in liquid, i.e., casseroling or poaching, seems to be the one style veal takes without reservations. If you want to cook a joint of veal successfully by any other method, rid yourself of the attitude that it is the younger brother of beef, and instead treat it like poultry—a delicate meat that will dry out and become tasteless unless you protect it by supplementing its own fat and juices, and using gentle temperatures.

Like poultry, too, it must be roasted until the juices run just golden and no more. To take it any further would reduce the meat to shreds and destroy its delicate elusive flavour beyond recall. And like poultry, veal has a remarkable versatility, and a positive passion for being flattered with herbs, lemon or garlic, anchovies and olives, cream, dry white wine or vermouth, marinades of all kinds, and delicate stuffings.

How to choose veal

Here is where you stop thinking of veal as a bird. Buying a tender chicken presents no problems—though finding one with any flavour might—but you have to tread carefully when choosing veal.

Look for milk-fed veal. It will have a delicate pink, almost white colour and be finely grained, firm and smooth, with white, satiny fat. Darker meat should be avoided at all costs. It comes from an older animal which has been fed on grain and grass, and has no business to be on the veal counter at all, for at this stage of its development it is neither veal nor beef, but an extremely tough and uninteresting adolescent.

Some different cuts of veal

Fillet Escalopes are cut across the grain from this expensive joint. When preparing for roasting, it is best to lard this joint or cover with a thin layer of fat to prevent it drying out.

Knuckle Lower part of the leg. Excellent for boiling or for stewing pieces and pie pieces. It can also be boned and stuffed and then braised. The knuckle is full of marrow. Very good for stock or for jellied veal or veal moulds.

Shin Wonderful for stocks and broths. This inexpensive cut can be sawn across the bone to make individual servings for Italian *osso buco*.

Loin Sold as one joint with bone, or boned and stuffed, or as separate loin chops with or without kidney. I like to roast the loin until half done, then cut it into thick chump chops with kidney; flavour chops with salt, pepper, rosemary and bay leaf, baste with olive oil and bake in the oven in small earthenware dishes. Deliciously tender and moist.

Best end of neck May be roasted or braised. Can be divided into cutlets. Usually grilled, fried, braised or stewed.

Shoulder Sold on the bone, or stuffed and rolled. When knuckle is removed, the remaining 'oyster' makes a good roasting piece. This cut is excellent for *blanquette de veau*, or for a veal *gulyas* or stew. Small pieces of boneless shoulder are used for pies, stew and fricassées.

Breast The breast is not used often enough. I like this economical cut stuffed, and either roasted, braised or steamed. It is also suitable for stewing, pot-roasting and boiling. I also use it with an equal quantity of shoulder for a *blanquette de veau*.

Calf's kidney Delicious sautéed with bacon, avocado pear or onions.

Pie veal Many butchers sell scraps of veal cut up ready to use for hot and cold veal pies. These are usually small pieces from shoulder, breast and leg.

Veal must never be overcooked; for maximum flavour and succulence, there should still be a hint of pink in the beige meat, even though the juices run clear. If using a meat thermometer, I like to take the temperature to 165°F. (75°C.), i.e., 5 degrees Fahrenheit under the temperature usually recommended.

Roast Beef with Roast Potatoes

IMPERIAL	METRIC
1 2-lb. joint rolled sirloin	1 900-g. joint rolled sirloin
coarsely ground black pepper	coarsely ground black pepper
2 lb. potatoes	900 g. potatoes
4 tablespoons dripping or butter	4 tablespoons dripping or butter
salt	salt

1. Preheat oven to fairly hot (425°F., 220°C., Gas Mark 7).

2. Wipe joint clean with a damp cloth and season generously with coarsely ground black pepper.

3. Peel potatoes. Cut them into even-sized chunks. Wash and dry them thoroughly.

4. Heat dripping or butter in a roasting tin and brown joint thoroughly on all sides over a steady heat.

5. Remove tin from heat. Add potatoes and turn them over in the resulting fat until thoroughly coated. Sprinkle potatoes with salt and freshly ground black pepper.

6. Stand a rack over potatoes and lay joint on it. (If you have no suitable rack, lay the beef in the centre of the tin and push potatoes back so that they do not crowd it.)

7. Roast beef until done to your liking, turning the oven down to 325°F., 170°C., Gas Mark 3 after 15 minutes' roasting, allowing 15 minutes per lb. (450 g.) for rare, 25 minutes per lb. for medium and 35 to 37 minutes per lb. for a well-done joint. Baste meat once or twice and turn potatoes over so that they absorb flavours and cook evenly.

8. Remove roasting tin from the oven. Season beef with salt and more freshly ground black pepper if necessary. Transfer beef to a well-heated serving platter and leave to rest for 15 minutes in a warm place—the warming compartment of the oven with the door ajar is a good place.

9. Meanwhile, turn oven up to 425°F. again and return the tin of potatoes to it for 15 minutes to finish cooking and crisp the surface.

10. Serve roast potatoes with the beef. They are quite delicious.

Serves 4–6

Chef's tip:
When roasting a small joint of beef, you can put the potatoes in with the meat from the start and reckon on them being ready by the time meat is rare. Otherwise, start the beef and add the potatoes no more than an hour before calculated end of cooking time.

Roast Beef with Yorkshire Pudding

IMPERIAL	METRIC
1 5-lb. rib roast of beef	1 2¼-kg. rib roast of beef
coarsely ground black pepper	coarsely ground black pepper
4 tablespoons butter	4 tablespoons butter
Yorkshire pudding:	*Yorkshire pudding:*
4 oz. plain flour	100 g. plain flour
salt	salt
2 eggs	2 eggs
¼ pint milk	1¼ dl. milk

1. Preheat oven to fairly hot (425°F., 220°C., Gas Mark 7).

2. To prepare Yorkshire pudding, sift flour and a pinch of salt into a bowl; make a well in the centre. Break in eggs; add 2 tablespoons milk, work to a smooth paste with a wooden spoon. Slowly add remaining milk, beating vigorously. Put on one side until ready to use.

3. Season roast generously with coarsely ground black pepper; spread all over with butter. Lay it on a rack over a roasting tin.

4. Roast beef for 15 minutes, then lower temperature to 325°F., 170°C., Gas Mark 3 and continue to roast, basting occasionally. Allow 16 minutes per lb. (450 g.) for rare beef, 25 minutes per lb. for medium and 31 to 32 minutes per lb. for well done.

5. Thirty to 40 minutes before the end of cooking time, lift rack with joint and pour Yorkshire pudding batter into pan underneath. Continue cooking and both meat and Yorkshire pudding will be ready at the same time.

6. When roast is ready, transfer it to the serving dish; then leave it for 15 to 20 minutes in the turned-off oven with the door ajar—this resting of the meat makes it easier to carve and gives you time for last minute preparations of gravy, etc.

Serves 6–8

Chef's tip:
You can cook Yorkshire puddings in individual moulds if you prefer; use some fluted round tins 3 to 3½ inches (7½ to 9 cm.) in diameter across the top. Time them to go in the oven when you remove the roast beef, allowing the latter 15 to 20 minutes to 'settle' before carving.

Grilled Steak au Poivre

IMPERIAL	METRIC
1 8-oz. rump steak	1 225-g. rump steak
9 black peppercorns	9 black peppercorns
salt	salt
tomatoes and finely chopped parsley or sprigs of watercress, to garnish	tomatoes and finely chopped parsley or sprigs of watercress, to garnish
Garlic butter:	*Garlic butter:*
1 oz. garlic cloves	25 g. garlic cloves
2 oz. softened butter	50 g. softened butter
½ teaspoon finely chopped parsley	½ teaspoon finely chopped parsley
salt	salt

1. To make garlic butter, peel the garlic cloves; drop them into a pan of boiling water and simmer for 8 to 10 minutes. Drain well and pat dry.

2. Crush cloves to a paste in a mortar. Add the butter and pound until smooth. Add finely chopped parsley.

3. Season to taste with salt. Shape into a neat brick, wrap up tightly in plastic film and chill until ready to serve.

4. Take steak out of refrigerator well in advance of cooking it. Nick fat in several places to prevent steak curling up as it cooks.

5. Crush peppercorns coarsely in a mortar, or place them between two sheets of greaseproof paper and crush with a rolling pin.

6. Pat peppercorns firmly into both sides of steak; then leave at room temperature for a further 30 minutes to develop flavours.

7. Light grill at maximum temperature and let it heat for 20 minutes before cooking steak.

8. Grill steak as suggested in Chef's tip or until cooked to your liking.

9. Transfer to a hot plate; sprinkle with salt and serve immediately, with a pat of garlic butter and garnished with finely chopped parsley or sprigs of watercress, and tomatoes.

Serves 1

Chef's tip:
The following timings will give you a good guide as to how long to grill the steaks to the degree of doneness you prefer. For a steak just over 1 inch (2½ cm.) thick, allow 2 to 3 minutes for blue; 3½ minutes for rare; 5 minutes for medium; and 6 to 7 minutes for well done.

Steak Diane

IMPERIAL	METRIC
6 thin frying steaks, about 4 oz. each	6 thin frying steaks, about 100 g. each
salt and freshly ground black pepper	salt and freshly ground black pepper
4 tablespoons butter	4 tablespoons butter
6 tablespoons sherry	6 tablespoons sherry
3 tablespoons brandy	3 tablespoons brandy
1 tablespoon finely chopped chives or spring onion tops	1 tablespoon finely chopped chives or spring onion tops

1. The steaks should be very thin. Pound them out if necessary, and season both sides with salt and freshly ground black pepper.

2. Melt half the butter in a large sauté pan and sear steaks three at a time on both sides over a high heat, 30 to 45 seconds per side. Return all steaks to pan. Remove from heat.

3. Add sherry and brandy to the pan; stand back and set alight with a match. Remove steaks from the pan when flames die down, and keep hot.

4. Bring cooking juices to the boil again and reduce slightly. Add remaining butter and chives or spring onion tops, and simmer, stirring, for 2 minutes longer.

5. Pour over steaks and serve immediately.

Serves 3–6, according to appetite

Chef's tip:
This dish can be prepared effectively at the table in a chafing dish, much in the style of crêpes suzette. Do dip your meat battener into cold water before each flattening whack. If bashed with a dry implement the flesh splits up and breaks.

Boeuf Stroganoff

IMPERIAL	METRIC
1 lb. rump steak	450 g. rump steak
3 tablespoons flour	3 tablespoons flour
salt	salt
4 tablespoons butter	4 tablespoons butter
2 oz. finely chopped onion	50 g. finely chopped onion
3 oz. white button mushrooms, thinly sliced	75 g. white button mushrooms, thinly sliced
1 tablespoon tomato paste	1 tablespoon tomato paste
½ pint beef stock	3 dl. beef stock
1 5-oz. carton sour cream	1 142-g. carton sour cream
1 tablespoon dry sherry	1 tablespoon dry sherry
freshly ground black pepper	freshly ground black pepper

1. Pound meat out thinly with a moistened meat bat and cut diagonally across the grain into neat strips about ¼ inch (½ cm.) wide and 2 inches (5 cm.) long.

2. Combine 1 tablespoon flour with ½ teaspoon salt in a plastic bag; add strips of meat, close the bag securely and shake to coat meat strips with seasoned flour.

3. Melt half the butter in a large, deep frying pan and when very hot brown beef rapidly on all sides. The strips should remain very juicy and pink inside. Remove from pan and keep hot.

4. In the same fat, sauté finely chopped onion until soft and golden. Add thinly sliced mushrooms and continue to simmer, stirring, until tender, for about 3 to 4 minutes longer. Remove onions and mushrooms from pan and reserve.

5. Melt remaining butter in the pan and stir in remaining flour. Cook over a low heat for about 3 minutes, stirring and scraping with a wooden spoon to dislodge any pieces of meat or onion stuck to pan.

6. Add tomato paste and beef stock, and bring to the boil slowly, stirring to make a smooth sauce. Then continue to simmer, stirring occasionally, until sauce is rich and thick.

7. Fold in meat, onions and mushrooms; stir in sour cream and sherry, and correct seasoning, adding freshly ground black pepper and more salt if necessary. Reheat briefly and serve immediately with a bowl of plain boiled rice.

Serves 4

Chef's tip:
This dish may appear to be expensive, since only best quality beef is suitable, but you will find that you need allow much less meat per person than you would if serving straight grilled or fried steak.

Marinated Beef Brochettes

IMPERIAL	METRIC
1¼ lb. tender rump steak	550 g. tender rump steak
1 teaspoon paprika	1 teaspoon paprika
salt and freshly ground black pepper	salt and freshly ground black pepper
½ teaspoon fennel seeds	½ teaspoon fennel seeds
juice of 1½ lemons	juice of 1½ lemons
grated rind of 1 lemon	grated rind of 1 lemon
olive oil	olive oil
1 large red sweet pepper	1 large red sweet pepper
18 button mushrooms	18 button mushrooms
12 button onions	12 button onions
12 stuffed olives	12 stuffed olives
6 thin slices smoked streaky bacon, halved	6 thin slices smoked streaky bacon, halved
3 small gherkins, halved	3 small gherkins, halved
6 small firm tomatoes	6 small firm tomatoes

1. Cut beef into 1-inch (2½-cm.) cubes, removing fat and gristle. Put in a large bowl. Sprinkle with paprika and salt and freshly ground black pepper.

2. Crush fennel seeds to bring out their flavour. Add them to beef together with the juice and grated rind of 1 lemon and 1 tablespoon olive oil. Toss; leave to marinate for 3 hours.

3. Core pepper and remove seeds; cut into twelve pieces.

4. Clean mushrooms and trim stems; sprinkle with remaining lemon juice.

5. Light grill, set at maximum, to allow it 20 minutes' preheating.

6. Assemble brochettes. Divide marinated beef cubes among six skewers, alternating them with all remaining ingredients except tomatoes (i.e., three mushrooms, two onions, two olives, two pieces each pepper and bacon, and a half-gherkin per skewer).

7. Brush brochettes and tomatoes generously with olive oil.

8. Arrange tomatoes in the grill pan together with brochettes, and grill, turning skewers frequently to ensure that they cook evenly: 6 to 8 minutes for rare, 8 to 10 for medium rare, and 10 to 15 for well done.

9. When brochettes are done to your liking, transfer them to a heated serving dish and garnish with grilled tomatoes. Serve immediately.

Serves 6

Chef's tip:
If you prefer to have your meat rare it may be better to blanch both the onions and the red sweet pepper for a few minutes before threading them onto the skewers. This ensures that they do not remain too raw with the shorter cooking time.

Pepper Cheese Beef Olives

Steak and Kidney Pudding

IMPERIAL	METRIC
4 neat slices rump or buttock steak, about 6 oz. each	4 neat slices rump or buttock steak, about 175 g. each
1 2½-oz. pack Boursin au Poivre cheese	1 70-g. pack Boursin au Poivre cheese
2 tablespoons plain flour	2 tablespoons plain flour
salt and freshly ground black pepper	salt and freshly ground black pepper
1 tablespoon butter	1 tablespoon butter
1 tablespoon olive oil	1 tablespoon olive oil
¼ pint hot beef stock	1½ dl. hot beef stock
1 teaspoon soy sauce	1 teaspoon soy sauce
2 tablespoons double cream	2 tablespoons double cream
gherkin and finely chopped parsley, to garnish (optional)	gherkin and finely chopped parsley, to garnish (optional)

1. Flatten each slice of steak out thinly with a moistened meat mallet and cut it into two rectangles, roughly 5 by 4 inches (12 by 10 cm.). Trim off any really uneven scraps.

2. Spread each piece of meat with pepper cheese. Roll it up tightly, starting from one of the narrower ends, and secure it with a small toothpick.

3. Coat beef rolls lightly and evenly with seasoned flour.

4. Combine butter and olive oil in a deep, heavy frying pan, large enough to take beef rolls in one layer.

5. Brown beef rolls thoroughly on all sides in hot fat, transferring them to a plate with a slotted spoon as they are done.

6. When all the rolls have been browned, return them to the frying pan. Pour over hot stock mixed with soy sauce and bring to simmering point.

7. Lower heat to a simmer. Cover pan tightly and cook gently for 10 minutes, shaking pan occasionally to prevent rolls sticking to the bottom.

8. When beef rolls are tender, transfer to a heated serving dish with a slotted spoon. Remove toothpicks and keep rolls hot while you finish sauce.

9. Boil pan juices until reduced by about a half, stirring and scraping up any crusty bits stuck to bottom of pan. Remove from heat. Stir in cream and season to taste with salt and freshly ground black pepper.

10. Strain sauce through a sieve over beef olives. Garnish with gherkin and parsley if you like and serve. Plain boiled or steamed rice is a good accompaniment.

Serves 4

IMPERIAL	METRIC
1½ lb. buttock or rump steak	675 g. buttock or rump steak
8 oz. ox kidney	225 g. ox kidney
seasoned flour	seasoned flour
butter	butter
1 medium-sized onion, finely chopped	1 medium-sized onion, finely chopped
¼ teaspoon dried thyme	¼ teaspoon dried thyme
¼ teaspoon marjoram	¼ teaspoon marjoram
2 teaspoons soy sauce	2 teaspoons soy sauce
2 tablespoons port	2 tablespoons port
a little rich beef stock	a little rich beef stock
Suet crust:	*Suet crust:*
12 oz. plain flour	350 g. plain flour
4 teaspoons baking powder	4 teaspoons baking powder
1 teaspoon salt	1 teaspoon salt
freshly ground black pepper	freshly ground black pepper
6 oz. freshly grated or packaged suet	175 g. freshly grated or packaged suet

1. Trim excess fat from meat and kidney; cut meats into fairly small pieces and toss in seasoned flour.

2. Butter a 1¾-pint (1-litre) pudding bowl.

3. To make the suet crust, sift flour, baking powder and salt into a bowl. Add a little freshly ground black pepper and suet. Stir in approximately 12 tablespoons cold water to make a soft, but not sticky dough.

4. Place dough on a floured surface and knead lightly. Roll out to a round, large enough to line bowl. Cut out a quarter of the circle to make a lid. Use rest of suet crust to line pudding bowl.

5. Place meats in lined bowl, sprinkling with chopped onion and herbs, as you go.

6. Pour a mixture of soy sauce and port over meat before placing suet crust lid on top.

7. Cover pudding with a buttered sheet of greaseproof paper, pleated down the centre (this allows pudding room to rise). Cover this with a cloth or foil and tie firmly in position with string.

8. Steam pudding, covered, over or in simmering water for 4½ to 5 hours.

9. When cooked, cut a small hole in top of pudding and top up with a little rich beef stock.

10. Serve pudding in its bowl, wrapped in a clean cloth or napkin.

Serves 6

Basic Beef Stew

IMPERIAL

2 lb. stewing beef
4 oz. butter
4 Spanish onions, thinly
   sliced
salt and freshly ground
   black pepper

METRIC

900 g. stewing beef
100 g. butter
4 Spanish onions, thinly
   sliced
salt and freshly ground
   black pepper

1. If you intend to use the oven, preheat it to cool (225°F., 110°C., Gas Mark $\frac{1}{4}$).

2. Cut beef into 1-inch (2$\frac{1}{2}$-cm.) cubes, discarding excess fat and gristle.

3. In a heavy casserole, melt half the butter and sauté thinly sliced onions over a moderate heat until soft and a rich golden brown.

4. Add beef cubes; mix well and season to taste with salt and freshly ground black pepper.

5. Add remaining butter in a lump. Cover casserole tightly and bake in the oven for 2 hours, or until meat is meltingly tender and onions have disintegrated into a thick brown sauce. Alternatively, simmer the casserole on top of the stove over the lowest possible heat for the same length of time, using an asbestos mat to protect it if it starts cooking too fast.

6. Skim sauce; correct seasoning and serve.

Serves 6

Baked Beef and Onions

IMPERIAL

12 oz. cold roast beef
2 Spanish onions, thinly
   sliced
1 tablespoon butter
1 tablespoon oil
4 tablespoons beef gravy,
   or 2 tablespoons jellied
   meat juices from
   roasting tin diluted
   with 2 tablespoons
   water
2 oz. sharp Cheddar
   cheese, grated

METRIC

350 g. cold roast beef
2 Spanish onions, thinly
   sliced
1 tablespoon butter
1 tablespoon oil
4 tablespoons beef gravy,
   or 2 tablespoons jellied
   meat juices from
   roasting tin diluted
   with 2 tablespoons
   water
50 g. sharp Cheddar
   cheese, grated

1. Preheat oven to moderately hot (400°F., 200°C., Gas Mark 6).

2. Slice cold roast beef and arrange slices in a shallow 10- by 6-inch (25- by 15-cm.) ovenproof dish.

3. Sauté sliced onions in butter and oil until a rich golden colour and meltingly tender. Remove from pan with a slotted spoon and spread evenly over beef slices.

4. Moisten dish with beef gravy or diluted juices from the roasting tin and sprinkle with grated cheese.

5. Bake for 15 to 20 minutes, or until beef is hot and topping is bubbling and golden brown.

Serves 3–4

Chef's tip:
Do not be concerned that this recipe does not seem to contain much liquid. Although you start with little or no liquid at all, you will finish with a rich abundant sauce, thanks to the moisture provided by the onions.

Chef's tip:
Here is a dish which is good enough to warrant keeping back some of the Sunday joint specially for it. You can make it go further by slicing some leftover boiled potatoes and laying them over the beef before adding the onions.

Sliced Beef in Aspic

IMPERIAL	METRIC
8 slices rare roast beef	8 slices rare roast beef
$\frac{1}{2}$ teaspoon thyme	$\frac{1}{2}$ teaspoon thyme
$\frac{1}{2}$ teaspoon basil	$\frac{1}{2}$ teaspoon basil
salt and freshly ground black pepper	salt and freshly ground black pepper
thin slices cooked carrot	thin slices cooked carrot
button onions, boiled and sliced	button onions, boiled and sliced
leaves of chervil, tarragon or parsley	leaves of chervil, tarragon or parsley
1 pint liquid aspic	6 dl. liquid aspic
2–3 tablespoons Madeira	2–3 tablespoons Madeira
1 teaspoon Worcestershire sauce	1 teaspoon Worcestershire sauce
cayenne pepper	cayenne pepper

1. Arrange overlapping slices of cold rare beef in a shallow serving dish. Sprinkle with thyme and basil, and season to taste with salt and freshly ground black pepper.

2. Garnish beef slices with rows of sliced carrot and button onions; decorate with sprigs of chervil, tarragon or parsley.

3. Heat aspic until quite liquid. Remove from heat and stir in Madeira, Worcestershire sauce and a dash of cayenne pepper, to taste. Flavours should be quite strong as they weaken considerably on cooling. Cool until aspic is syrupy and on the point of setting.

4. Spoon a thin coating of Madeira aspic over beef slices, taking care not to dislodge garnish. Chill until set.

5. When first coating of aspic is firm, repeat with a second layer. Pour leftover aspic into a shallow plate. Chill both for about 2 hours, or until quite firm.

6. When ready to serve, chop leftover aspic up roughly and use it to decorate the dish. Serve cold but not chilled.

Serves 4

Chef's tip:
To give this dish a more professional appearance turn the leftover aspic out of the shallow plate onto two or three thicknesses of wet greaseproof paper. Using a wet knife cut the aspic into regular square or diamond shapes and use to decorate dish.

Beef Salad

IMPERIAL	METRIC
$\frac{3}{4}$–1 lb. cold roast beef	350–450 g. cold roast beef
1 oz. fat salt pork, finely diced	50 g. fat salt pork, finely diced
$\frac{1}{2}$ large green sweet pepper, cored, seeded and diced	$\frac{1}{2}$ large green sweet pepper, cored, seeded and diced
1 canned red pimento, cut into strips	1 canned red pimento, cut into strips
2 oz. cooked green peas	50 g. cooked green peas
4 oz. cooked long-grain rice	100 g. cooked long-grain rice
salt and freshly ground black pepper	salt and freshly ground black pepper
3 tablespoons olive oil	3 tablespoons olive oil
2 tablespoons wine vinegar	2 tablespoons wine vinegar
1 tablespoon lemon juice	1 tablespoon lemon juice
3 tablespoons chicken stock	3 tablespoons chicken stock
2 tablespoons finely chopped parsley	2 tablespoons finely chopped parsley
$\frac{1}{2}$ teaspoon dried chervil	$\frac{1}{2}$ teaspoon dried chervil
$\frac{1}{4}$–$\frac{1}{2}$ teaspoon dried tarragon	$\frac{1}{4}$–$\frac{1}{2}$ teaspoon dried tarragon

1. Cut roast beef into strips about 1 inch ($2\frac{1}{2}$ cm.) long and $\frac{1}{4}$ inch ($\frac{1}{2}$ cm.) thick, discarding fat and gristle.

2. Sauté diced fat salt pork in a small, heavy pan until fat runs and little cubes turn golden brown.

3. In a large bowl, combine beef with diced green pepper, strips of red pimento, peas and rice. Toss gently with a fork until well mixed. Season lightly with salt and freshly ground black pepper.

4. Add remaining ingredients to the pan containing salt pork. Mix well; bring to the boil over a moderate heat and pour over salad.

5. Toss again until well mixed. Correct seasoning if necessary and serve.

Serves 4

Chef's tip:
This is a good salad for playing the game of substitutes and using up leftovers; use cold meat from the weekend joint, any cold rice—I have used leftover saffron rice very successfully. Fresh green and red peppers can be used, or canned pimento with haricot verts instead of green peppers, etc.

Basic Roast Veal

IMPERIAL	METRIC
1 joint of veal	1 joint of veal
salt and freshly ground black pepper	salt and freshly ground black pepper
softened butter	softened butter
½ pint chicken stock	3 dl. chicken stock
1 tablespoon flour	1 tablespoon flour
Coating (optional):	*Coating (optional):*
1 egg, beaten	1 egg, beaten
6 tablespoons fine white breadcrumbs	6 tablespoons fine white breadcrumbs
2 tablespoons freshly grated Parmesan	2 tablespoons freshly grated Parmesan

1. Preheat oven to slow (325°F., 170°C., Gas Mark 3).

2. Season joint generously with salt and freshly ground black pepper. Spread all over with 2–3 tablespoons softened butter. Place joint in roasting tin and insert a meat thermometer, if available, through the thickest part.

3. The following cooking times apply to joints of average quality; a rolled joint will take longer as there is a thicker expanse of meat to penetrate.
   When roasting *loin* of veal, allow 20 minutes per lb. (450 g.) and for *best end of neck*, 25 minutes per lb. A *leg* will need 30 minutes per lb. and for *brisket* allow 40 minutes per lb. These cooking times will provide you with a well-done, but still very juicy joint.

4. If you wish to coat the joint, increase oven temperature to moderately hot (400°F., 200°C., Gas Mark 6) 15 minutes before the projected end of cooking time.

5. Remove joint from the oven. Brush with beaten egg and pat on a mixture of breadcrumbs and grated Parmesan.

6. Return joint to the oven until meat is cooked through and thermometer reads 165°F. (74°C.). Coating should be crisp and lightly coloured.

7. Transfer the joint to a heated serving dish and allow to 'settle' at the door of the turned-off oven.

8. To make gravy, pour off excess fat from roasting tin. Add chicken stock and bring to the boil on top of the stove, stirring and scraping bottom and sides of tin clean with a wooden spoon.

9. Blend 1 tablespoon each butter and flour together smoothly to make a beurre manié. Add to simmering sauce in small pieces; stir and simmer until sauce has thickened slightly. Correct seasoning. Serve in a sauceboat with veal.

Serves 4–6

Roast Veal with Rosemary and Garlic

IMPERIAL	METRIC
1 veal roast to serve 4–6	1 veal roast to serve 4–6
1 fat clove (or 2 small cloves) garlic	1 fat clove (or 2 small cloves) garlic
2 teaspoons rosemary needles	2 teaspoons rosemary needles
salt and freshly ground black pepper	salt and freshly ground black pepper
2–3 tablespoons softened butter	2–3 tablespoons softened butter
¼ pint dry white wine	1½ dl. dry white wine
¼ pint chicken stock	1½ dl. chicken stock
1 tablespoon butter	1 tablespoon butter
1 tablespoon flour	1 teaspoon flour

1. Preheat oven to slow (325°F., 170°C., Gas Mark 3).

2. With the point of a sharp, narrow-bladed knife, make about twenty slits all over surface of veal.

3. Peel garlic and cut lengthwise into twenty thin slivers.

4. Push a sliver of garlic, together with a few rosemary needles, deep down into each slit you made in the veal.

5. Season joint with salt and freshly ground black pepper, and spread it with softened butter.

6. Roast as directed in the preceding recipe, basting frequently.

7. Make gravy as directed in the preceding recipe, substituting dry white wine for half the chicken stock, and serve with the veal.

Serves 4–6

Chef's tip:
Look for milk-fed veal. It will be a delicate pink, almost white, finely grained with firm white, satiny fat. Avoid darker meat—this comes from older animals fed on grain and grass; avoid too, veal that looks 'blown up' which is usually the result of excessive bleeding to lighten the meat's colour.

Côtes de Veau à la Normande

Sautéed Veal Scallopini with Lemon and Herbs

IMPERIAL	METRIC
6 veal cutlets, about 4 oz. each	6 veal cutlets, about 100 g. each
salt and freshly ground black pepper	salt and freshly ground black pepper
1 oz. flour	25 g. flour
3 oz. butter	75 g. butter
6 shallots, finely chopped	6 shallots, finely chopped
¼ pint Calvados	1½ dl. Calvados
12 oz. white button mushrooms, sliced	350 g. white button mushrooms, sliced
½ pint single cream	3 dl. single cream
4 tablespoons chicken stock or dry white wine	4 tablespoons chicken stock or dry white wine

1. Pound cutlets out thinly; season with salt and freshly ground black pepper, and dust with flour.

2. Sauté cutlets in 2 oz. (50 g.) butter for about 5 minutes on each side, or until just tender. (Take care not to dry them out by overcooking.) Remove from pan and keep hot in a shallow, heated serving dish.

3. Add remaining butter to pan, and when it has melted, sauté shallots over a moderate heat until soft and lightly coloured, about 5 minutes.

4. Stir in all but 1 tablespoon of the Calvados and simmer, stirring, until reduced by half. Then add sliced mushrooms, cream and chicken stock or dry white wine, bring to the boil and simmer gently for further 10 minutes.

5. Season sauce to taste with salt and freshly ground black pepper, and stir in remaining 1 tablespoon Calvados.

6. Smother veal cutlets with rich sauce and serve immediately.

Serves 6

IMPERIAL	METRIC
Per portion:	*Per portion:*
4 oz. boneless veal, loin or fillet, sliced ¼ inch thick	100 g. boneless veal, loin or fillet, sliced ½ cm. thick
salt and freshly ground black pepper	salt and freshly ground black pepper
1 teaspoon olive oil	1 teaspoon olive oil
3 teaspoons butter	3 teaspoons butter
pinch each marjoram or oregano and thyme	pinch each marjoram or oregano and thyme
1 tablespoon finely chopped parsley	1 tablespoon finely chopped parsley
lemon juice	lemon juice
2 thin slices lemon	2 thin slices lemon

1. Season veal slices on both sides with salt and freshly ground black pepper. Batten out slightly with a meat mallet or the side of a rolling pin. Cut slices into squares (roughly 2-inch or 5-cm.).

2. Heat olive oil with 2 teaspoons butter in a frying pan. When fat froths, add herbs and leave over a moderate heat for a minute longer.

3. Add squares of veal in one layer; cook in hot fat for 1 minute on each side, or until cooked through but still juicy. Remove pan from heat.

4. Transfer veal to a heated dish with a slotted spoon.

5. Add remaining butter to the frying pan, together with a squeeze of lemon juice, 1 or 2 teaspoons water and the lemon slices. Heat gently, scraping surface of pan clean with a wooden spoon.

6. Lay lemon slices on top of veal. Sprinkle with pan juices and serve immediately.

Chef's tip:
Calvados is a brandy made from cider in the department of Calvados in the Normandy region of France; hence the name of the recipe. So if you do not have any Calvados you can substitute an ordinary brandy, but taste as you go.

Chef's tip:
A very simple, logical point, but one which most people fail to think of: damp or wet meat will not brown, so dry it on kitchen paper before attempting to brown it in any way, especially for a dish like this.

Wiener Schnitzel

Schnitzel Holstein

IMPERIAL	METRIC
2 veal cutlets, about 10 oz. each, boned, or 4 thin slices veal fillet	2 veal cutlets, about 275 g. each, boned, or 4 thin slices veal fillet
1 oz. plain flour	25 g. plain flour
1 egg, beaten	1 egg, beaten
3 oz. fine dry breadcrumbs	75 g. fine dry breadcrumbs
2 oz. butter	50 g. butter
2 tablespoons olive oil	2 tablespoons olive oil
salt and freshly ground black pepper	salt and freshly ground black pepper
4 anchovy fillets	4 anchovy fillets
4 stuffed olives	4 stuffed olives
1 lemon, cut in wedges	1 lemon, cut in wedges

1. If boned cutlets are used, cut each one into two thin slices, slanting the knife so that you cut as much *across* the grain as possible. Lay pieces of veal between two sheets of greaseproof paper and pound them out thinly.

2. Dust each slice (Schnitzel) with flour. Dip on both sides in beaten egg, draining off excess, and coat with fine dry breadcrumbs, patting them on firmly with a palette knife or the palm of your hand. Chill in the refrigerator for at least ½ hour to 'set' coating.

3. Use one very large frying pan or two smaller ones which will hold the Schnitzel comfortably in one layer. Heat butter with olive oil until foaming. Sprinkle lightly with salt and freshly ground black pepper.

4. Add Schnitzel and fry over a steady, moderate heat for 3 to 5 minutes on each side, turning them once, until breadcrumb casing is crisp and golden, and the veal inside cooked but still very juicy.

5. Transfer Schnitzel to a large, heated serving dish. Place an anchovy-wrapped olive in the centre of each one and garnish the dish with lemon wedges. Serve immediately.

Serves 4

IMPERIAL	METRIC
4 Wiener Schnitzel (see preceding recipe)	4 Wiener Schnitzel (see preceding recipe)
3 oz. butter	75 g. butter
1 teaspoon olive oil	1 teaspoon olive oil
¼ pint stock	1½ dl. stock
juice of ½ lemon	juice of ½ lemon
½–1 teaspoon jellied meat juices (optional)	½–1 teaspoon jellied meat juices (optional)
salt and freshly ground black pepper	salt and freshly ground black pepper
Garnish:	*Garnish:*
4 fried eggs	4 fried eggs
8 anchovy fillets	8 anchovy fillets
few capers	few capers

1. Prepare Wiener Schnitzel up to and including step 2, and chill in the refrigerator for at least ½ hour to 'set' coating.

2. When ready to cook Schnitzel, heat 2 oz. (50 g.) butter with olive oil until foaming in a large frying pan, and fry Schnitzel over a steady, moderate heat, two at a time, until crisp and golden on the outside, and cooked through but still juicy inside, 3 to 5 minutes on each side. Transfer to a large, heated serving dish and keep hot while you finish sauce and prepare garnish.

3. To the juices remaining in the pan, add stock, remaining butter, the lemon juice and jellied meat juices if available—leftover meat jelly from a roasting tin is ideal. Bring to the boil over a high heat, scraping bottom and sides of pan thoroughly with a wooden spoon, and simmer for 1 minute, stirring. Season to taste with freshly ground black pepper, and a little salt if necessary, taking into account the saltiness of the anchovy garnish.

4. Pour pan juices over Schnitzel. Trim fried eggs to a neat shape and place one on top of each Schnitzel. Lay two anchovy fillets in a criss-cross on each egg. Sprinkle with a few capers and serve immediately.

Serves 4

Chef's tip:
Persuade your butcher to cut slices of veal escalope *across* the grain from a leg of veal. Or, alternatively, use a boned veal cutlet and pound out to the required thinness without shredding; or, sliced fillet. A Schnitzel should be thin but not transparent or you will end up with a fried breadcrumb sandwich.

Chef's tip:
Move as quickly as you can once the Schnitzel have been fried. Remember that they will go on cooking whilst keeping hot in the oven so do not leave them hanging around too long or else they will be dry and tasteless.

Pot-roasted Veal with Chicory Garnish

IMPERIAL	METRIC
2½–3 lb. rolled loin of veal (boned weight)	1–1⅓ kg. rolled loin of veal (boned weight)
1 tablespoon olive oil	1 tablespoon olive oil
5 tablespoons butter	5 tablespoons butter
8 oz. button onions, peeled	225 g. button onions, peeled
salt and freshly ground black pepper	salt and freshly ground black pepper
6 small heads chicory	6 small heads chicory
¼ pint double cream	1½ dl. double cream
1 tablespoon flour	1 tablespoon flour
lemon juice	lemon juice
chopped parsley, to garnish	chopped parsley, to garnish

1. Preheat oven to moderate (350°F., 180°C., Gas Mark 4).

2. Select a heavy, flameproof casserole just large enough to hold the rolled joint of veal. Heat oil in it, together with 2 tablespoons butter, and brown veal on all sides over a steady, moderate heat.

3. Cover casserole tightly; transfer to the oven and pot-roast for 1½ hours or until tender, turning joint over occasionally. After the first 45 minutes, pack onions around meat, adding salt and freshly ground black pepper.

4. Meanwhile, wash chicory carefully and trim the stems, which contain most of the bitterness characteristic of chicory. Bring a pan of salted water to the boil; drop in chicory and boil for 20 minutes. Drain and squeeze lightly in a cloth to extract remaining moisture. Put aside.

5. About 15 minutes before veal is ready, melt 2 tablespoons butter in a shallow pan. Lay heads of chicory in it side by side; cover and cook over a moderate heat for 10 minutes, shaking pan so that chicory colours lightly all over.

6. When veal is cooked, discard strings or skewers which held it together and transfer joint to a large, heated platter. Garnish with button onions and chicory, and keep hot.

7. Place casserole over a moderate heat. Add cream and bring to the boil, scraping base and sides of pan to incorporate into the sauce all the bits stuck there.

8. Knead flour to a smooth paste with the remaining tablespoon of butter to make a beurre manié. Beat enough of it into sauce, a small piece at a time, to thicken it. Bring to the boil again; simmer for a final 2 to 3 minutes and season to taste with salt, freshly ground black pepper and a few drops of lemon juice.

9. Spoon some of the sauce over meat and vegetables and garnish with parsley. Serve veal in thickish slices, with vegetables, and remaining sauce in a heated sauceboat.

Serves 6

Casseroled Veal with Olives

IMPERIAL	METRIC
4 veal chops	4 veal chops
flour	flour
3 tablespoons butter	3 tablespoons butter
salt and freshly ground black pepper	salt and freshly ground black pepper
½ pint dry white wine	3 dl. dry white wine
8 oz. button mushrooms	225 g. button mushrooms
juice of ½ lemon	juice of ½ lemon
6 oz. stuffed olives	175 g. stuffed olives
1 tablespoon finely chopped fresh tarragon	1 tablespoon finely chopped fresh tarragon
2 tablespoons double cream	2 tablespoons double cream
1–2 teaspoons cornflour (optional)	1–2 teaspoons cornflour (optional)

1. Dust veal chops with flour.

2. Melt 2 tablespoons butter in a wide, deep frying pan or shallow casserole, and sauté veal chops for 2 to 3 minutes, or until golden brown on both sides. Season to taste with salt and freshly ground black pepper.

3. Put aside 4 tablespoons wine and pour remainder over chops. Bring to the boil very slowly; cover and simmer over the lowest possible heat for 15 minutes.

4. Meanwhile, wipe mushrooms clean and trim stems. Cut mushrooms in two or three if they are large, but leave small ones whole. Toss with lemon juice to prevent cut surfaces discolouring.

5. Melt remaining butter in a frying pan and sauté mushrooms for 4 to 5 minutes without letting them brown. Then moisten with remaining wine and simmer for 5 minutes.

6. When veal chops have cooked for 15 minutes, add mushrooms, together with their cooking juices, and stuffed olives, cover pan again and simmer very gently for a further 10 minutes, or until chops are tender and garnish is hot again.

7. Transfer chops to a heated serving dish. Garnish with mushrooms and olives, and sprinkle with finely chopped tarragon. Keep hot.

8. Stir double cream into sauce and bring to the boil, scraping bottom and sides of pan clean with a wooden spoon. Correct seasoning. If sauce is very thin, thicken it by stirring in a little cornflour worked to a smooth paste with a few tablespoons of the sauce, and simmering it for 2 or 3 minutes longer.

9. Spoon some of the sauce over chops and garnish, and serve remainder in a heated sauceboat.

Serves 4

Veal Czarina

IMPERIAL	METRIC
2 13-oz. cans asparagus tips	2 368-g. cans asparagus tips
2 lb. boned loin of veal	900 g. boned loin of veal
3 tablespoons butter	3 tablespoons butter
1 small onion, finely chopped	1 small onion, finely chopped
2 tablespoons flour	2 tablespoons flour
$\frac{1}{4}$ pint sour cream	$1\frac{1}{2}$ dl. sour cream
lemon juice	lemon juice
parsley	parsley
freshly ground black pepper	freshly ground black pepper

1. Drain juice from cans of asparagus tips and reserve.

2. Cut veal into 1-inch (2½-cm.) cubes, discarding any fat or gristle.

3. Melt 2 tablespoons butter in a deep frying pan or heavy casserole without letting it colour. Add pieces of veal and sauté gently on all sides until golden.

4. Add finely chopped onion and sauté for a few minutes longer. Do not season meat as asparagus juices will probably contribute enough salt.

5. Sprinkle veal and onions with flour and cook for another minute, taking great care not to let ingredients brown.

6. Moisten with ½ pint (3 dl.) of the reserved asparagus juice; stir well, cover and simmer for 15 to 20 minutes or until veal is tender.

7. Wrap the asparagus from one can in a neat foil parcel with 1 tablespoon butter and heat in the oven until warmed through.

8. Purée remaining asparagus in a blender or rub through a fine sieve.

9. Stir purée into the veal together with sour cream, a squeeze of lemon juice and chopped parsley. Taste for seasoning—you may only want to add a little freshly ground black pepper. Simmer for 7 to 8 minutes longer.

10. Transfer veal to a heated serving dish. Pour over sauce. Arrange warmed asparagus stems attractively in small bunches around side of dish and serve immediately.

Serves 4–6

Chef's tip:

You can use fresh asparagus when it is at its cheapest from May to July. Use 2 lb. mature asparagus; cook tips and stems in separate pans of simmering water, tips for 8 minutes, stems 3 to 5 minutes more. Use cooking liquor in recipe. Purée tips and reserve stems for garnish.

Blanquette de Veau

IMPERIAL	METRIC
5 oz. butter	150 g. butter
2½ lb. boned veal shoulder, cut into 1-inch cubes	1¼ kg. boned veal shoulder, cut into 2½-cm. cubes
2 pints chicken stock	generous litre chicken stock
2 carrots, chopped	2 carrots, chopped
1 leek, white parts only, coarsely chopped	1 leek, white parts only, coarsely chopped
1 small stalk celery, coarsely chopped	1 small stalk celery, coarsely chopped
bouquet garni	bouquet garni
6 oz. small button mushrooms, thinly sliced	175 g. small button mushrooms, thinly sliced
juice of 1 lemon	juice of 1 lemon
24 button onions	24 button onions
salt and freshly ground black pepper	salt and freshly ground black pepper
1 oz. flour	25 g. flour
2 egg yolks	2 egg yolks
4 tablespoons double cream	4 tablespoons double cream
1 tablespoon finely chopped parsley	1 tablespoon finely chopped parsley

1. Melt 2 oz. (50 g.) butter in a heavy pan; sauté veal cubes without letting them colour.

2. Add stock; bring to the boil and add coarsely chopped vegetables and bouquet garni. Cover and simmer over a low heat for 1¼ hours, or until veal is tender.

3. In another pan, toss mushrooms over a low heat in melted butter, with a few drops of lemon juice to preserve their colour. Cover and simmer gently until softened.

4. Melt another 1 oz. (25 g.) butter in a pan and sauté button onions until golden, adding 2 tablespoons stock from pan of veal. Season to taste with salt and pepper.

5. When veal is tender, drain and remove pieces and keep hot. Strain pan juices into a bowl.

6. Melt remaining butter in the rinsed out pan; add flour and stir over a low heat for 2 or 3 minutes to make a pale roux. Gradually add strained pan juices and bring to the boil, stirring until sauce is smooth; simmer for 2 or 3 minutes. Add mushrooms to sauce; simmer for 10 minutes.

7. Beat egg yolks with cream and 1 tablespoon lemon juice. Beat in a few tablespoons of the hot sauce; pour back into pan and stir over a low heat until sauce thickens. Do not allow to boil, or it may curdle.

8. Add veal to the sauce and heat through for a few minutes longer, taking the same care not to let pan come to boiling point. Serve blanquette immediately, garnished with finely chopped parsley, and accompanied by plain boiled rice.

Serves 4–6

Veal à la King

IMPERIAL	METRIC
1 lb. cold roast veal	450 g. cold roast veal
½ green sweet pepper, cored and seeded	½ green sweet pepper, cored and seeded
2 oz. butter	50 g. butter
1 oz. flour	25 g. flour
½ pint hot chicken stock	3 dl. hot chicken stock
¼ pint double cream	1½ dl. double cream
4 oz. button mushrooms	100 g. button mushrooms
2 tablespoons diced canned red pimento	2 tablespoons diced canned red pimento
1 teaspoon lemon juice	1 teaspoon lemon juice
salt and freshly ground black pepper	salt and freshly ground black pepper
1 egg yolk	1 egg yolk

1. Cut veal and green pepper into ⅓-inch (¾-cm.) dice.

2. Melt half the butter in a heavy pan. Blend in flour smoothly with a wooden spoon and stir over a low heat for 2 minutes to make a pale roux. Gradually add hot chicken stock to roux, stirring vigorously to prevent flour lumping. Stir in cream.

3. When sauce is thick and smooth, add veal and bring to the boil over a low heat, stirring. Simmer gently for 30 minutes, stirring from time to time to prevent veal sticking to bottom of pan.

4. Wipe mushrooms clean. Trim stems and slice mushrooms.

5. Melt remaining butter in a frying pan, and sauté green pepper and mushrooms over a moderate heat for 8 to 10 minutes until soft and golden.

6. Stir contents of frying pan into veal mixture, together with red pimento, lemon juice, and salt and freshly ground black pepper, to taste.

7. Beat egg yolk lightly with a fork.

8. When veal mixture comes to simmering point again, remove pan from heat and add lightly beaten egg yolk, stirring vigorously to prevent it curdling. Continue to stir until sauce thickens slightly—there is no need to return pan to the stove as egg will cook sufficiently from the heat of the sauce.

9. Serve hot on a bed of boiled white rice.

Serves 3–4

Chef's tip:
White sauces should always be made in a heavy-bottomed enamelled, stainless steel or tin-lined copper saucepan. If a thin pan is used, the sauce may scorch on the base of the pan. Aluminium tends to discolour a white sauce, especially one with wine or egg.

Cold Curried Veal

IMPERIAL	METRIC
8 oz. cold roast veal	225 g. cold roast veal
2 crisp eating apples	2 crisp eating apples
1 green sweet pepper	1 green sweet pepper
4 stalks celery, thinly sliced	4 stalks celery, thinly sliced
¼ pint double cream	1½ dl. double cream
salt	salt
Curry sauce:	*Curry sauce:*
1 shallot, finely chopped	1 shallot, finely chopped
2 tablespoons butter	2 tablespoons butter
2 tablespoons flour	2 tablespoons flour
2 teaspoons curry paste	2 teaspoons curry paste
1 tablespoon mango chutney	1 tablespoon mango chutney
1 teaspoon tomato paste	1 teaspoon tomato paste
¾ pint milk	4 dl. milk
salt	salt
lemon juice	lemon juice

1. Prepare sauce, which must be allowed to cool. In a heavy pan, sauté finely chopped shallot in butter for 3 to 4 minutes until soft and transparent.

2. Blend in flour with a wooden spoon to make a roux, and simmer for 1 minute longer.

3. Add curry paste, mango chutney and tomato paste; mix well.

4. Gradually add milk, stirring vigorously to prevent flour lumping.

5. Bring the sauce to the boil, stirring, and simmer gently for 30 minutes, stirring occasionally.

6. Rub sauce through a fine sieve into a bowl. Season to taste with salt and a few drops of lemon juice, and allow to cool.

7. Meanwhile, cut veal into ⅓-inch (¾-cm.) dice. Peel, core and cut apples into ⅓-inch dice. Seed and core pepper, and cut into ⅓-inch dice.

8. In a bowl, toss diced ingredients with thinly sliced celery.

9. Blend double cream into cold curry sauce.

10. Mix sauce with veal mixture; correct seasoning and chill lightly until ready to serve.

Serves 4

Chef's tip:
Another version of this dish is to substitute ½ pint (3 dl.) thick lemon mayonnaise for the sauce. Flavour with 2 tablespoons curry paste and 1 tablespoon mango chutney, and combine with prepared ingredients—delicious and more suitable for a summer meal.

Pork and Lamb

Lamb

We produce some of the finest lamb in the world, as good as any that can be found in France, yet once again, it has been left to the French to show us how it should be roasted. They take it just far enough for the juices to run pink and not, as is the unhappy custom both in this country and the United States, until the meat is grey and dry, and practically falling away from the bone.

If you insist on serving lamb 'well-done', then at least be extra careful not to take it beyond the stage where the juices not only run clear, but virtually cease to flow altogether: 170°F. (77°C.) is quite enough, whatever your meat thermometer may advocate.

I enjoy roasting lamb. It is less of a hit-and-miss affair than beef, providing you follow the rules. Lamb positively welcomes being flavoured with a whole range of herbs, garlic, wine or lemon juice, used lightly or strongly as the mood takes one. And there is such a variety of cuts to choose from, including some of the cheapest ones, for roasting plain, or for boning and stuffing with a savoury, sour or sweet mixture, according to your fancy.

How to choose lamb

Unlike beef, good lamb should have a fine texture, the meat lean and lightly pink, the fat firm, almost brittle, and white with a blush of pink. Look for a high proportion of meat to bone and fat—and always demand that the butcher turn the joint over so that you can examine it from all sides. Human nature being what it is, you will almost certainly have been shown the joint to its best advantage. Check that the fat is evenly distributed and not thick.

To prepare lamb for roasting

Remove joint from the refrigerator and wipe it clean with a damp cloth. Cut away any loose lumps of excess fat, leaving the meat protected with an even layer over the surface. Pare off any official marks that have been stamped on. The 'fell' or tough, papery outer skin is left on when roasting to help keep the joint in shape.

Next, for the simplest seasoning of all, rub the meat vigorously with a cut clove of garlic; season generously with salt and freshly ground black pepper, and spread with softened butter—4 tablespoons should be enough for a large joint—and sprinkle with a little dried rosemary.

Pork

There can never be any excuse for buying a 'pig in a poke', since the quality of pork can safely be judged by appearance alone.

Look for pale pink meat with a fine grain, firm to the touch and smooth in texture. The fat, too, should be on the firm side and pearly white in colour, and there should be plenty of it. The bones should be tinged with pink where they have been cut. Avoid dark meat, flabby meat, a coarse texture and/or hard white bones. These are sure indications of an older animal. Most important of all, remember that fresh pork should have *no* smell.

When it comes to indicating cuts that can be roasted, the answer is again simple: any cut of pork can be roasted provided that (*a*) it is fat enough, and (*b*) there is enough meat on it to make roasting worthwhile. A lean piece of belly pork, for example, makes an economical and hearty roast for the family, but a very fat one will give you little but crackling— and fat.

When buying a pork roast, allow one good-sized chop, 6–8 oz. (175–225 g.) boned and rolled meat, or 8–12 oz. (225–350 g.) meat on the bone per person, a little more if the meat is very fat or has a greater than average proportion of bone.

Pork joints, especially those that are awkward to carve on the bone, may be boned and rolled with stuffing like any other meat. Loins should be chined by a butcher. Pork is practically self-basting pro-vided the fat stays on top so that it can run down the sides of the joint as it melts, but take a look at it and spoon over some of the pan juices occasionally. If the crackling appears to be browning too fast, protect it with a *loose* covering of foil.

Roast Pork with Herbs

IMPERIAL	METRIC
1 loin of pork, about 2 lb., chined	1 loin of pork, about 900 g., chined
4 tablespoons softened butter	4 tablespoons softened butter
1½ tablespoons French mustard	1½ tablespoons French mustard
1 bay leaf, crumbled	1 bay leaf, crumbled
½ teaspoon dried thyme	½ teaspoon dried thyme
salt and freshly ground black pepper	salt and freshly ground black pepper

1. Preheat oven to hot (450°F., 230°C., Gas Mark 8).

2. With the point of a sharp knife, make incisions all over the joint about 1 inch (2½ cm.) deep.

3. Blend butter with French mustard, crumbled bay leaf and thyme.

4. Season pork with salt and freshly ground black pepper and spread with mustard butter, making sure it goes deep into the incisions.

5. Roast in the usual way, lowering heat to 300°F., 150°C., Gas Mark 2 after the first 15 minutes. Serve with tomato halves scooped out and filled with cooked peas.

Serves 4–6

Roast Loin of Pork à la Boulangère

IMPERIAL	METRIC
2 lb. potatoes, peeled and thinly sliced	1 kg. potatoes, peeled and thinly sliced
1 large Spanish onion, shredded	1 large Spanish onion, shredded
3 tablespoons finely chopped parsley	3 tablespoons finely chopped parsley
$\frac{1}{2}$ teaspoon dried savory	$\frac{1}{2}$ teaspoon dried savory
salt and freshly ground black pepper	salt and freshly ground black pepper
$\frac{1}{4}$ pint chicken stock	$1\frac{1}{2}$ dl. chicken stock
$\frac{1}{4}$ pint single cream	$1\frac{1}{2}$ dl. single cream
2 teaspoons French mustard	2 teaspoons French mustard
4 tablespoons butter	4 tablespoons butter
1 $2\frac{1}{2}$- to 3-lb. piece lean loin of pork (6 large chops), chined	1 $1\frac{1}{4}$- to $1\frac{1}{2}$-kg. piece lean loin of pork (6 large chops), chined

1. Preheat oven to moderately hot (400°F., 200°C., Gas Mark 6).

2. In a bowl, toss thinly sliced potatoes with shredded onion, chopped parsley, savory, and salt and freshly ground black pepper to taste.

3. Blend chicken stock with cream and mustard in another bowl; pour over potatoes and mix well.

4. Butter a large, shallow baking dish and cover bottom with raw potato slices, spreading them out in an even layer. Pour over any liquid remaining in the bowl.

5. Lay pork on top, fat side up; dot pork and potatoes with remaining butter and roast for about 2 hours, or until pork is thoroughly cooked and potatoes are tender and crisp on top. (Test potatoes under the joint particularly carefully as they usually take longest to become tender.)

6. Divide loin into chops and serve very hot with potatoes, straight from the baking dish.

Serves 6

Chef's tip:
It is very important to select a lean joint of pork for this dish, otherwise the potatoes will become heavy and saturated with grease. If you feel the dish needs skimming of fat, do so immediately you take it out of the oven, before the potatoes have had a chance to absorb it.

Roast Pork Italian Style

IMPERIAL	METRIC
2 fat cloves garlic	2 fat cloves garlic
3 tablespoons finely chopped Spanish onion	3 tablespoons finely chopped Spanish onion
2 tablespoons olive oil	2 tablespoons olive oil
1 3-lb. piece loin of pork, rind removed	1 $1\frac{1}{3}$-kg. piece loin of pork, rind removed
about 1 teaspoon rosemary needles	about 1 teaspoon rosemary needles
salt and freshly ground black pepper	salt and freshly ground black pepper
1 large or 2 small bay leaves, crumbled	1 large or 2 small bay leaves, crumbled

1. Preheat oven to moderate (375°F., 190°C., Gas Mark 5).

2. Peel garlic and cut each clove into six slivers.

3. Mix finely chopped onion with olive oil.

4. With a thick skewer, pierce pork loin deeply in twelve places. Push a garlic sliver, a little chopped onion mixture and three or four rosemary needles into each hole.

5. Season joint all over with salt and freshly ground black pepper; sprinkle with crumbled bay leaves and lay it in a roasting tin.

6. Pour about $\frac{1}{2}$ inch (1 cm.) boiling water around the pork. Transfer to the oven and roast for about 35 minutes per lb., or until meat is thoroughly cooked, but still moist and tender.

7. To serve, transfer joint to a heated serving dish and divide into chops. Skim fat from pan juices and serve juices with the roast.

Serves 6

Chef's tip:
Ask your butcher to remove the rind and about half of the fat from a loin of pork, and chine it to make the carving of it easier; or do it yourself with a large sharp knife. A 3-lb. ($1\frac{1}{3}$-kg.) piece of loin of pork will be about six chops.

Roast Loin of Pork with Apricots and Prunes

Pork Chops with Apple Rings

IMPERIAL	METRIC
1 3-lb. loin of pork, in one piece	1 1⅓-kg. loin of pork, in one piece
4 oz. plump dried prunes	100 g. plump dried prunes
4 oz. dessert apricots	100 g. dessert apricots
2 oz. sugar	50 g. sugar
salt and freshly ground black pepper	salt and freshly ground black pepper
¼ teaspoon dried thyme	¼ teaspoon dried thyme
2 tablespoons softened butter	2 tablespoons softened butter

1. Preheat oven to moderately hot (400°F., 200°C., Gas Mark 6).

2. Remove skin from loin of pork, taking some of the fat with it if too thick.

3. Put prunes and apricots in a pan with sugar and 1 pint (6 dl.) water. Bring to the boil, cover and simmer for 20 minutes, or until fruits are soft but still firm, removing lid halfway through cooking time. Drain fruits. Stone prunes carefully.

4. Score loin of pork lengthwise at 1-inch (2½-cm.) intervals to a depth of 1½ inches (3¾ cm.). Season meat generously with salt and freshly ground black pepper, and rub with thyme.

5. Fill scores with prunes and apricots in alternating bands.

6. Tie joint securely at intervals with several bands of string. Place it in a roasting tin lined with foil and spread top with softened butter.

7. Roast for 1½ to 2 hours, or until cooked through, adding 1 or 2 tablespoons boiling water occasionally to prevent pan juices burning. If bands of fruit caramelise too quickly, lower oven temperature slightly or cover joint with crumpled foil.

8. Transfer joint to a heated serving dish and serve glazed with the rich pan juices.

Serves 6

IMPERIAL	METRIC
4 pork chops, 1 inch thick	4 pork chops, 2½ cm. thick
salt and freshly ground black pepper	salt and freshly ground black pepper
2 large crisp tart dessert apples	2 large crisp tart dessert apples
2 tablespoons demerara sugar	2 tablespoons demerara sugar
2 tablespoons butter	2 tablespoons butter
4 tablespoons apple juice or 2 tablespoons each apple juice and water	4 tablespoons apple juice or 2 tablespoons each apple juice and water
parsley, to garnish	parsley, to garnish

1. Trim excess fat from pork chops. Chop up fat and place in a frying pan over a moderate heat until fat has melted and pieces are shrivelled and crisp.

2. Dry chops with absorbent paper. Season generously with salt and freshly ground black pepper.

3. Remove fat bits from pan with a slotted spoon. Add chops and fry over a moderately high heat for 5 minutes on each side.

4. Meanwhile, core apples and slice into thick rings. Toss with sugar.

5. When chops are well browned on both sides and practically cooked through, remove them from the pan. Keep hot.

6. Add butter to the pan and, when it has melted, sauté apples for 2 to 3 minutes until coloured on both sides and beginning to soften.

7. Bury chops among the apple rings and continue to fry for a further 4 to 5 minutes, or until chops are cooked through, turning once. Some of the apple slices will start off under the chops—see that you transpose them with those on top when you turn the chops.

8. Remove pan from heat. Arrange chops on a heated serving dish and garnish with sautéed apple. Keep hot.

9. Add apple juice (or apple juice and water) to the pan. Return to a moderate heat and bring to the boil, scraping surface of pan clean with a wooden spoon. Taste and add salt or freshly ground black pepper if necessary. Pour over chops and serve immediately, garnished with parsley.

Serves 4

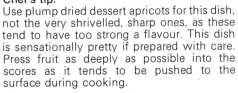

Chef's tip:
Use plump dried dessert apricots for this dish, not the very shrivelled, sharp ones, as these tend to have too strong a flavour. This dish is sensationally pretty if prepared with care. Press fruit as deeply as possible into the scores as it tends to be pushed to the surface during cooking.

Chef's tip:
The only way to tell if chops, steaks, etc., are done to your liking is actually to take a look and see, and the only way to do that is to take a sharp knife and make a cut through meat and open it up to see. (You can always serve yourself the cut chop or steak.)

Pork and Prune Brochettes

IMPERIAL	METRIC
3 strips pork fillet (about 1 lb.)	3 strips pork fillet (about 450 g.)
¼ pint olive oil	1½ dl. olive oil
juice of 1 lemon	juice of 1 lemon
3 shallots, thinly sliced	3 shallots, thinly sliced
2 tablespoons pickling spice	2 tablespoons pickling spice
1 teaspoon dried sage	1 teaspoon dried sage
salt and freshly ground black pepper	salt and freshly ground black pepper
24 large plump prunes	24 large plump prunes
12 thin slices smoked streaky bacon	12 thin slices smoked streaky bacon

1. Cut the pork into large cubes.

2. Combine next five ingredients in a large bowl, adding salt and freshly ground black pepper, to taste.

3. Marinate pork cubes in this mixture for at least 1 hour, turning them occasionally to ensure that they remain evenly coated.

4. At the same time, cover prunes with 2 pints (a generous litre) warm water and leave to swell and soften for 1 hour.

5. Cut each slice of bacon in half lengthwise.

6. When ready to cook brochettes, pour prunes with their soaking liquid into a saucepan; bring to the boil and simmer for 10 to 15 minutes, or until prunes are soft but not disintegrating.

7. In the meantime, drain pork cubes thoroughly.

8. Drain cooked prunes; with a sharp knife slit down one side and remove stones. Wrap each prune in a half-slice of bacon.

9. Turn on grill, set at maximum, to allow it about 20 minutes' preheating.

10. Thread pork cubes onto skewers alternately with bacon-wrapped prunes. Continue until pork and prunes are used up, dividing them equally between skewers.

11. Cook brochettes under preheated grill for 10 to 15 minutes, turning them frequently and lowering the heat to moderate after the first turn. Pork should be well cooked but not dry.

12. Sprinkle brochettes with salt and freshly ground black pepper, and serve immediately with pan juices, if any, poured over the top.

Serves 4

Pork Pie with Sage Scone Topping

IMPERIAL	METRIC
1½–2 lb. boned shoulder of pork	675–900 g. boned shoulder of pork
seasoned flour	seasoned flour
2 tablespoons olive oil	2 tablespoons olive oil
2 tablespoons lard	2 tablespoons lard
1 large Spanish onion, coarsely chopped	1 large Spanish onion, coarsely chopped
4 stalks celery, thinly sliced	4 stalks celery, thinly sliced
¾ pint chicken stock	4 dl. chicken stock
2 teaspoons Worcestershire sauce	2 teaspoons Worcestershire sauce
1 small bay leaf	1 small bay leaf
3 large potatoes, peeled and cut into 1-inch cubes	3 large potatoes, peeled and cut into 2½-cm. cubes
1 8-oz. packet frozen peas	1 226-g. packet frozen peas
1 sugar lump	1 sugar lump
salt and freshly ground black pepper	salt and freshly ground black pepper
chopped parsley	chopped parsley
Sage scone topping:	*Sage scone topping:*
1 recipe butter scones (see page 110)	1 recipe butter scones (see page 110)
1 teaspoon dried sage	1 teaspoon dried sage
freshly ground black pepper	freshly ground black pepper

1. Cut shoulder of pork into 1½-inch (3¾-cm.) cubes and toss meat in seasoned flour.

2. Heat 1 tablespoon each of olive oil and lard in a large, heavy casserole (ideally, 9½ to 10 inches (23 to 25 cm.) in diameter and of about 6-pint (3½-litre) capacity). Fry meat over a moderately high heat, turning frequently until golden brown all over. When ready, drain and remove meat.

3. Add remaining oil and lard to casserole and sauté onion and celery. Cook for 10 minutes, stirring occasionally.

4. Return meat to casserole; add stock, Worcestershire sauce and bay leaf. Cover and simmer very gently for 1 hour.

5. After 1 hour, add cubed potatoes; cover and simmer for a further 30 minutes.

6. Meanwhile, make the topping. Prepare butter scones, adding sage and freshly ground black pepper to dry ingredients. Preheat oven to hot (425°F., 220°C., Gas Mark 7).

7. Remove casserole from heat; discard bay leaf. Stir in frozen peas and sugar lump. Season to taste with salt and freshly ground black pepper. Top with a circle of overlapping butter scones around inside edge of casserole.

8. Bake for 15 to 20 minutes until butter scones are well risen and golden. Sprinkle with chopped parsley; serve.

Serves 4–6

Boiled Ham Pot with Cornmeal Dumplings

IMPERIAL	METRIC
1 ham hock	1 ham hock
1 small plump roasting chicken	1 small plump roasting chicken
2 Spanish onions, quartered	2 Spanish onions, quartered
6 carrots, cut into chunks	6 carrots, cut into chunks
10 small potatoes, peeled	10 small potatoes, peeled
salt and freshly ground black pepper	salt and freshly ground black pepper
2 heads firm cabbage, quartered	2 heads firm cabbage, quartered
Cornmeal dumplings:	*Cornmeal dumplings:*
5 oz. cornmeal	150 g. cornmeal
5 oz. self-raising flour	150 g. self-raising flour
$\frac{1}{2}$ teaspoon salt	$\frac{1}{2}$ teaspoon salt
2 tablespoons butter	2 tablespoons butter
1 egg, beaten	1 egg, beaten
4 tablespoons milk	4 tablespoons milk

1. In a heavy, 8-pint ($4\frac{1}{2}$-litre) saucepan or flameproof casserole, simmer ham hock and chicken in water to cover for 1 to $1\frac{1}{4}$ hours, or until tender.

2. Add quartered onions, carrots and potatoes. Taste stock and season with salt and freshly ground black pepper (ham hock may already be salty enough). Simmer for 20 minutes longer.

3. Cut cabbage into wedges and add to pot. Simmer for 10 minutes.

4. Prepare cornmeal dumplings. Sift cornmeal, flour and salt into a bowl. Rub in butter until mixture resembles fine breadcrumbs; add beaten egg and enough of the milk to make a soft dough.

5. Drop rounded teaspoonfuls of cornmeal batter into the simmering stock. Cover and cook gently until dumplings are firm and well risen, 10 to 15 minutes. Serve hot.

Serves 8

Chef's tip:
Make sure that the vegetables are cooked just to the point of doneness. Ham hocks vary in saltiness, so taste particularly carefully before adding salt to the stock. Simmer stock very gently once you have added the dumplings or they will disintegrate because of the boiling action.

Glazed Gammon Steaks

IMPERIAL	METRIC
4 gammon steaks, about $\frac{1}{3}$ inch thick	4 gammon steaks, about $\frac{3}{4}$ cm. thick
4 oz. Gruyère cheese, finely grated	100 g. Gruyère cheese, finely grated
2 tablespoons double cream	2 tablespoons double cream
2 teaspoons Dijon mustard	2 teaspoons Dijon mustard
freshly ground black pepper	freshly ground black pepper
chopped parsley, to garnish	chopped parsley, to garnish

1. Cook gammon steaks on one side under a preheated moderate grill for 5 minutes.

2. Meanwhile, blend grated Gruyère, double cream and mustard to a stiff, spreadable paste. Season lightly with freshly ground black pepper.

3. Turn gammon steaks over and continue to grill for a further 5 minutes.

4. Spread steaks with cheese paste and slip back under the grill for a final 5 minutes, or until topping is bubbling and golden brown. Serve immediately, garnished with chopped parsley.

Serves 4

Chef's tip:
To save on washing up, line your grill pan with foil to protect it. This cheese paste is also delicious on toast for a quick snack. Toast bread on one side, turn and toast lightly on the other; spread thinly with butter and then with cheese paste; grill until golden on top.

Ham Steaks en Papillote

IMPERIAL	METRIC
4 tablespoons butter	4 tablespoons butter
2 tablespoons finely chopped onion	2 tablespoons finely chopped onion
8 button mushrooms, finely chopped	8 button mushrooms, finely chopped
$\frac{1}{2}$–1 tablespoon lemon juice	$\frac{1}{2}$–1 tablespoon lemon juice
2 tablespoons Madeira	2 tablespoons Madeira
2 tablespoons tomato paste	2 tablespoons tomato paste
2 tablespoons finely chopped parsley	2 tablespoons finely chopped parsley
4 ham steaks, sliced $\frac{1}{4}$ inch thick	4 ham steaks, sliced $\frac{1}{2}$ cm. thick
sprigs of watercress, to garnish	sprigs of watercress, to garnish

1. Preheat oven to moderate (375°F., 190°C., Gas Mark 5).

2. In a small pan, heat butter until frothy. Add finely chopped onion and mushrooms; sprinkle with lemon juice and cook over a low heat for 8 to 10 minutes, stirring frequently, until pale golden.

3. Remove pan from heat. Stir in Madeira, tomato paste and parsley.

4. Cut four squares of foil large enough to envelop ham steaks completely.

5. Spread each slice of ham with an eighth of the prepared mixture; lay each ham slice in the centre of a square of foil, spread side down. Then spread other side with the remaining mixture.

6. Seal foil packets neatly and carefully so that no juices escape during cooking. Arrange them on a baking sheet.

7. Bake packets for 15 minutes; then flip them over with a spatula and bake for 10 minutes longer.

8. Serve ham slices with the foil wrapping undone, and garnished with sprigs of watercress.

Serves 4

Chef's tip:
Wrap ham steaks very loosely in foil, dull side on the inside. Only wrap foil tightly when storing food, then the foil acts as a preservative and completely insulates one smell from another when stored in the refrigerator. If wrapped tightly for baking, food is successfully insulated against the heat.

Ham and Cheese Fritters

IMPERIAL	METRIC
$1\frac{1}{2}$ oz. butter	40 g. butter
$1\frac{1}{2}$ oz. flour	40 g. flour
$\frac{1}{2}$ pint milk	3 dl. milk
4 oz. Cheddar cheese, freshly grated	100 g. Cheddar cheese, freshly grated
salt and freshly ground black pepper	salt and freshly ground black pepper
pinch cayenne	pinch cayenne
pinch freshly grated nutmeg	pinch freshly grated nutmeg
3 oz. sliced lean cooked ham, diced	75 g. sliced lean cooked ham, diced
oil for deep-frying	oil for deep-frying
flour	flour
1–2 eggs, beaten	1–2 eggs, beaten
dry white breadcrumbs	dry white breadcrumbs

1. Make a thick white sauce with the butter, flour and milk. Beat in grated Cheddar; season lightly with salt and generously with freshly ground black pepper, and add a pinch each of cayenne and freshly grated nutmeg.

2. Fold in diced ham.

3. Oil a large plate or baking sheet and spread out cheese sauce in an even layer about $\frac{1}{4}$ inch ($\frac{1}{2}$ cm.) thick, smoothing it with the side of a broad-bladed knife. Chill in the refrigerator for 2 hours.

4. Heat a pan of oil for deep-frying to 350°F. (177°C.); then lower heat so that temperature holds as steady as possible.

5. Cut cheese and ham mixture, which should be quite solid, into small rectangles (about twenty-four in all). Coat them lightly with flour, dip in beaten egg and coat with breadcrumbs.

6. Drop rectangles into fat, a few at a time so that the temperature does not fall too abruptly. Let them rise to the surface; fry for 1 minute; then flip over and fry for a further 1 or 2 minutes, until fritters are golden brown and crisp all over.

7. Remove with a slotted spoon and drain thoroughly on paper towels. Serve immediately.

Serves 4–6

Chef's tip:
These fritters should be crisp and golden on the outside, with a creamy centre. It is very important to keep the temperature of the oil steady—if you let it fall below 325°F. (163°C.) the fritters will start disintegrating and become heavy with fat.

Bacon and Mushroom Omelette

IMPERIAL	METRIC
5½ oz. butter	150 g. butter
6 oz. smoked bacon, diced	175 g. smoked bacon, diced
2 Spanish onions, thinly sliced	2 Spanish onions, thinly sliced
8 oz. button mushrooms, thinly sliced	225 g. button mushrooms, thinly sliced
salt and freshly ground black pepper	salt and freshly ground black pepper
8 eggs	8 eggs
parsley, to garnish	parsley, to garnish

1. Melt 2 oz. (50 g.) butter in a large, heavy frying pan and sauté diced bacon and sliced onions until onions are soft and golden.

2. Add thinly sliced mushrooms and sauté for 3 minutes longer. Season generously with salt and freshly ground black pepper; remove from the heat and keep hot.

3. Beat eggs lightly in a bowl, adding 1 oz. (25 g.) butter in small pieces. Season with a pinch each of salt and freshly ground black pepper—the filling is already highly seasoned.

4. Melt 2 oz. butter in a large, thick-bottomed omelette pan; pour in egg mixture and proceed as for chicken liver omelette (see page 67), steps 6 to 8. Just before folding it, arrange bacon and mushroom filling down centre; then fold omelette in two.

5. Slip omelette out onto a heated serving dish; brush top with remaining butter on the point of a knife and serve immediately, garnished with a sprig of parsley.

Serves 2 as a substantial main course

Chef's tip:
Buy the bacon in one piece if possible, so that you can dice it into cubes. The cardinal rule when making omelettes is to have the diners ready, seated at the table—make them wait for the omelette, not the omelette wait for the diners; there is a split second's difference between a good and a bad omelette.

Ham Hash

IMPERIAL	METRIC
4 medium-sized potatoes (about 1¼ lb.)	4 medium-sized potatoes (about 575 g.)
salt	salt
8 oz. cooked ham	225 g. cooked ham
1 small onion, quartered	1 small onion, quartered
½ green sweet pepper, seeded and cored	½ green sweet pepper, seeded and cored
freshly ground black pepper	freshly ground black pepper
¼ teaspoon thyme	¼ teaspoon thyme
2 tablespoons butter	2 tablespoons butter
1 tablespoon olive oil	1 tablespoon olive oil
onion rings and a sprig of parsley, to garnish	onion rings and a sprig of parsley, to garnish

1. Boil potatoes in salted water. Drain thoroughly and toss in the dry pan over a moderate heat to evaporate excess moisture.

2. Put potatoes, cooked ham, onion and green pepper through the coarse blade of a mincer. (Or chop them up together very finely indeed.) Season to taste with salt and freshly ground black pepper; add thyme and mix well.

3. Heat butter and oil together in a heavy, 8-inch (20-cm.) frying pan. Add hash mixture; shape into an even cake with a spatula or the back of a spoon, and cook over a moderate heat for 5 minutes, or until cake is crisp and golden underneath.

4. Brown top under a hot grill for 3 to 4 minutes.

5. Garnish with onion rings and a sprig of parsley. Serve immediately, cut into thick wedges.

Serves 2–4

Chef's tip:
A mincer is an extremely valuable piece of equipment to have when using up leftovers, for a dish such as the one above. Mine also gets employed for making coarse breadcrumbs, marmalade, all variety of meat loaves, mincing fish for mousses, etc.

French Ham Crêpes with Cheese Cream

IMPERIAL	METRIC
8 thin crêpes, 4–5 inches in diameter	8 thin crêpes, 10–13 cm. in diameter
4 tablespoons cream cheese	4 tablespoons cream cheese
5 tablespoons sour cream	5 tablespoons sour cream
8 tablespoons double cream	8 tablespoons double cream
salt and freshly ground black pepper	salt and freshly ground black pepper
8 very thin slices cooked ham	8 very thin slices cooked ham
1 oz. Gruyère cheese, freshly grated	25 g. Gruyère cheese, freshly grated

1. Prepare crêpes in advance.

2. In a bowl, combine cream cheese with sour cream and beat until smoothly blended. Gradually beat in double cream. Season to taste with salt and freshly ground black pepper, and chill until ready to serve.

3. To assemble crêpes, lay crêpes out flat on a board and spread them evenly with a third of the cream mixture. Cover each crêpe with a slice of ham; then spread ham with half of the remaining cream.

4. Roll each crêpe up quite tightly and arrange them side by side in a shallow heatproof dish.

5. Spread with remaining cream mixture and sprinkle with grated Gruyère.

6. Just before serving, slip the dish of crêpes under a pre-heated, moderately hot grill for 3 to 4 minutes, or until crêpes are hot through, with a bubbling, golden topping. Serve immediately.

Serves 4 as an appetizer

Chef's tip:
The most satisfactory way to make thin crêpes is to pour a little mixture into the heated pan, swirl the pan quickly so the base is coated with mix, then quickly pour off any liquid surplus; trim off the trail up the side of the pan.

Roast Lamb

IMPERIAL	METRIC
1 leg of lamb, weighing about 3½–4 lb.	1 leg of lamb, weighing about 1½–1¾ kg.
1 fat clove garlic or 2 smaller cloves (optional)	1 fat clove garlic or 2 smaller cloves (optional)
4 tablespoons softened butter	4 tablespoons softened butter
1 teaspoon rosemary needles, crushed	1 teaspoon rosemary needles, crushed
juice of 1 lemon	juice of 1 lemon
salt and freshly ground black pepper	salt and freshly ground black pepper
To finish gravy:	*To finish gravy:*
½ pint lamb or beef stock	3 dl. lamb or beef stock
1 tablespoon butter	1 tablespoon butter
1 tablespoon flour	1 tablespoon flour
salt and freshly ground black pepper	salt and freshly ground black pepper

1. Preheat oven to moderately hot (400°F., 200°C., Gas Mark 6).

2. Check weight of joint and calculate roasting time, allowing 23 minutes per lb. for very pink, 27 minutes per lb. for *rosé* and 31 minutes per lb. for well done. Wipe joint clean with a damp cloth.

3. Peel garlic if used and cut lengthwise into about twenty thin slivers.

4. With the point of a sharp knife, make the same number of deep slits all over surface of meat. Push a sliver of garlic deep into each slit.

5. In a small bowl, beat butter and rosemary with a wooden spoon, gradually adding lemon juice and a generous seasoning of salt and freshly ground black pepper.

6. Spread seasoned butter evenly over meat. Lay it in a rack over a roasting tin (or directly in the tin if the joint will support itself), fat side up.

7. Roast lamb, basting occasionally, not frequently.

8. When roast is cooked to your liking, transfer it to a hot serving platter and leave to 'set' for 15 to 20 minutes at the door of the oven before carving.

9. Meanwhile, skim most of the fat from the roasting tin. Place tin over direct heat; add stock and bring to the boil, stirring and scraping bottom and sides of tin vigorously with a wooden spoon to dislodge the crusty morsels.

10. Mash butter and flour to a smooth paste. Add to the tin in tiny pieces, stirring until they have dissolved in the gravy. Season, then bring to the boil and simmer for 2 or 3 minutes until gravy has thickened. Strain, pour into a heated sauceboat and serve with the lamb.

Serves 6

Roast Leg of Lamb in Parsley Crust

Carré d'Agneau Persillé

IMPERIAL	METRIC
2 tablespoons olive oil	2 tablespoons olive oil
2 cloves garlic, peeled	2 cloves garlic, peeled
½ teaspoon crushed rosemary needles	½ teaspoon crushed rosemary needles
salt and freshly ground black pepper	salt and freshly ground black pepper
1 boned and rolled leg of lamb, about 3½ lb.	1 boned and rolled leg of lamb, about 1½ kg.
2 oz. fine stale bread-crumbs	50 g. fine stale bread-crumbs
3–4 tablespoons finely chopped parsley	3–4 tablespoons finely chopped parsley
little melted butter	little melted butter

1. In a mortar, pound olive oil, garlic and rosemary to a paste. Season generously with salt and freshly ground black pepper.

2. Wipe lamb with a damp cloth. Spread all over with garlic mixture and leave to absorb flavours for 3 hours.

3. Preheat oven to cool (300°F., 150°C., Gas Mark 2). Place lamb in the oven. Calculate roasting time, allowing 23 minutes per lb. for very pink, 28 minutes per lb. for *rosé* and 37 minutes per lb. for well done.

4. Mix breadcrumbs and parsley together in a bowl.

5. Thirty minutes before lamb is due to come out of the oven, spoon off enough of the roasting juices to mix breadcrumbs and parsley to a paste, if need be adding a little melted butter to make it of a spreading consistency.

6. Spread this paste over lamb and return to the oven for the final 30 minutes to finish cooking and brown the crust.

7. Finish gravy as in preceding recipe. Pour into a hot sauceboat and serve with the lamb.

Serves 6

IMPERIAL	METRIC
2 best ends of neck of young lamb, about 1 lb. each	2 best ends of neck of young lamb, about 450 g. each
4 tablespoons softened butter	4 tablespoons softened butter
salt and freshly ground black pepper	salt and freshly ground black pepper
4 oz. fresh white breadcrumbs	100 g. fresh white breadcrumbs
4 tablespoons finely chopped parsley	4 tablespoons finely chopped parsley
½ teaspoon dried marjoram	½ teaspoon dried marjoram
½ teaspoon dried thyme	½ teaspoon dried thyme
finely grated rind of ½ lemon	finely grated rind of ½ lemon
grilled tomatoes, to garnish	grilled tomatoes, to garnish
sprigs of parsley, to garnish	sprigs of parsley, to garnish

1. Preheat oven to moderately hot (400°F., 200°C., Gas Mark 6).

2. Spread best ends with half the butter and season generously with salt and freshly ground black pepper. Place in roasting tin.

3. Roast best ends for 15 minutes. Remove from oven and allow to cool.

4. Meanwhile, make a paste with breadcrumbs, finely chopped herbs, grated lemon rind and the remaining butter.

5. Coat joints of lamb thickly with this mixture, patting it on firmly.

6. Return lamb to the oven and roast for a further 35 to 40 minutes for *rosé*, 10 minutes longer if you prefer it well done. Baste occasionally towards the end of cooking time.

7. Serve garnished with whole grilled tomatoes and sprigs of parsley.

Serves 4–6

 Chef's tip:
Have the butcher bone and roll a leg of lamb; the bone will add another 1 lb. or more to its weight. Transfer roast to a hot serving platter then let it stand at the open door of the turned-off oven for 15 to 20 minutes before carving.

 Chef's tip:
Ask your butcher to chine the best ends and to scrape the tops of the bones clean. After grating lemon (or orange) rinds, use a pastry brush to whisk off the rind which would otherwise remain stuck to the grater.

Lamb Chops with Almonds

IMPERIAL	METRIC
2 tablespoons butter	2 tablespoons butter
1 tablespoon oil	1 tablespoon oil
8 baby lamb chops	8 baby lamb chops
salt and freshly ground black pepper	salt and freshly ground black pepper
4 tablespoons slivered blanched almonds	4 tablespoons slivered blanched almonds
6–8 tablespoons Madeira or port	6–8 tablespoons Madeira or port
parsley, to garnish	parsley, to garnish

1. Heat butter and oil in a large frying pan and sauté lamb chops until lightly browned on both sides and cooked to your liking. Season generously with salt and freshly ground black pepper. Transfer to a heated serving dish and keep hot.

2. Pour off half the fat in the frying pan; add slivered almonds and sauté over a moderately high heat until golden brown. Take care not to burn them.

3. Add Madeira or port and stir rapidly over a moderate heat, scraping bottom and sides of pan clean with a wooden spoon, until sauce sizzles.

4. Pour almonds and sauce over chops; garnish with parsley and serve immediately.

Serves 4

Chef's tip:
Allow 3 to 4 minutes each side for chops including an initial 2 minutes at high heat on each side. This is a simple, easy recipe which will live up to even the most glamorous of occasions.

Lamb Patties in Bacon Collars

IMPERIAL	METRIC
1 Spanish onion, very finely chopped	1 Spanish onion, very finely chopped
1 clove garlic, very finely chopped or crushed	1 clove garlic, very finely chopped or crushed
2 tablespoons butter	2 tablespoons butter
2 tablespoons olive oil	2 tablespoons olive oil
2 oz. soft white bread-crumbs	50 g. soft white bread-crumbs
3–4 tablespoons cold milk	3–4 tablespoons cold milk
1¼ lb. lean minced lamb	575 g. lean minced lamb
3 tablespoons finely chopped parsley	3 tablespoons finely chopped parsley
¼ teaspoon dried marjoram	¼ teaspoon dried marjoram
1 tablespoon tomato ketchup	1 tablespoon tomato ketchup
1 egg	1 egg
salt and freshly ground black pepper	salt and freshly ground black pepper
flour	flour
6–8 slices fat bacon	6–8 slices fat bacon

1. Simmer finely chopped onion and garlic in half the butter and 1 tablespoon olive oil until soft and a rich golden colour. Put aside to cool.

2. Soak breadcrumbs in milk for 5 minutes; then squeeze lightly to remove excess moisture.

3. Put minced lamb in a large bowl. Add cooled sautéed onions and garlic, soaked breadcrumbs, the herbs, tomato ketchup and the egg, and knead vigorously by hand until thoroughly blended. Season with salt and freshly ground black pepper.

4. Divide mixture into six equal-sized portions. Shape them into balls and roll lightly in flour. Dry your hands, flour them lightly and pat balls into cylinders about 2 inches (5 cm.) in diameter and 2½ inches (6 cm.) high.

5. Lay bacon slices on a board and stretch each one out very thinly with the back of a knife.

6. Wrap a strip of bacon round the middle of each patty and secure it in place with thin string, tying it tightly.

7. Heat remaining butter and oil in a frying pan, large enough to take patties. Fry patties slowly until cooked through, about 30 minutes in all.

8. Discard strings. Transfer patties to a heated serving dish and serve very hot.

Serves 6

Lamb in Greek Pastry

IMPERIAL	METRIC
6 large lamb cutlets	6 large lamb cutlets
salt and freshly ground black pepper	salt and freshly ground black pepper
1 tablespoon butter	1 tablespoon butter
1 tablespoon olive oil	1 tablespoon olive oil
6 sheets (about 5 oz.) Greek *phyllo* pastry	6 sheets (about 150 g.) Greek *phyllo* pastry
melted butter	melted butter
3 oz. pâté de foie gras, cut into 6 small rounds	75 g. pâté de foie gras, cut into 6 small rounds
Mushroom duxelles:	*Mushroom duxelles:*
1 tablespoon butter	1 tablespoon butter
½ Spanish onion, very finely chopped	½ Spanish onion, very finely chopped
2 oz. mushrooms, very finely chopped	50 g. mushrooms, very finely chopped
2 oz. cooked ham, very finely chopped	50 g. cooked ham, very finely chopped
salt and freshly ground black pepper	salt and freshly ground black pepper

1. Season lamb cutlets with salt and freshly ground black pepper, and brown them in a mixture of butter and olive oil for 2 to 3 minutes on each side. Remove from pan, cool.

2. Meanwhile, prepare mushroom duxelles. Melt butter in a pan and sauté onion until soft. Add mushrooms and continue to sauté gently until soft. Stir in ham; season to taste with salt and freshly ground black pepper. Cool.

3. Preheat oven to fairly hot (425°F., 220°C., Gas Mark 7).

4. Take one sheet of Greek pastry at a time and fold it in half to make a rectangle. Brush lightly all over with melted butter. Place a round of pâté in the centre; cover with 1 tablespoon mushroom duxelles and lay a sautéed lamb cutlet on top so that the nut of the cutlet covers duxelles. Fold nearside edge of pastry up over the cutlet and the two sides in towards the centre. Brush again with melted butter and twist pastry round cutlet neatly to seal it completely. Lay on a baking sheet, seam side down, and brush all over with melted butter.

5. Bake parcels for 25 to 30 minutes, or until well puffed and golden brown. Serve immediately.

Serves 6

Chef's tip:
Greek pastry or *phyllo* is an almost transparent, paper-like pastry. It can be bought from Cypriot shops in tightly rolled, standard-size sheets sealed in cellophane. Keep the pastry covered as much as possible while you work as it becomes brittle and useless if left exposed to the air for any time.

Marinated Lamb Brochettes

IMPERIAL	METRIC
1½ lb. shoulder of lamb	675 g. shoulder of lamb
8 oz. button mushrooms	225 g. button mushrooms
4 small firm tomatoes	4 small firm tomatoes
3 tablespoons olive oil	3 tablespoons olive oil
salt and freshly ground black pepper	salt and freshly ground black pepper
Marinade:	*Marinade:*
2 cloves garlic, crushed	2 cloves garlic, crushed
2 tablespoons finely chopped parsley	2 tablespoons finely chopped parsley
juice of 1 orange	juice of 1 orange
¼ pint white wine	1½ dl. white wine
3 tablespoons wine vinegar	3 tablespoons wine vinegar
1 teaspoon coarse salt	1 teaspoon coarse salt
1 tablespoon sugar	1 tablespoon sugar
6 black peppercorns	6 black peppercorns
freshly ground black pepper	freshly ground black pepper
pinch dried basil	pinch dried basil
3 sprigs fresh thyme or ½ teaspoon dried thyme	3 sprigs fresh thyme or ½ teaspoon dried thyme
2 bay leaves, crumbled	2 bay leaves, crumbled
To flame:	*To flame:*
1 teaspoon thyme	1 teaspoon thyme
3 tablespoons brandy	3 tablespoons brandy

1. Cut lamb into 1-inch (2½-cm.) cubes and put them in a large bowl. Add all the marinade ingredients and toss thoroughly to coat lamb evenly. Leave to marinate in a cool place for at least 3 hours, preferably longer, tossing meat occasionally to keep it well coated.

2. Half an hour before you are ready to cook brochettes, wash or wipe mushrooms clean and trim off stem ends. Cut tomatoes in half.

3. Light grill, set at maximum, to allow it about 20 minutes' preheating.

4. Drain lamb. Thread cubes onto four large skewers alternately with mushrooms, spearing a tomato half onto the beginning and end of each skewer.

5. Arrange brochettes on the grill pan. Brush all over with olive oil, and season to taste with salt and freshly ground black pepper.

6. Grill for 10 to 12 minutes, or until brochettes are done, turning skewers so that they cook evenly.

7. Arrange brochettes on a heated, flameproof serving dish. Sprinkle with crumbled thyme.

8. Just before serving, flame with brandy. Serve as soon as the flames have died down.

Serves 4

Basic Lamb Stew

IMPERIAL	METRIC
1½ lb. lean boned stewing lamb	675 g. lean boned stewing lamb
salt and freshly ground black pepper	salt and freshly ground black pepper
flour	flour
1 tablespoon oil	1 tablespoon oil
1 tablespoon butter	1 tablespoon butter
1 pint chicken (cube) stock	6 dl. chicken (cube) stock
1 clove garlic, very finely chopped	1 clove garlic, very finely chopped
4 medium-sized carrots	4 medium-sized carrots
6–8 button onions	6–8 button onions
3–4 small potatoes	3–4 small potatoes
3 small white turnips, halved	3 small white turnips, halved
8 oz. frozen peas	225 g. frozen peas
2 tablespoons finely chopped parsley	2 tablespoons finely chopped parsley

1. Cut lamb into 1- to 1½-inch (2½- to 3½-cm.) cubes, discarding fat and gristle. Toss in seasoned flour until well coated.

2. Heat oil and butter in a heavy pan or flameproof casserole and sauté lamb cubes over a steady heat until richly browned all over.

3. Stir in stock and garlic, and season to taste with salt and freshly ground black pepper.

4. Bring to the boil and lower heat; cover pan and simmer gently for 1½ hours, or until meat is almost tender.

5. Meanwhile, scrape carrots; halve them if they are thick and cut them into 2-inch (5-cm.) lengths. Peel button onions. Peel and halve potatoes and turnips.

6. Add prepared vegetables to the stew and simmer, uncovered, for about 20 minutes, or until they, in their turn, are practically cooked.

7. Finally, stir in frozen peas and finely chopped parsley and simmer until tender, about 5 minutes. Correct seasoning and serve.

Serves 4

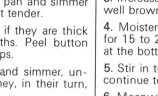

Chef's tip:
To coat meat in seasoned flour, place the seasoned flour in a plastic or strong paper bag. Add the cubed meat a small quantity at a time; grasp the paper bag, firmly closed, and jump the meat up and down in the flour until well coated; no fuss, no mess.

Agnello al Forno

IMPERIAL	METRIC
3 lb. boned leg of lamb (a 4-lb. joint on the bone)	1⅓ kg. boned leg of lamb (a 1¾-kg. joint on the bone)
salt and freshly ground black pepper	salt and freshly ground black pepper
2 sprigs fresh rosemary, finely chopped, or 1 teaspoon crushed dried rosemary	2 sprigs fresh rosemary, finely chopped, or 1 teaspoon crushed dried rosemary
4 tablespoons butter	4 tablespoons butter
6 tablespoons olive oil	6 tablespoons olive oil
2 Spanish onions, finely shredded	2 Spanish onions, finely shredded
½ pint dry white wine or stock	3 dl. dry white wine or stock
1 14-oz. can Italian peeled tomatoes, chopped	1 396-g. can Italian peeled tomatoes, chopped
2 lb. new potatoes	900 g. new potatoes
chopped parsley, to garnish	chopped parsley, to garnish

1. Cut lamb into 1-inch (2½-cm.) cubes, discarding excess fat and sinew, and pat dry. Season to taste with salt and freshly ground black pepper, and sprinkle with rosemary.

2. In a wide, shallow, heatproof casserole, melt butter and oil, and simmer onions over a moderate heat for 4 or 5 minutes until soft and transparent.

3. Increase heat slightly, add cubes of lamb and sauté until well browned on all sides.

4. Moisten with wine or stock; lower heat and simmer for 15 to 20 minutes until there is barely any moisture left at the bottom of the casserole.

5. Stir in tomatoes, together with juices from the can, and continue to simmer, uncovered, for 30 minutes.

6. Meanwhile, preheat oven to moderate (375°F., 190°C., Gas Mark 5), and scrape or peel potatoes.

7. When lamb has been cooking for 30 minutes, add potatoes, spooning pan juices over them until well coated, and transfer casserole to the oven.

8. Bake for about 1 hour, carefully turning contents of casserole over from time to time, until potatoes are brown and soft and lamb is tender. Serve hot, straight from the casserole, garnished with chopped parsley.

Serves 6

Irish Hotpot

IMPERIAL	METRIC
1½ lb. scrag end of mutton	675 g. scrag end of mutton
1 lb. potatoes	450 g. potatoes
8 oz. Spanish onions	225 g. Spanish onions
salt and freshly ground black pepper	salt and freshly ground black pepper
parsley, to garnish	parsley, to garnish

1. Cut neck of mutton into serving pieces.

2. Peel potatoes and slice them ⅛ inch (3 mm.) thick.

3. Peel onions and slice thinly.

4. In a flameproof 3-pint (1¾-litre) casserole or pan, layer ingredients as follows: first some potato slices, then a layer of meat, onions, potato slices, etc., seasoning each layer with salt and freshly ground black pepper, and ending with a layer of potatoes.

5. Pour in 1–1¼ pints (6–7 dl.) cold water to cover; bring to the boil and skim off scum with a slotted spoon.

6. Cover casserole tightly and leave to simmer over the lowest heat possible for 1½ to 2 hours, or until all the ingredients are very tender and imbued with each others' flavour.

7. Garnish and serve straight from the casserole.

Serves 4

Chef's tip:
Middle neck of lamb or mutton can also be used for this stew. For a more elaborate version of the classic dish, use 3 lb. (1⅓ kg.) shoulder of mutton, 1 lb. (450 g.) onions, 2 lb. (900 g.) potatoes, 2 stalks celery and 8 oz. (225 g.) carrots. Layer the vegetables with the meat and proceed as above.

Algerian Stuffed Courgettes

IMPERIAL	METRIC
12 fat courgettes, about 5 inches long	12 fat courgettes, about 13 cm. long
salt	salt
12 oz. cold roast lamb	350 g. cold roast lamb
2 oz. long-grain rice	50 g. long-grain rice
3–4 tablespoons finely chopped parsley	3–4 tablespoons finely chopped parsley
1 large Spanish onion, grated	1 large Spanish onion, grated
1 teaspoon cinnamon	1 teaspoon cinnamon
2 tablespoons gravy from roast	2 tablespoons gravy from roast
freshly ground black pepper	freshly ground black pepper
2 eggs	2 eggs
Tomato sauce:	*Tomato sauce:*
2 lb. tomatoes or 2 14-oz. cans peeled tomatoes	900 g. tomatoes or 2 396-g. cans peeled tomatoes
1 Spanish onion, finely chopped	1 Spanish onion, finely chopped
3–4 tablespoons finely chopped parsley	3–4 tablespoons finely chopped parsley
2 cloves garlic, finely chopped	2 cloves garlic, finely chopped
6–8 tablespoons olive oil	6–8 tablespoons olive oil
paprika, cayenne pepper and salt	paprika, cayenne pepper and salt

1. Make tomato sauce. If using fresh tomatoes, cover with boiling water for 1 minute; drain and peel. Cut in half, remove seeds and chop flesh coarsely. (Canned tomatoes should be drained, seeded and coarsely chopped.)

2. Mix sauce ingredients in a large pan with 1 pint (6 dl.) water. Season generously with paprika, cayenne and salt. Bring slowly to the boil and simmer, uncovered, for 1 hour.

3. Preheat oven to very slow (300°F., 150°C., Gas Mark 2).

4. Trim off stem ends of courgettes and slice in half lengthwise; scoop out seeds and most of the pulp with a teaspoon, taking care not to break through shells. Sprinkle insides lightly with salt and leave upside down to drain.

5. To make filling, put minced lamb in a bowl. Add rice, parsley, onion and cinnamon; mix in gravy and season with salt and freshly ground black pepper. Bind with eggs.

6. Stuff half the courgettes with meat mixture, leaving room for rice to expand. Re-form with remaining halves.

7. Place them side by side in a wide, shallow pan and pour tomato sauce over. Cover casserole and bake for 1 hour, or until courgettes are tender and stuffing, especially rice, well cooked. Add a little hot water from time to time. Serve hot.

Serves 4–6

Chicken and Other Birds

Chicken, ducks, turkey and all the other farm-reared birds that the French clarify under the general heading *volailles* make wonderful eating.

The chicken, particularly, is one of the easiest birds to prepare, and one of the most popular. Whether it is roasted, poached, braised, barbecued or fried, served in a cream or a curry sauce, or casseroled in red or white wine, it is one of the most versatile natural ingredients in our kitchen today.

You'll find many delicious ways of dealing with chickens and the other birds in this chapter. But to my way of thinking, nothing can compare with a tender young spring chicken, marinated in a little dry white wine and olive oil with a touch of chopped onion and bay leaf—or a little honey, lemon juice and soy sauce—and grilled until its skin crackles crisply. Served with a tossed green salad, it is a dish fit for a king.

Poussins can be grilled or spit roasted whole over the open fire or on a rôtisserie spit in the oven. But if the birds are a little larger—2 lb. (900 g.) drawn weight—split them down the middle and grill half a chicken for each guest. If larger, divide the bird into joints before grilling.

To halve a chicken

Lay the chicken on its back with its head towards you, and with a strong, sharp knife, cut right down between the breasts, starting at the vent, then slipping the knife down one side of the breast bone, right through the rib cage and finally through the wishbone. Open the carcass out and chop it away from the backbone on both sides. This will leave you with two sides of chicken plus the backbone, which can be discarded or used to make a stock.

Chop off the tip of each wing and leg at the first joint—all these do is burn up to a frazzle under the grill, so you may as well get rid of them from the start and add them to your stock pot.

To grill a half chicken

1. Preheat your grill as usual, and at the same time turn on the oven set at moderately hot (400°F., 200°C., Gas Mark 6).

2. Season half-chicken all over with salt and freshly ground black pepper; brush it generously with the usual mixture of half butter and half olive oil, and lay it outside up on the rack of your grill pan, which you have lined with double-thickness foil.

3. Slide pan under the grill so that chicken is 3 inches (7½ cm.) from heat and grill for 10 minutes, basting occasionally with its own juices plus a little more butter and oil if necessary. Then turn chicken and grill it on the other side for another 10 minutes.

4. Transfer foil lining and chicken to a baking tray and give it about 10 minutes in the oven to finish cooking.

5. Test for doneness by cutting in at the drumstick. The meat should come away from the bone without any trouble, and the juices that pour out should be a clear golden colour.

To grill chicken joints

Breast and wing joints (about 9 oz. or 250 g.) should be grilled as above for 8 minutes on each side; leg joints (about 6 oz. or 175 g.) need a further minute or two. In neither case do you need to use the oven to finish cooking.

To marinate chicken

A marinade does a lot for chicken. Here are a few combinations:

Marinade I Add 2 cloves of finely chopped garlic and 2 crumbled bay leaves to 6 tablespoons each of olive oil and dry white wine. Brush mixture over chicken halves or chicken joints and marinate them in mixture, turning them one or twice, for at least 2 hours. Grill as above.

Marinade II Combine ½ Spanish onion, finely chopped, with 2 level tablespoons each finely chopped parsley and chervil, 1 level teaspoon powdered cumin, ½ level teaspoon salt and a generous pinch of cayenne pepper. Add ¼ pint (1½ dl.) olive oil or melted butter and marinate chicken as above before grilling.

Marinade III Combine 4 tablespoons each olive oil and dry sherry with 1 clove garlic and ¼ Spanish onion, finely chopped. Add 4 level tablespoons finely chopped parsley, 1 level teaspoon dried oregano and salt and pepper to taste. Marinate and grill as above.

Roast Chicken

IMPERIAL	METRIC
1 3- to 3½-lb. roasting chicken, with giblets	1 1⅓- to 1½-kg. roasting chicken, with giblets
4 oz. butter	100 g. butter
½ teaspoon mixed dried herbs	½ teaspoon mixed dried herbs
salt and freshly ground black pepper	salt and freshly ground black pepper
flour	flour
watercress, to garnish	watercress, to garnish
Giblet stock:	*Giblet stock:*
2 teaspoons butter	2 teaspoons butter
1 carrot, thickly sliced	1 carrot, thickly sliced
1 medium-sized onion, quartered	1 medium-sized onion, quartered
1 stalk celery, coarsely chopped	1 stalk celery, coarsely chopped
bouquet garni	bouquet garni

1. Preheat oven to fairly hot (425°F., 220°C., Gas Mark 7).

2. Cut off chicken wing tips. Reserve with giblets to make a giblet stock for gravy.

3. To make stock, sauté vegetables gently in 2 teaspoons butter for 5 minutes. Add giblets and wing tips. Sauté for a further 10 minutes. Cover with 1 pint (6 dl.) water; add bouquet garni and simmer for 1 hour. Strain and make up to ½ pint (3 dl.) with water if necessary.

4. Beat butter together with herbs and salt and freshly ground black pepper, to taste.

5. Carefully loosen breast skin of chicken by slipping hand under skin, gradually working down, over, and around breast. Use one third of seasoned butter to spread under breast skin of bird.

6. Truss chicken firmly into a neat shape with skewers and string. Spread remaining seasoned butter over breast.

7. Lay chicken on one side in roasting tin. Roast for 15 minutes. Turn bird on its other side; roast for a further 15 to 20 minutes.

8. Reduce oven temperature to 350°F., 180°C., Gas Mark 4 and turn bird on its back. Dust breast with flour and baste with 3–4 tablespoons boiling water.

9. Roast for a further 25 minutes or until chicken is tender.

10. When cooked, remove trussing, drain bird and place on a heated serving dish. Garnish vent with watercress.

11. Skim fat from roasting tin; add giblet stock. Boil for 5 minutes to reduce stock to about ¼ pint (1½ dl.). Stir in 1 tablespoon butter. Season and pour into a heated sauceboat.

Serves 4

Chicken in a Basket

IMPERIAL	METRIC
2 3-lb. frying chickens	2 1⅓-kg. frying chickens
salt and freshly ground black pepper	salt and freshly ground black pepper
2 teaspoons dried tarragon	2 teaspoons dried tarragon
2 teaspoons crushed dried rosemary needles	2 teaspoons crushed dried rosemary needles
4 tablespoons finely chopped parsley	4 tablespoons finely chopped parsley
1 teaspoon finely grated lemon rind	1 teaspoon finely grated lemon rind
5 oz. plain flour	150 g. plain flour
3 eggs	3 eggs
4 oz. fine dry bread-crumbs	100 g. fine dry bread-crumbs
oil for deep-frying	oil for deep-frying
parsley sprigs and lemon wedges, to garnish	parsley sprigs and lemon wedges, to garnish
potato chips, to serve	potato chips, to serve

1. Cut each chicken into eight pieces, two from each leg and two from each breast. Season with salt and freshly ground black pepper.

2. Mix next five ingredients in a bowl and season generously with salt and freshly ground black pepper.

3. In another bowl, beat eggs lightly with 3–4 tablespoons cold water.

4. Put breadcrumbs in a wide, shallow dish.

5. Coat each chicken joint with flour mixture and dip in beaten egg, allowing excess to drain off. Repeat this process once more then coat with breadcrumbs. Chill for about 1 hour to allow coating to 'set' firmly.

6. Heat oil for deep-frying to 350°F. (177°C.) (or until a cube of bread fries golden brown within 60 seconds).

7. Deep-fry three or four chicken joints at a time for 20 to 25 minutes, or until juices run clear when chicken is pricked deeply with a skewer, and breadcrumb coating is crisp and brown.

8. Drain on absorbent paper. Cooked chicken joints will retain their crispness if kept hot in a moderate oven (350°F., 180°C., Gas Mark 4) while remainder is prepared.

9. Arrange chicken pieces in individual baskets lined with thick paper napkins. Garnish each portion with a sprig of parsley and a wedge of lemon. Pile in chips beside them or serve separately. Serve immediately.

Serves 8

Oven-fried Chicken Parmesan

IMPERIAL	METRIC
1 3½-lb. frying chicken	1 1½-kg. frying chicken
1 egg	1 egg
2 tablespoons milk	2 tablespoons milk
3 oz. fresh white bread-crumbs	75 g. fresh white bread-crumbs
1½ oz. Parmesan, freshly grated	40 g. Parmesan, freshly grated
salt and freshly ground black pepper	salt and freshly ground black pepper
seasoned flour	seasoned flour
4 tablespoons butter	4 tablespoons butter
4 tablespoons olive oil	4 tablespoons olive oil
sprigs of watercress, to garnish	sprigs of watercress, to garnish
triangles of fried bread	triangles of fried bread

1. Divide chicken into eight neat pieces; wipe each piece dry with a cloth.

2. Beat egg lightly with milk in a large, deep dish or shallow bowl. Combine breadcrumbs and grated Parmesan in another shallow dish, adding a generous sprinkling of salt and freshly ground black pepper. Put seasoned flour in a third dish.

3. Dust chicken pieces lightly with seasoned flour. Coat each piece with beaten egg; then roll in breadcrumb mixture, patting it on firmly. Chill for about an hour to allow coating to 'set'.

4. Preheat oven to moderately hot (400°F., 200°C., Gas Mark 6).

5. Melt butter and oil in a roasting tin on top of the stove. When it is sizzling, arrange chicken pieces in the tin side by side and spoon fat over them. Transfer tin to oven and bake, turning pieces once or twice, for 30 to 35 minutes, or until they are tender and a crusty golden brown.

6. Serve very hot on a large serving dish, garnished with sprigs of watercress, and triangles of bread fried until golden in combined butter and oil.

Serves 4

Southern Fried Chicken with Gravy

IMPERIAL	METRIC
1 frying chicken, about 3 lb.	1 frying chicken, about 1⅓ kg.
salt and freshly ground black pepper	salt and freshly ground black pepper
seasoned flour	seasoned flour
lard for frying (about 2 lb.)	lard for frying (about 900 g.)
1 oz. butter	25 g. butter
1 oz. flour	25 g. flour
¼ pint milk	1½ dl. milk
¼ pint single cream	1½ dl. single cream
parsley, to garnish	parsley, to garnish

1. Divide chicken into quarters. Season to taste with salt and freshly ground black pepper, then roll each piece in seasoned flour, making sure it is well coated. Shake off excess flour.

2. Select a deep, wide frying pan with a lid (or use a wide, heavy saucepan instead). Melt lard in it to a depth of 2 inches (5 cm.) or more.

3. When lard is hot, add chicken pieces in one layer; cover pan and cook over a low heat for 10 minutes. Then remove lid; raise heat under pan and sauté chicken pieces until nicely browned on both sides and cooked through, about 10 to 12 minutes longer.

4. Prepare sauce. Melt butter in a saucepan and blend in flour. Cook for 1 minute, stirring, taking great care not to let flour colour.

5. Add milk gradually; bring to the boil and simmer, stirring constantly, until sauce is smooth and thick, and no longer tastes of raw flour. Season to taste with salt and freshly ground black pepper.

6. Add cream; correct seasoning if necessary, and stir over a low heat until sauce is hot again but not boiling.

7. Serve fried chicken pieces with a little of the sauce poured over them, and the remainder in a heated sauceboat. Garnish with parsley.

Serves 4

Chef's tip:
For speed and ease in working, organise a 'conveyor belt' assembly line for coating chicken; have chicken ready at one end to dip in seasoned flour, followed by beaten egg and milk, followed by Parmesan/bread-crumb mixture, one straight after the other.

Chef's tip:
This is a classic American dish from the Deep South which is traditionally served with corn fritters and fried bananas. When preparing this dish for more than four people, you will find it easier to work with two pans, but make sure that they are deep ones.

Poulet à la Crème

IMPERIAL	METRIC
1 3½-lb. roasting chicken	1 1½-kg. roasting chicken
butter	butter
salt and freshly ground black pepper	salt and freshly ground black pepper
20–24 button onions	20–24 button onions
1 teaspoon sugar	1 teaspoon sugar
4 egg yolks	4 egg yolks
½ pint double cream	3 dl. double cream
lemon juice	lemon juice
chopped parsley, to garnish	chopped parsley, to garnish

1. Cut chicken into eight serving pieces, two from each breast and two from each leg.

2. Melt 3 oz. (75 g.) butter in a heavy sauté pan or deep frying pan and sauté chicken pieces gently without letting them brown.

3. Season to taste with salt and freshly ground black pepper, and moisten with about ¼ pint (1½ dl.) hot water. Cover pan and simmer gently until chicken is tender, about 20 minutes.

4. Meanwhile, peel onions; put them in a small pan with 1 tablespoon butter, 1 teaspoon sugar and barely enough water (about ¼ pint) to cover. Bring to the boil and simmer for 15 minutes, or until onions are tender and liquid has evaporated. Then continue to cook, stirring constantly, until onions are richly and evenly glazed.

5. When chicken is tender, beat egg yolks lightly and combine them with cream.

6. Transfer chicken pieces to a heated serving dish, using a slotted spoon. Keep hot.

7. Add glazed onions to the pan. Stir in cream and egg yolks, and cook over a very low heat until they have amalgamated with pan juices to form a rich sauce. Take great care not to let sauce boil, or egg yolks will curdle.

8. Correct seasoning with a few drops of lemon juice and more salt or freshly ground black pepper if necessary. Spoon sauce and button onions over chicken, and serve immediately, garnished with chopped parsley.

Serves 4

Chef's tip:
Egg whites can be kept in the refrigerator for several days without deteriorating—in fact, they beat up far more when slightly stale. If you have forgotten how many egg whites you put away for later use, measure 1 egg white to equal 1 oz. (25 g.).

Paprika Chicken Brochettes

IMPERIAL	METRIC
2 Spanish onions, coarsely chopped	2 Spanish onions, coarsely chopped
¼ pint olive oil	1½ dl. olive oil
1 tablespoon dried thyme	1 tablespoon dried thyme
2 bay leaves	2 bay leaves
paprika	paprika
salt and freshly ground black pepper	salt and freshly ground black pepper
4 small courgettes	4 small courgettes
1 3½-lb. chicken	1 1½-kg. chicken
4 small tomatoes, halved and seeded	4 small tomatoes, halved and seeded

1. In a bowl, combine coarsely chopped onions with olive oil, thyme, bay leaves, ½ teaspoon paprika, and salt and freshly ground black pepper, to make marinade.

2. Wash courgettes; trim both ends and cut courgettes into ½-inch (1-cm.) slices. Add them to the marinade.

3. Wipe chicken clean. Remove wings and legs, and with a sharp knife cut away all the meat in large pieces. In the same way, remove meat from breasts and the two oysters in the back. Cut meat into chunks, making them all as even as possible. Add them to the bowl, spoon marinade over them several times and leave to marinate for 2 hours.

4. Light grill, set at maximum, to allow it about 20 minutes' preheating.

5. When ready to grill brochettes, drain chicken and courgettes, reserving marinade. Thread pieces of tomato, chicken and courgette alternately onto four skewers, dividing ingredients evenly between them.

6. Arrange brochettes in grill pan and brush generously with marinating oil. Sprinkle with a little more paprika.

7. Grill brochettes for about 20 minutes, or until chicken is well cooked, lowering the heat to moderate after the first 5 minutes, and turning the skewers at least twice to ensure that they cook evenly. Serve immediately.

Serves 4

Chef's tip:
If you have any small pieces of chicken, thread them onto the skewers two or three at a time. These brochettes are also excellent barbecued over a charcoal fire. Serve them with saffron rice and a mixed green salad.

Chicken and Ham Croquettes

IMPERIAL	METRIC
2 tablespoons butter	2 tablespoons butter
2 tablespoons flour	2 tablespoons flour
$\frac{1}{4}$ pint milk	$1\frac{1}{2}$ dl. milk
$\frac{1}{4}$ pint single cream	$1\frac{1}{2}$ dl. single cream
12 oz. cooked chicken, finely chopped	350 g. cooked chicken, finely chopped
2 oz. cooked ham, finely chopped	50 g. cooked ham, finely chopped
2 tablespoons freshly grated Parmesan	2 tablespoons freshly grated Parmesan
2 egg yolks, lightly beaten	2 egg yolks, lightly beaten
salt and freshly ground black pepper	salt and freshly ground black pepper
To coat croquettes:	*To coat croquettes:*
flour	flour
1 egg	1 egg
2 tablespoons milk	2 tablespoons milk
4 oz. fine stale breadcrumbs	100 g. fine stale breadcrumbs

1. Melt butter in a heavy pan; blend in flour with a wooden spoon and stir over a low heat for 1 minute to make a pale roux.

2. Gradually add milk, followed by cream, stirring vigorously to avoid lumps. Bring to the boil and simmer over a low heat for 3 minutes, stirring.

3. Remove pan from heat. Add finely chopped chicken and ham, grated Parmesan and lightly beaten egg yolks. Mix; season to taste with salt and freshly ground black pepper; cool and chill for at least $\frac{1}{2}$ hour.

4. Flour your hands and divide mixture into eight portions. Shape into croquettes and chill for 15 minutes.

5. Beat egg thoroughly with milk in a shallow dish. Have two other dishes ready, one with more flour, the other with fine dry breadcrumbs.

6. Dust each croquette with flour; dip in egg mixture, allowing excess to drain back into dish, and coat with breadcrumbs.

7. Heat a pan of oil for deep-frying to 375°F. (190°C.), and deep-fry croquettes for about 3 minutes, or until crisp and golden. Drain on absorbent paper and serve immediately.

Serves 3–4

Chef's tip:
If you have stale bread use it to make breadcrumbs rather than throw it away. Keep the breadcrumbs in an airtight plastic container in the refrigerator and they will keep almost indefinitely. Please do not use the shop-bought breadcrumbs like orange grit.

Chicken Liver Omelette

IMPERIAL	METRIC
3 eggs	3 eggs
salt and freshly ground black pepper	salt and freshly ground black pepper
freshly grated Parmesan	freshly grated Parmesan
butter	butter
Chicken liver filling:	*Chicken liver filling:*
2 oz. chicken livers	50 g. chicken livers
12 small, thin onion rings	12 small, thin onion rings
pinch dried sage	pinch dried sage
1 teaspoon port	1 teaspoon port
1 teaspoon butter	1 teaspoon butter

1. Prepare chicken liver filling before making the omelette. Clean livers carefully, removing any green parts or small pieces of membrane, and put them in a bowl with onion rings, a small pinch each of salt, freshly ground black pepper and sage, and a sprinkling of port. Toss lightly and leave for about 30 minutes to allow flavours to develop.

2. Melt butter in a small, heavy frying pan, and when very hot, tip in contents of bowl. Sauté over a high heat for 3 to 5 minutes until juices have evaporated, onion rings are brown and tender, and livers are well browned on the outside but still very pink in the middle.

3. Turn livers and onion rings out onto a plate lined with absorbent paper. Separate them out; slice livers and cut them into small squares. Keep warm.

4. Break eggs into a bowl. Add a teaspoon of cold water; season to taste with salt, freshly ground black pepper and Parmesan. Stir with a fork until well mixed.

5. Melt $\frac{1}{2}$–1 tablespoon butter in the omelette pan over a high heat, swirling it around so that bottom and sides of pan are entirely coated.

6. As soon as foaming subsides and butter is on the point of changing colour, pour in eggs all at once.

7. As soon as eggs are in, take the handle of the pan in your left hand and start shaking it back and forth over the heat. At the same time, scrape bottom of pan with a large fork held flat in your right hand, back and forth several times in one direction, then back and forth at right angles, and bringing in the sides so that eggs cook evenly. Continue working like this for a few seconds, with both hands on the move. Then discard the fork and allow the bottom to set for a few seconds longer. You should feel the omelette slipping freely over the pan, but the surface should still be soft and moist.

8. Just before folding the omelette, scatter chicken livers down the centre. Fold the omelette in three and turn out onto a heated plate. Brush top with butter; garnish with sautéed onion rings and serve immediately.

Serves 1–2

Chicken Mayonnaise with Black Olives

IMPERIAL	METRIC
12 oz. cold cooked chicken meat	350 g. cold cooked chicken meat
4 oz. drained canned tuna	100 g. drained canned tuna
1 head lettuce	1 head lettuce
4 stalks celery, sliced	4 stalks celery, sliced
3 hard-boiled eggs, chopped	3 hard-boiled eggs, chopped
¼ pint thick, home-made mayonnaise	1½ dl. thick, home-made mayonnaise
lemon juice	lemon juice
salt and freshly ground black pepper	salt and freshly ground black pepper
celery salt	celery salt
4 tablespoons stoned and thinly sliced black olives	4 tablespoons stoned and thinly sliced black olives
parsley, to garnish	parsley, to garnish

1. Cut chicken and tuna into neat, ⅓-inch (¾-cm.) dice.

2. Wash and dry lettuce leaves and shred finely.

3. Combine chicken, tuna and shredded lettuce in a bowl with sliced celery and chopped hard-boiled eggs. Mix lightly to avoid crushing ingredients.

4. Dilute mayonnaise by beating in lemon juice—or part lemon juice part water if it begins to taste too lemony. Season quite generously with salt, freshly ground black pepper and celery salt. Stir in sliced black olives.

5. Pour mayonnaise dressing over salad ingredients. Toss lightly until ingredients are thoroughly coated; correct seasoning if necessary and serve, garnished with parsley.

Serves 4–6

Chicken Ham Salad

IMPERIAL	METRIC
1 lb. cooked chicken	450 g. cooked chicken
6 oz. cooked ham	175 g. cooked ham
4 stalks celery, thinly sliced	4 stalks celery, thinly sliced
1 large green sweet pepper, seeded, cored and finely diced	1 large green sweet pepper, seeded, cored and finely diced
2 tablespoons finely chopped parsley	2 tablespoons finely chopped parsley
4 teaspoons finely chopped chives or spring onion tops	4 teaspoons finely chopped chives or spring onion tops
2 large oranges	2 large oranges
2 eating apples	2 eating apples
¼ pint lemon mayonnaise	1½ dl. lemon mayonnaise
6–8 drops Tabasco	6–8 drops Tabasco
generous pinch cinnamon	generous pinch cinnamon
salt and freshly ground black pepper	salt and freshly ground black pepper
lettuce leaves, chopped chives and parsley, to garnish	lettuce leaves, chopped chives and parsley, to garnish

1. Cut cooked chicken and ham into ½-inch (1-cm.) cubes, and combine in a large bowl with sliced celery, diced green pepper and finely chopped herbs.

2. Peel oranges, removing every scrap of white pith. Cut each segment out of its membrane; divide in half and add to the bowl.

3. Peel and core apples, and cut into ½-inch dice. Add to the bowl and toss well.

4. Fold in mayonnaise and season to taste with Tabasco, a good pinch of cinnamon, and salt and freshly ground black pepper.

5. Serve chilled on a bed of lettuce leaves, sprinkled with additional chopped chives and parsley.

Serves 4–6

Chef's tip:
Don't panic if your mayonnaise curdles. Start again with another 2 egg yolks, and whisk them until thick, then gradually add the failed mayonnaise drop by drop. You will lessen the chance of curdling if you start with all the ingredients at room temperature.

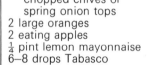

Chef's tip:
A simple way to make a mayonnaise if you have a blender or an electric hand beater is to combine 2 egg yolks with a tablespoon of wine vinegar or lemon juice and ½ teaspoon each of dry mustard and salt. Beat or blend until well mixed and then gradually beat in approximately ½ pint (3 dl.) olive oil in a thin trickle.

Chicken Fruit Salad

IMPERIAL	METRIC
1 large, crisp lettuce, or 2 smaller ones	1 large, crisp lettuce, or 2 smaller ones
12 oz. cooked chicken	350 g. cooked chicken
2 oranges	2 oranges
4 tablespoons sour cream	4 tablespoons sour cream
2 tablespoons double cream	2 tablespoons double cream
salt and freshly ground black pepper	salt and freshly ground black pepper
2 bananas	2 bananas

1. Separate lettuce leaves; wash them carefully and pat each leaf dry in a clean cloth. Roll up in a damp cloth and leave in the vegetable drawer of the refrigerator to crisp up until needed.

2. Cut chicken into ½-inch (1-cm.) dice or large slivers.

3. Just before serving, slice peel and pith from oranges with a razor-sharp knife. Cut out segments over a plate to catch juices, picking out pips as you come across them.

4. Beat sour cream and double cream together with a fork. Beat in juice of oranges and season to taste with salt and freshly ground black pepper.

5. To assemble salad, pour creamy dressing into a salad bowl. Break lettuce leaves into the bowl in fairly large pieces (don't cut them with a knife), and lay orange segments on top.

6. Peel bananas and slice into rounds; scatter over top of salad, together with chicken.

7. Quickly toss ingredients together so that they are completely coated with dressing.

8. Correct seasoning and serve at once.

Serves 4–6

Chef's tip:
If you cannot get any sour cream (this is a *commercially* soured cream, not a cream that has simply 'gone off') stir a little lemon juice into fresh cream and leave for a few minutes. Milk can be soured in the same way.

Turkey Ring Mould

IMPERIAL	METRIC
butter	butter
12 oz. cooked turkey	350 g. cooked turkey
1 medium-sized onion, grated	1 medium-sized onion, grated
4 oz. water biscuits, finely crushed	100 g. water biscuits, finely crushed
4 tablespoons diced canned red pimento	4 tablespoons diced canned red pimento
1 stalk celery, finely diced	1 stalk celery, finely diced
1–2 tablespoons finely chopped parsley	1–2 tablespoons finely chopped parsley
¼ pint milk	1½ dl. milk
¼ pint turkey or chicken stock (cube)	1½ dl. turkey or chicken stock (cube)
2 eggs, beaten	2 eggs, beaten
¾ teaspoon salt	¾ teaspoon salt
freshly ground black pepper	freshly ground black pepper
½ pint hot, well-flavoured white sauce, to serve	3 dl. hot, well-flavoured white sauce, to serve
sprigs of watercress, to garnish	sprigs of watercress, to garnish

1. Preheat oven to moderate (350°F., 180°C., Gas Mark 4).

2. Butter a 2-pint (1-litre), plain ring mould and a square of foil large enough to cover top.

3. Cut cooked turkey meat into small dice.

4. In a small pan, heat 1 tablespoon butter until frothy but not coloured. Add grated onion and simmer gently until soft and golden. Scrape contents of pan into a large bowl.

5. Add diced turkey and remaining ingredients and mix well.

6. Pack mixture into ring mould. Level off top and cover tightly with buttered foil.

7. Stand ring mould in a deep baking dish or roasting tin. Place it just inside the oven door and pour enough hot water into tin to come two-thirds of the way up side of mould.

8. Bake for 50 minutes, or until mixture is firm to the touch.

9. To serve, slip the tip of a knife around sides of mould and turn out onto a heated serving dish. Spoon the hot, white sauce over the turkey ring, garnish centre of ring with sprigs of watercress and serve immediately.

Serves 4

Chef's tip:
A hot water bath, or a 'bain-marie', is used either to cook the food very gently in the oven, or to keep the contents of saucepans hot and ready to serve.

Turkey Divan

IMPERIAL	METRIC
1 9-oz. packet frozen broccoli, cooked	1 255-g. packet frozen broccoli, cooked
3 tablespoons freshly grated Parmesan	3 tablespoons freshly grated Parmesan
12 oz. cooked turkey, cut into $\frac{1}{3}$-inch cubes	350 g. cooked turkey, cut into $\frac{3}{4}$-cm. cubes
Cream sauce:	*Cream sauce:*
3 tablespoons butter	3 tablespoons butter
3 tablespoons flour	3 tablespoons flour
$\frac{1}{2}$ pint milk	3 dl. milk
1 chicken stock cube	1 chicken stock cube
freshly ground black pepper	freshly ground black pepper
$\frac{1}{4}$ pint single cream	$1\frac{1}{2}$ dl. single cream
2–3 tablespoons medium dry sherry	2–3 tablespoons medium dry sherry
2 egg yolks	2 egg yolks
2 tablespoons thick or whipped cream	2 tablespoons thick or whipped cream
salt	salt

1. Preheat oven to moderate (350°F., 180°C., Gas Mark 4).

2. Drain cooked broccoli thoroughly and arrange neatly over the base of a heatproof, oval, 2-pint (1-litre) dish. Sprinkle with 1 tablespoon grated Parmesan.

3. To make cream sauce, melt butter in a heavy pan. Blend in flour and cook over a low heat for 2 to 3 minutes, stirring constantly, to make a pale roux.

4. Gradually add milk, stirring vigorously to prevent lumps forming. Add crumbled stock cube and a little freshly ground black pepper, bring to the boil and simmer, stirring, for 2 to 3 minutes until sauce has thickened.

5. Stir in single cream. Bring just to boiling point again and remove from heat.

6. Beat in sherry and egg yolks, and when thoroughly blended, stir in thick (or whipped) cream. Taste and add salt and more freshly ground black pepper if necessary.

7. Spoon half of sauce over broccoli. Arrange turkey on top and cover with remaining sauce. Sprinkle with remaining Parmesan.

8. Bake for 30 minutes, or until dish is hot through and sauce is bubbling and golden brown on top. Serve immediately.

Serves 4

Chef's tip:
If you do not have any medium dry sherry, use a slightly smaller quantity of dry martini in the recipe. To prevent sauce from forming a skin on top if it has to wait around at all after boiling, slip a sheet of buttered grease-proof paper right down on top of the sauce.

Turkey Tetrazzini

IMPERIAL	METRIC
1 lb. cold cooked turkey	450 g. cold cooked turkey
8 oz. spaghetti	225 g. spaghetti
salt	salt
1 tablespoon olive oil	1 tablespoon olive oil
butter	butter
4 oz. blanched slivered almonds	100 g. blanched slivered almonds
$\frac{1}{2}$ teaspoon lemon juice	$\frac{1}{2}$ teaspoon lemon juice
8 oz. button mushrooms, thinly sliced	225 g. button mushrooms, thinly sliced
2 tablespoons flour	2 tablespoons flour
$\frac{3}{4}$ pint turkey or chicken (cube) stock	$2\frac{1}{2}$ dl. turkey or chicken (cube) stock
$\frac{1}{2}$ pint hot double cream	3 dl. hot double cream
3 tablespoons dry white wine	3 tablespoons dry white wine
freshly ground black pepper	freshly ground black pepper
2 tablespoons freshly grated Parmesan	2 tablespoons freshly grated Parmesan

1. Cut turkey into neat strips.

2. Cook spaghetti in boiling salted water until tender but still *al dente*, about 12 minutes.

3. Meanwhile, heat olive oil with 2 tablespoons butter in a large, wide pan. Add slivered almonds and sauté over a moderate heat until golden, stirring constantly. Remove from pan with a slotted spoon and drain on absorbent paper.

4. Add lemon juice to fat remaining in pan; sauté sliced mushrooms gently for 5 minutes until lightly coloured.

5. When spaghetti is cooked, drain well and return to the (dry) saucepan. Add almonds and mushrooms. Mix well.

6. Preheat oven to moderate (375°F., 190°C., Gas Mark 5).

7. In another, heavy pan, melt 3 tablespoons butter. Stir in flour; cook over a low heat for 2 to 3 minutes, stirring.

8. Gradually add stock, stirring vigorously; bring to the boil and simmer gently for 8 to 10 minutes, stirring occasionally.

9. Stir hot cream into sauce. Add wine and season to taste with salt and freshly ground black pepper.

10. Pour half of sauce into spaghetti mixture; mix well. Fold turkey meat into remaining sauce.

11. Generously butter a large, deep heatproof serving dish.

12. Place spaghetti mixture in dish. Hollow out a well in the centre and fill with sauced turkey. Sprinkle all over with freshly grated Parmesan.

13. Bake dish for 20 minutes, or until thoroughly hot and lightly browned on top. Serve immediately.

Serves 6

Duckling with Turnips

IMPERIAL	METRIC
1½ lb. young turnips	675 g. young turnips
1 4-lb. oven-ready duck	1 1¾-kg. oven-ready duck
salt and freshly ground black pepper	salt and freshly ground black pepper
2 tablespoons flour	2 tablespoons flour
4 tablespoons butter	4 tablespoons butter
1 tablespoon castor sugar	1 tablespoon castor sugar
1½ pints chicken stock	scant litre chicken stock
bouquet garni	bouquet garni
1 Spanish onion, quartered	1 Spanish onion, quartered
parsley, to garnish	parsley, to garnish

1. Peel and quarter turnips. Cover with cold salted water; bring to the boil; simmer for 5 minutes and drain.

2. Wipe duck clean both inside and out. Rub all over with salt and freshly ground black pepper and dust with 1 tablespoon flour.

3. Select a heavy casserole large enough to take duck and turnips comfortably. Melt butter in it and, when hot, brown duck thoroughly on all sides. Remove duck from casserole.

4. Add turnips; sprinkle with sugar and sauté in fat remaining in casserole for 3 to 4 minutes until lightly coloured. Remove from casserole.

5. Blend remaining flour into fat left in casserole and when smooth, gradually add chicken stock, stirring and scraping bottom and sides of casserole clean with a wooden spoon. Bring to the boil, stirring occasionally; add bouquet garni and quartered onion and season to taste with salt and freshly ground black pepper.

6. Return duck to casserole and spoon sauce over the top. Cover tightly and simmer very gently for 1½ hours, turning duck occasionally so that it cooks evenly.

7. Add sautéed turnips to casserole and continue to simmer for a further 30 to 40 minutes, or until both duck and turnips are meltingly tender.

8. To serve, transfer duck to a heated serving dish; surround with turnips and keep hot.

9. Skim sauce and boil it briskly for 15 minutes, or until reduced to nearly one third of its original volume.

10. Strain some of the sauce over duck and turnips. Serve the rest in a heated sauceboat. Garnish duck and turnips with parsley. Serve immediately.

Serves 4

Duck en Daube

IMPERIAL	METRIC
2 tender, oven-ready ducks, about 4½ lb. each	2 tender, oven-ready ducks, about 2 kg. each
salt and freshly ground black pepper	salt and freshly ground black pepper
2 bay leaves	2 bay leaves
½ teaspoon dried thyme	½ teaspoon dried thyme
2 stalks celery, finely chopped	2 stalks celery, finely chopped
4 carrots, thinly sliced	4 carrots, thinly sliced
2 large Spanish onions, halved and thinly sliced	2 large Spanish onions, halved and thinly sliced
4 fl. oz. brandy	1 dl. brandy
¾–1 pint dry red wine	4–6 dl. dry red wine
8 oz. fat bacon in one piece, cut into small dice	225 g. fat bacon in one piece, cut into small dice
12 oz. mushrooms, sliced	350 g. mushrooms, sliced
butter	butter
bouquet garni	bouquet garni
½ pint beef stock	3 dl. beef stock
2 cloves garlic, chopped	2 cloves garlic, chopped
2 tablespoons flour	2 tablespoons flour

1. Cut each duck into eight serving pieces: two from each leg and two from each breast. Place in a large earthenware bowl. Sprinkle with salt and freshly ground black pepper; add herbs, vegetables, brandy and red wine; mix well. Leave duck to marinate in this mixture for at least 2 hours.

2. Remove duck from marinade and dry pieces thoroughly. Reserve marinade for later use.

3. In a large, deep frying pan, sauté diced bacon in its own fat until golden. Remove bacon to a large, heatproof casserole with a slotted spoon.

4. Brown duck pieces all over in fat remaining in pan and add to the casserole, together with pan juices and fat. Cover and cook over a moderately high heat for 15 minutes.

5. Meanwhile, sauté sliced mushrooms in 3–4 tablespoons butter until soft and golden.

6. Add mushrooms to casserole with marinade and vegetables, bouquet garni, beef stock and garlic. Bring to the boil over a low heat and simmer very gently, with the lid half on, for 1½ hours, or until pieces of duck are tender.

7. When duck is cooked, remove bouquet garni and bay leaves. Skim fat from sauce.

8. Mash flour with softened butter to make a smooth paste and add to the simmering sauce in tiny pieces. Cook for 3 to 4 minutes longer, stirring, until sauce is smooth and thickened. Correct seasoning and serve, accompanied by rice or puréed potatoes.

Serves 8

Duck and Orange Salad

IMPERIAL	METRIC
1 roast duck	1 roast duck
4 shallots, finely chopped	4 shallots, finely chopped
2 stalks celery, sliced	2 stalks celery, sliced
olive oil	olive oil
wine vinegar	wine vinegar
salt and freshly ground black pepper	salt and freshly ground black pepper
crumbled rosemary	crumbled rosemary
4 small oranges	4 small oranges
lettuce leaves	lettuce leaves
8–10 black olives, stoned	8–10 black olives, stoned

1. Bone roast duck completely, keeping meat in large chunks wherever possible. Cut meat into neat dice. Combine in a bowl with finely chopped shallots and sliced celery.

2. Make a vinaigrette with olive oil and vinegar (3 parts oil to 1 part vinegar—see basic vinaigrette page 99). Season to taste with salt and freshly ground black pepper, and flavour with rosemary.

3. Pour dressing over duck meat and vegetables. Toss lightly until thoroughly coated and leave to absorb flavours for 2 hours.

4. Meanwhile, peel oranges and divide into segments (see grapefruit mint salad, step 2, page 15), catching any juices that escape on a plate.

5. Just before serving, add orange sections and their juices to bowl and mix lightly. If salad seems dry, add more dressing. Correct seasoning if necessary.

6. Line a serving bowl with lettuce leaves. Heap salad in the centre and garnish with stoned black olives, halved if they are large.

Serves 4–6

Chef's tip:
If you wonder why shallots are sometimes called for in recipes, and not just plain onions, it is because there *is* a difference in the flavours. Shallots have a flavour nearer that of garlic than onion. Never let shallots brown or they will become bitter.

Pheasants with Chestnuts

IMPERIAL	METRIC
3 lb. chestnuts	1⅓ kg. chestnuts
3 pints chicken stock	1¾ litres chicken stock
2 sugar lumps	2 sugar lumps
1 tablespoon olive oil	1 tablespoon olive oil
6 tablespoons butter	6 tablespoons butter
2 plump pheasants, trussed	2 plump pheasants, trussed
salt and freshly ground black pepper	salt and freshly ground black pepper
freshly grated nutmeg	freshly grated nutmeg
6–8 tablespoons milk	6–8 tablespoons milk
6–8 tablespoons dry vermouth	6–8 tablespoons dry vermouth
sprigs of watercress, to garnish	sprigs of watercress, to garnish

1. Nick skins of chestnuts. Drop them into boiling water and boil for 5 minutes. Drain, cool and peel chestnuts, taking off both tough outer peel and the paper-like skin underneath.

2. Pour stock into a pan; add chestnuts and sugar lumps and simmer for 30 minutes, or until chestnuts are tender but not disintegrating. Drain, reserving stock.

3. Heat oil with 2 tablespoons butter in a heavy casserole just large enough to take pheasants side by side, and brown pheasants on all sides over a steady, moderate heat. Pour in reserved stock, cover tightly and simmer pheasants over a very low heat for 25 minutes, or until tender, turning them occasionally.

4. Meanwhile, pick out twelve of the best chestnuts for garnish and purée remainder.

5. Put the chestnut purée in a heavy pan and beat in remaining butter over a low heat. Season to taste with salt and freshly ground black pepper, and a pinch of nutmeg. Stir in milk and vermouth; mix well and simmer, stirring frequently, for 5 minutes longer, or until purée is smooth and thick. Keep hot.

6. To serve, turn chestnut purée into a deep, heated serving dish. Drain pheasants; remove trussing threads and place pheasants on top of purée. Quickly reheat whole chestnuts in remaining stock and arrange them around pheasants.

7. Strain stock through a fine sieve; skim if necessary and taste for seasoning. Reduce slightly if the flavour requires strengthening and serve in a heated sauceboat. Garnish pheasants with watercress and serve immediately.

Serves 6

Chef's tip:
You may not like the idea of peeling chestnuts and decide to substitute canned chestnut purée, but I should warn you that the flavour will not be nearly as good.

Roast Partridge

IMPERIAL	METRIC
1 plump young partridge, dressed	1 plump young partridge, dressed
Per bird:	*Per bird:*
butter	butter
salt and freshly ground black pepper	salt and freshly ground black pepper
lemon juice	lemon juice
barding strips of fat salt pork or unsmoked bacon	barding strips of fat salt pork or unsmoked bacon
flour	flour
stock and wine, for sauce	stock and wine, for sauce
sprigs of watercress, to garnish	sprigs of watercress, to garnish

1. Preheat oven to fairly hot (425°F., 220°C., Gas Mark 7).

2. Clean partridge carefully, wiping it both inside and out with a damp cloth—there is a danger of it tasting slightly bitter if all traces of the intestines are not cleaned out. Partridge should not be washed. However, if you have the bird's liver, wash it and pat it dry.

3. Take a piece of butter the size of a nutmeg and work it with salt, freshly ground black pepper and a squeeze of lemon juice. Put into the cavity of the bird with its liver.

4. Truss partridge. Cover breast with a paper-thin slice of barding pork fat or slices of fat unsmoked bacon, and tie in place with string. Spread bird with a tablespoon of butter.

5. Lay partridge in a roasting tin—not too large, so that cooking juices do not spread over too large an area—and roast until tender but still very juicy. The time will depend very much on the age of the bird and its size: a young and tender one will be ready in 25 to 30 minutes, while an older one will need closer to 45. Baste frequently with pan juices throughout cooking time, otherwise there is a danger of the flesh being on the dry side.

6. Ten minutes before the end of cooking time, untie barding fat and discard it. Dredge breast of partridge with flour and return to the oven to finish cooking and brown breast.

7. Transfer partridge to a hot serving dish and remove trussing threads or skewers. Keep hot while making a gravy with pan juices, a little stock and a splash of wine.

8. Garnish partridge with a bunch of watercress and serve with its gravy, a bread sauce and game chips.

Allow ½ roast partridge per person

Chef's tip:
If you dislike strongly-flavoured game, partridge is the answer. A young partridge will have pale, yellow-brown feet and a paler plucked flesh than an older bird.

Partridge with Apple and Black Grapes

IMPERIAL	METRIC
2 3-oz. packets Philadelphia cream cheese	2 85-g. packets Philadelphia cream cheese
salt and freshly ground black pepper	salt and freshly ground black pepper
2 oven-ready young partridges	2 oven-ready young partridges
4 tablespoons butter	4 tablespoons butter
1 tablespoon olive oil	1 tablespoon olive oil
3 cooking or crisp tart dessert apples, peeled, cored and diced	3 cooking or crisp tart dessert apples, peeled, cored and diced
12 oz. black grapes, halved and seeded	350 g. black grapes, halved and seeded
2 tablespoons brandy	2 tablespoons brandy

1. Preheat oven to hot (450°F., 230°C., Gas Mark 8).

2. Pound cheeses smoothly with salt and freshly ground black pepper, to taste, and stuff half into each partridge. Truss partridges.

3. Melt 1 tablespoon butter with the oil in a heavy casserole just large enough to take partridges comfortably. Brown them on all sides over a steady heat; then transfer casserole to the oven and roast, uncovered, for 10 minutes. This cooking time applies only to young birds—if you are not sure about the age increase the cooking time at this stage. You must not increase the time at step 5 or the apples and grapes will disintegrate.

4. Meanwhile, toss diced apples in remaining butter over a high heat until golden but not mushy.

5. Remove casserole from the oven. Smother partridges in apples; add grapes and sprinkle with brandy. Cover casserole and return to the oven for a further 10 minutes.

6. Transfer partridges to a heated serving dish and spoon apples, grapes and cooking juices over them. Serve immediately.

Serves 2–4

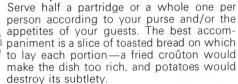

Chef's tip:
Serve half a partridge or a whole one per person according to your purse and/or the appetites of your guests. The best accompaniment is a slice of toasted bread on which to lay each portion—a fried croûton would make the dish too rich, and potatoes would destroy its subtlety.

Pigeons with Green Peas

IMPERIAL	METRIC
2 plump, tender pigeons, dressed	2 plump, tender pigeons, dressed
1 tablespoon butter	1 tablespoon butter
1 tablespoon olive oil	1 tablespoon olive oil
1 4-oz. piece fat unsmoked bacon, diced	1 100-g. piece fat unsmoked bacon, diced
10 button onions, peeled	10 button onions, peeled
1 tablespoon flour	1 tablespoon flour
$\frac{1}{2}$ pint light chicken stock	3 dl. light chicken stock
bouquet garni	bouquet garni
salt and freshly ground black pepper	salt and freshly ground black pepper
8 oz. fresh shelled or frozen peas	225 g. fresh shelled or frozen peas

1. Wipe pigeons clean both inside and out with a damp cloth. Tie legs together with string. Pass a wooden cocktail stick or small skewer through one wing, straight through the body and out through the other wing to hold them together.

2. In a heavy, heatproof casserole large enough to hold pigeons comfortably, melt butter and oil and sauté pigeons until well browned on all sides, about 10 minutes. Remove pigeons to a plate.

3. Add diced bacon and whole button onions to fat remaining in the pan, and continue to sauté gently until both are golden, about 10 minutes. Remove onions to another plate.

4. Sprinkle diced bacon and fat with flour, blending it in thoroughly with a wooden spoon. Gradually stir in chicken stock. Bring to the boil, stirring, and simmer for 2 to 3 minutes until sauce has thickened.

5. Return pigeons to the casserole, spooning sauce over them. Add bouquet garni and season lightly with salt and freshly ground black pepper. Reduce heat to a bare simmer and cover casserole.

6. Cook pigeons very gently for $1\frac{1}{2}$ to 2 hours, or until very tender, turning them over in the sauce from time to time to keep them moist.

7. Halfway through the cooking time, return button onions to the casserole.

8. Twenty minutes before end of cooking time, stir in peas.

9. Just before serving, split pigeons in half lengthwise. Reform them and arrange them in the centre of a heated serving dish. Surround with peas and onions, and serve immediately.

Serves 4

Pigeons aux Lentilles à la Provençale

IMPERIAL	METRIC
2 plump, tender pigeons, dressed	2 plump, tender pigeons, dressed
3 tablespoons butter	3 tablespoons butter
3 tablespoons olive oil	3 tablespoons olive oil
2 Spanish onions, finely chopped	2 Spanish onions, finely chopped
$\frac{1}{2}$ pint chicken stock	3 dl. chicken stock
bouquet garni	bouquet garni
salt and freshly ground black pepper	salt and freshly ground black pepper
8 oz. large brown lentils, soaked overnight	225 g. large brown lentils, soaked overnight
2 oz. fat salt pork, finely diced	50 g. fat salt pork, finely diced
1–2 carrots, cut in chunks	1–2 carrots, cut in chunks
$\frac{1}{4}$ teaspoon thyme	$\frac{1}{4}$ teaspoon thyme
$\frac{1}{2}$ bay leaf	$\frac{1}{2}$ bay leaf
4 thick slices fat unsmoked bacon	4 thick slices fat unsmoked bacon

1. Preheat oven to slow (325°F., 170°C., Gas Mark 3).

2. Prepare pigeons as described in preceding recipe step 1.

3. In a heavy, ovenproof casserole, melt 2 tablespoons each butter and olive oil; sauté birds until well browned all over, about 10 minutes. Remove to a plate.

4. In fat remaining in casserole, simmer half the finely chopped onions until soft and golden brown, stirring frequently.

5. Return pigeons to casserole. Add stock, bouquet garni and salt and freshly ground black pepper. Cover and transfer casserole to the oven; bake for 1 hour, or until pigeons are cooked but still firm. Drain soaked lentils thoroughly.

6. In a heavy saucepan, melt remaining butter and olive oil; sauté remaining onion gently for 5 minutes. Add salt pork and carrot, and continue to sauté gently for about 10 minutes longer. Add drained lentils; cook over a low heat for a further 5 minutes, stirring frequently.

7. Add 1 pint (6 dl.) water to lentil mixture, together with herbs and seasoning, to taste. Bring to the boil and lower heat to simmering point. Cover and cook for 15 minutes, or until lentils have softened but are still firm, and not mushy. Remove pan from heat and leave, covered, until needed.

8. When pigeons are cooked, remove them from casserole. Discard trussing threads and skewers and split them in half lengthwise. Cut bacon slices into thin strips.

9. Combine lentils with juices in casserole. Bury pigeons in lentils and add bacon. Mixture will be rather liquid.

10. Return casserole to the oven for a further $1\frac{1}{2}$ hours, or until pigeons are very tender. Serve very hot.

Serves 4

Spit-roasted Quails with Juniper Butter

Quails in Potato Nests

IMPERIAL	METRIC
salt and freshly ground black pepper	salt and freshly ground black pepper
4 dressed quails	4 dressed quails
4 oz. butter	100 g. butter
½ teaspoon lemon juice	½ teaspoon lemon juice
juniper berries	juniper berries

1. Mix a little salt and freshly ground black pepper on a saucer. Dip your finger in it and rub the quails all over, both inside and out.

2. Beat butter and lemon juice together.

3. Crush juniper berries with a rolling pin; then chop them finely with a knife.

4. Measure 1 tablespoon chopped juniper berries into butter mixture. Mix well and season to taste with salt and freshly ground black pepper.

5. Put a small knob of juniper butter in the body cavity of each quail. Spread quails all over with the remainder. Arrange them on a plate and leave at the bottom of the refrigerator to absorb flavours for 2 hours.

6. If using an oven rôtisserie, preheat it to fairly hot (425°F., 220°C., Gas Mark 7). Fashion a long, narrow trough from double-thick aluminium foil to catch juices from quails as they revolve, and lay it beneath the spit.

7. Thread quails lengthwise onto a spit and spit-roast for 15 to 20 minutes, or until juices run clear when they are pierced with a thin skewer around the inside leg area where the meat is thickest.

8. Transfer quails to a heated serving dish. Spoon over some of the buttery juices from the foil container and serve immediately.

Serve 1 or 2 quails per person

Chef's tip:
Juniper butter imparts a wonderful 'foresty' flavour to little birds. Use it with guinea fowl as well—it is quite delicious. Do not try catching the spit-roasting juices in a pan—they are likely to burn.

IMPERIAL	METRIC
6 plump dressed quails	6 plump dressed quails
1 tablespoon olive oil	1 tablespoon olive oil
butter	butter
1 large clove garlic	1 large clove garlic
about 2 lb. potatoes	about 900 g. potatoes
salt and freshly ground black pepper	salt and freshly ground black pepper
Marinade:	*Marinade:*
6–8 tablespoons dry white wine	6–8 tablespoons dry white wine
1 tablespoon finely chopped onion	1 tablespoon finely chopped onion
4 sage leaves, crumbled	4 sage leaves, crumbled
1 bay leaf, crumbled	1 bay leaf, crumbled
salt and freshly ground black pepper	salt and freshly ground black pepper

1. Combine marinade ingredients in a bowl, adding salt and freshly ground black pepper, to taste.

2. Add quails; coat them thoroughly and leave them to marinate for 4 to 6 hours, turning occasionally.

3. Drain quails thoroughly, reserving marinade. Pat them dry with absorbent paper.

4. Select a heavy pan or heatproof casserole that will take the quails comfortably in one layer. In it, heat oil with 2 tablespoons butter. When butter is foaming, brown quails in it, allowing 4 minutes in all: 1 minute on their backs, 1 minute on each side, and 1 minute on their breasts.

5. Strain marinade over quails. Cover pan tightly and cook for about 10 minutes, or until quails are tender. Remove pan from heat and leave quails to cool in their cooking juices.

6. When ready to make potato nests, preheat oven to moderately hot (400°F., 200°C., Gas Mark 6).

7. Rub six shallow, ovenproof gratin dishes 6 inches (15 cm.) in diameter with cut garlic and butter them.

8. Peel potatoes and slice them to the thickness of a 10-pence piece. Dry slices thoroughly with absorbent paper.

9. Line bases and sides of gratin dishes with a single layer of overlapping potato slices. Brush with a little melted butter and sprinkle with salt and freshly ground black pepper.

10. Bake potato-lined dishes for 15 to 20 minutes, or until potatoes are tinged with brown and feel soft when pierced with a skewer.

11. Lay a quail in the centre of each dish and spoon over a little of its cooking juices, allowing it to dribble onto potatoes underneath. Return to oven for a final 7 minutes.

Serves 6

Pasta and Rice Dishes

Pasta

It's only a very gifted people that can take some flour, eggs, oil and a drop or two of water, and transform them into a bewitching variety of shapes and sizes: tubes and strings, ribbons and bows, frills, stars, spirals and sea-shells, and little envelopes stuffed full with rich fillings. True, the Chinese may claim the credit for actually inventing pasta, but Marco Polo introduced it into Europe, and pasta as we know it is the result of Italian inventiveness, a glorious monument of that nation's *joie de vivre* and hearty love of good food.

Not content with inventing well over a hundred different shapes, the Italians then proceeded to marry each one off to the right dressing—rich, thick sauces that would cling to ropes and ribbons, rather thinner ones to flow through and around tubed noodles, from neat little macaroni to great ribbed *rigatoni*.

Sometimes, for sheer relief, a plate of perfectly cooked, steaming noodles will be served with just a dollop of sweet butter and a bowl of freshly grated Parmesan, or a light dressing of fruity olive oil and garlic, or the pounded basil sauce beloved of the Genoese, *pesto alla Genovese*. Sometimes they are tossed with eggs and cream and freshly grated Parmesan until the heat of the noodles fuses these ingredients into a creamy sauce.

When to serve pasta

Outside Italy, most people think of pasta as an informal, quick and easy main dish for lunch or supper-time. And very good it is, too, preceded by an *antipasto* platter in the Italian manner, washed down with a bottle of Chianti and followed by a green salad and something very light for the sweet. But why not try slotting a pasta course between the appetizer or *antipasto* which, literally translated, means 'before the pasta', and the main course? This is what the Italians do with pasta and also rice, and if you follow their example and leave your meat dish unaccompanied by anything except a green vegetable or a salad, you need have no fear of overwhelming your guests.

* Always boil pasta in plenty of salted water— 6 pints (3½ litres) per lb. of pasta is a reasonable amount—otherwise the noodles may stick together.

* Long noodles or spaghetti should never be broken: hold a sheaf upright in the water, pressing gently against the base of the pan and, as you feel it soften, gradually curl it around in the pan until it is completely submerged.

* Always add pasta gradually to the pan so that the water remains at a rolling boil.

* Once the strands or shapes are all in, give them a good stir with a fork to separate them and dislodge any that have stuck to the bottom of the pan.

* Finally, never cook pasta too far in advance. But if you have to keep it hot for a little while before serving, set the colander over a saucepan containing an inch of boiling water and cover with a damp cloth.

Rice

The reason for the mystique that surrounds the cooking of rice escapes me. Nowadays, I find it easier (and quicker, too) to cook a pot of rice to fluffy perfection than to boil a common supermarket potato without fear of it falling apart. Rice is predictable, providing you use the right type for the right job. But learn the simple rules for cooking rice and stick to them. You will never be let down.

Serving rice as an accompaniment

Serve plain-boiled rice as an accompaniment when you want nothing to come in the way of the flavour of your main dish. It makes the ideal partner for creamed and delicately sauced dishes, providing an unobtrusive backdrop to other, more exciting flavours.

Whichever method of cooking you prefer— boiling, steaming or a simple pilaff—cooked rice should always be fluffy, each grain separate, cooked tender but still with a little 'bite' to it.

* A bowl of steaming, snowy-white rice needs no adornment, perhaps just a pat of fresh butter or a sprinkling of freshly grated Parmesan cheese or a little finely chopped green parsley.

* A *rice ring* also makes an attractive container for morsels of seafood or white meat in a creamy sauce; brush a ring mould generously with tasteless oil or melted butter; press the cooked rice into it lightly— there is no need to pack it in tightly. Cover top of mould tightly with foil and keep hot until needed by standing the mould in a baking dish with hot (not boiling) water to come halfway up sides. When ready to serve, turn out carefully onto a heated dish and fill centre as desired. A 2-pint (1-litre) ring mould will take 10 or 12 oz. (275 or 350 g.) rice (raw weight) depending on how firmly it is packed.

To cook rice

The same rules apply, whichever method you prefer for cooking rice:

* Use long-grain rice for boiled or steamed rice and leave short-grain for puddings and the Italian varieties for risottos.

* Cooked in a tightly covered pan, rice will absorb its own volume of liquid, water, stock or whatever. Some people prefer to add up to twice the volume. This certainly makes the rice more tender, but it also makes it more liable to overcook and disintegrate.

* Never stir cooked rice with a spoon. Use a long-pronged fork and fluff it gently with a straight, up-and-down motion to avoid crushing the grains.

* There is no need to wash or rinse rice. This practice, which was originally intended to rid the grains of floury starch and impurities, has been rendered obsolete by modern milling and marketing methods.

* If cooking rice by the covered method, avoid the temptation to lift off the lid every few minutes. Otherwise the vapour will escape instead of being forced into the grains to make them light and fluffy.

Spaghetti all'Amatriciana

IMPERIAL	METRIC
salt	salt
1 lb. spaghetti	450 g. spaghetti
2 tablespoons butter	2 tablespoons butter
freshly grated Parmesan	freshly grated Parmesan
Sauce:	*Sauce:*
4 oz. fat salt pork	100 g. fat salt pork
1 Spanish onion	1 Spanish onion
2 cloves garlic	2 cloves garlic
1 small red sweet pepper	1 small red sweet pepper
2 tablespoons olive oil	2 tablespoons olive oil
2 14-oz. cans Italian peeled tomatoes	2 396-g. cans Italian peeled tomatoes
2 tablespoons tomato paste	2 tablespoons tomato paste
salt and freshly ground black pepper	salt and freshly ground black pepper

1. To make the sauce, cut fat salt pork into ¼-inch (½-cm.) cubes.

2. Peel Spanish onion and garlic, and chop them finely.

3. Halve, core and seed red pepper, and cut into ¼-inch dice.

4. In a heavy saucepan, sauté fat salt pork, onion and garlic gently in olive oil until soft and golden, about 10 minutes.

5. Add canned tomatoes, together with their juices, tomato paste and diced red pepper. Mix well and season to taste with salt and freshly ground black pepper.

6. Bring to the boil, stirring; cover pan and simmer very gently, stirring occasionally, for 1 hour, or until ingredients are reduced to a thick sauce.

7. Meanwhile, bring a large pan of salted water to the boil.

8. When sauce has been cooking for about 45 minutes, add spaghetti to boiling water and cook until tender but not mushy.

9. As soon as spaghetti is ready, drain thoroughly in a colander.

10. To serve, heap spaghetti in a deep, well-heated serving dish. Dot with butter. Pour sauce over the top and serve immediately, with plenty of freshly grated Parmesan to sprinkle over each portion.

Serves 4

Chef's tip:
Never cook pasta too far in advance. But if you have to keep it hot for a little while before serving, set the colander over a saucepan containing an inch of boiling water and cover with a damp cloth until ready to serve.

Spaghetti alla Rusticana

IMPERIAL	METRIC
salt	salt
12 oz. spaghetti	350 g. spaghetti
6 tablespoons olive oil	6 tablespoons olive oil
2 cloves garlic, lightly crushed	2 cloves garlic, lightly crushed
8–10 large anchovy fillets	8–10 large anchovy fillets
1 teaspoon crushed oregano	1 teaspoon crushed oregano
2–3 tablespoons finely chopped parsley	2–3 tablespoons finely a chopped parsley
freshly ground black pepper	freshly ground black pepper
freshly grated Parmesan	freshly grated Parmesan

1. Bring a large pan of salted water to the boil and cook spaghetti until tender but still firm.

2. Meanwhile, heat oil in a frying pan and sauté crushed garlic cloves gently until golden brown. Discard garlic.

3. Add anchovies and cook over the lowest possible heat, stirring, until they have dissolved into a paste.

4. Add oregano and stir over a low heat for a few minutes longer.

5. Drain spaghetti thoroughly in a colander and pile it in a deep, heated serving dish.

6. Pour over anchovy sauce; sprinkle with finely chopped parsley and toss well at the table with a serving fork or spoon. Season to taste with freshly ground black pepper and a little salt if necessary.

7. Serve very hot, accompanied by a large bowl of freshly grated Parmesan.

Serves 4 as a first course

Chef's tip:
Drain noodles as soon as they are cooked. Overcooking will not make them any more tender, and if they are left standing around in water they turn pasty and unpleasant.

Sicilian Spaghetti

IMPERIAL	METRIC
salt	salt
1 lb. spaghetti	450 g. spaghetti
freshly grated Parmesan, to serve	freshly grated Parmesan, to serve
Sicilian sauce:	*Sicilian sauce:*
1 2-oz. can anchovy fillets in olive oil	1 57-g. can anchovy fillets in olive oil
¼ pint olive oil	1½ dl. olive oil
1 14-oz. can Italian peeled tomatoes	1 396-g. can Italian peeled tomatoes
8 tablespoons finely chopped parsley	8 tablespoons finely chopped parsley
1–2 cloves garlic, finely chopped	1–2 cloves garlic, finely chopped
2 oz. walnuts, chopped	50 g. walnuts, chopped
4 oz. button mushrooms, chopped	100 g. button mushrooms, chopped
salt and freshly ground black pepper	salt and freshly ground black pepper

1. Bring a large pan of salted water to the boil. Lower in spaghetti; bring back to the boil and simmer gently until cooked but still firm—*al dente*, as the Italians say.

2. Meanwhile, prepare sauce; drain off oil from can of anchovies into a measuring jug and make up to ¼ pint (1½ dl.) with olive oil. Pour into a pan; add anchovies and heat gently, stirring and mashing with a wooden spoon until anchovies are thoroughly blended with oil.

3. Drain tomatoes; press out seeds and chop tomatoes coarsely. Add to pan, together with finely chopped parsley and garlic, walnuts and mushrooms. Season to taste with salt if necessary and freshly ground black pepper, and continue to stir until sauce heats through without actually cooking ingredients.

4. Drain spaghetti thoroughly and heap in a heated serving dish.

5. Pour over hot sauce, and serve immediately, accompanied by a bowl of grated Parmesan; toss well at the table.

Serves 4

Chef's tip:
Never cover noodles while they are cooking; the pan is sure to boil over and you will have the devil's own job cleaning up the sticky mess. Go steady with the salt for this sauce —the anchovies will probably make the sauce salty enough.

Spaghetti with Black Olives

IMPERIAL	METRIC
salt	salt
8 oz. spaghetti	225 g. spaghetti
2–3 cloves garlic	2–3 cloves garlic
2–3 sprigs fresh basil	2–3 sprigs fresh basil
3 tablespoons olive oil	3 tablespoons olive oil
2 oz. butter, diced	50 g. butter, diced
4 oz. small black olives, stoned	100 g. small black olives, stoned
4 oz. Parmesan, freshly grated	100 g. Parmesan, freshly grated
freshly ground black pepper	freshly ground black pepper
chopped parsley, to garnish	chopped parsley, to garnish

1. Bring a large pan of salted water to the boil and cook spaghetti until tender but still firm.

2. Meanwhile, peel garlic cloves and strip leaves from basil sprigs. Put both in a mortar and pound to a purée; then gradually add olive oil, pounding or beating well between each addition as if making a mayonnaise.

3. When spaghetti is cooked, drain in a colander and transfer to a large, deep heated serving dish.

4. Stir in diced butter; add garlic and basil paste, black olives and freshly grated Parmesan, and toss lightly but thoroughly. Season with freshly ground black pepper, but taste carefully before adding salt, as the Parmesan may already have made the dish salty enough. Serve immediately, sprinkled with parsley.

Serves 3–4

Chef's tip:
This classic Italian dish of noodles with fresh basil is very different from trenette col pesto (see page 80). Always add pasta gradually to pan so that water remains at a rolling boil, and once strands are in give a good stir with a fork to separate or dislodge any that have stuck to base of pan.

Spaghetti alla Carbonara

IMPERIAL	METRIC
salt	salt
1 lb. spaghetti	450 g. spaghetti
3 oz. butter	75 g. butter
1–2 tablespoons olive oil	1–2 tablespoons olive oil
4 tablespoons finely chopped onion	4 tablespoons finely chopped onion
8 oz. back bacon, cut into thin strips	225 g. back bacon, cut into thin strips
6 egg yolks	6 egg yolks
¼ pint single cream	1½ dl. single cream
freshly grated Parmesan	freshly grated Parmesan
freshly ground black pepper	freshly ground black pepper
chopped parsley, to garnish	chopped parsley, to garnish

1. Bring a large pan of salted water to the boil and cook spaghetti until tender but not mushy.

2. Meanwhile, heat butter and olive oil together in a heavy, medium-sized pan. Add finely chopped onion and simmer until soft and golden but not brown.

3. Add bacon strips and continue to sauté gently for about 5 minutes.

4. In a bowl, beat egg yolks with cream and 8 tablespoons freshly grated Parmesan.

5. As soon as spaghetti is cooked, drain thoroughly in a colander. Return spaghetti to dry pan.

6. Remove bacon and onion mixture from heat. Beat in egg and cream mixture. Season to taste with salt and freshly ground black pepper.

7. Quickly pour this sauce over hot spaghetti and toss vigorously with a large fork and spoon so that heat of spaghetti 'cooks' the sauce into a creamy dressing. Taste and season with more salt or freshly ground black pepper if necessary.

8. Serve immediately, piled in a well-heated serving dish, with more freshly grated Parmesan to sprinkle over each portion. Garnish with chopped parsley.

Serves 6

Chef's tip:
Long noodles should never be broken; hold a sheaf upright in the bubbling, salted water pressing gently against the base of the pan and, as you feel it soften, gradually curl it around the pan until it is completely submerged.

Trenette col Pesto

IMPERIAL	METRIC
2 cloves garlic	2 cloves garlic
4 small bunches fresh basil	4 small bunches fresh basil
1 tablespoon toasted pine nuts	1 tablespoon toasted pine nuts
coarse sea salt	coarse sea salt
2 tablespoons freshly grated Parmesan	2 tablespoons freshly grated Parmesan
2 tablespoons freshly grated Pecorino	2 tablespoons freshly grated Pecorino
8 fl. oz. olive oil	2¼ dl. olive oil
freshly ground black pepper	freshly ground black pepper
3 medium-sized potatoes, peeled and diced	3 medium-sized potatoes, peeled and diced
8 oz. trenette or thin ribbon noodles	225 g. trenette or thin ribbon noodles
freshly grated Parmesan or Pecorino, to serve	freshly grated Parmesan or Pecorino, to serve

1. Pound first three ingredients to a paste in a mortar, adding coarse salt to taste. Beat in grated cheeses gradually, and when paste is smooth again, add olive oil a little at a time, as for mayonnaise. Season to taste with freshly ground black pepper, and more salt if necessary. (If you have an electric blender, add all the ingredients at the same time and blend at top speed for 1 minute.)

2. Bring a large pan of salted water to the boil. Add diced potatoes and noodles, bring to the boil again and cook briskly for 10 minutes, or until both are tender but not disintegrating.

3. Drain potatoes and noodles and place them in a deep, heated serving dish.

4. Pour over pesto sauce; toss quickly and serve immediately, accompanied by a large bowl of more grated Parmesan or Pecorino to sprinkle over the top.

Serves 4

Chef's tip:
Pesto originated in Genoa. The Genoese maintain that it should never be served other than with *trenette*, thin, ribbon noodles which can be found in Italian shops stocking a good variety of pasta. If Pecorino is not available, use all Parmesan.

Ribbon Noodles with Cream Sauce

Noodles with Almonds

IMPERIAL	METRIC
salt	salt
1 lb. ribbon noodles	450 g. ribbon noodles
4 tablespoons butter	4 tablespoons butter
2 raw egg yolks	2 raw egg yolks
6 tablespoons freshly grated Parmesan	6 tablespoons freshly grated Parmesan
6 tablespoons double cream	6 tablespoons double cream
freshly ground black pepper	freshly ground black pepper
additional butter and grated Parmesan, to serve	additional butter and grated Parmesan, to serve

1. Bring a large (6- to 8-pint, 3½- to 4½-litre) pan of salted water to the boil. Add noodles and cook until tender but still firm, *al dente* as the Italians say.

2. Drain noodles thoroughly in a colander and place them in a well-heated serving bowl or chafing dish.

3. Quickly add butter, egg yolks, grated Parmesan and cream.

4. Toss noodles in this mixture until their heat 'cooks' the egg and cream sauce. Season to taste with salt and freshly ground black pepper.

5. Serve immediately with additional quantities of butter and grated Parmesan.

Serves 4

IMPERIAL	METRIC
8 oz. ribbon noodles	225 g. ribbon noodles
salt	salt
4 tablespoons thinly sliced blanched almonds	4 tablespoons thinly sliced blanched almonds
4 tablespoons soft white breadcrumbs	4 tablespoons soft white breadcrumbs
3 tablespoons melted butter	3 tablespoons melted butter
freshly ground black pepper	freshly ground black pepper

1. Boil noodles in salted water until tender. Drain thoroughly in a colander; place in a deep, heated serving dish and keep hot.

2. While noodles are cooking, toss sliced almonds and breadcrumbs in melted butter and sauté gently until crisp and golden.

3. Top noodles with buttered almonds and breadcrumbs. Season to taste with salt and freshly ground black pepper, and toss again gently before serving.

Serves 4

Chef's tip:
Whilst noodles are cooking stir occasionally with a fork to keep strands separate. The cooking time will depend on whether noodles are fresh or dry: say 6 to 8 minutes for the former, 11 minutes plus for the latter, but keep trying a piece of noodle as it cooks.

Chef's tip:
To keep strands of noodles separate, add a few drops of olive oil to the water when boiling. Never rinse cooked noodles in cold water—this has little effect other than to wash out all the flavour.

Ribbon Noodles alla Bolognese

IMPERIAL	METRIC
salt	salt
1 lb. ribbon noodles (tagliatelle or fettuccine)	450 g. ribbon noodles (tagliatelle or fettuccine)
freshly grated Parmesan	freshly grated Parmesan
Bolognese sauce:	*Bolognese sauce:*
2 tablespoons butter	2 tablespoons butter
4 tablespoons olive oil	4 tablespoons olive oil
4 oz. fat salt pork or unsmoked bacon, finely chopped	100 g. fat salt pork or unsmoked bacon, finely chopped
1 Spanish onion, finely chopped	1 Spanish onion, finely chopped
2 carrots, finely chopped	2 carrots, finely chopped
1 stalk celery, finely chopped	1 stalk celery, finely chopped
8 oz. lean beef, minced	225 g. lean beef, minced
1 strip lemon peel	1 strip lemon peel
1 bay leaf	1 bay leaf
4 tablespoons tomato paste	4 tablespoons tomato paste
$\frac{1}{2}$ pint rich beef stock	3 dl. rich beef stock
$\frac{1}{4}$ pint dry white wine	$1\frac{1}{2}$ dl. dry white wine
salt and freshly ground black pepper	salt and freshly ground black pepper
freshly grated nutmeg	freshly grated nutmeg
4 tablespoons double cream	4 tablespoons double cream

1. Start by preparing Bolognese sauce. Heat butter and oil in a large, heavy pan and sauté salt pork or bacon, onion, carrots and celery over a moderate heat until golden brown, stirring occasionally.

2. Add minced beef and continue to sauté until evenly browned, crumbling it with a fork.

3. Stir in lemon peel, bay leaf, tomato paste, beef stock and dry white wine; season to taste with salt, freshly ground black pepper and a pinch of freshly grated nutmeg.

4. Cover pan and simmer gently for 30 minutes, stirring occasionally.

5. Remove lemon peel and bay leaf, and continue to simmer sauce, uncovered, for 30 minutes longer, or until slightly thickened.

6. Stir in cream and simmer gently for 2 to 3 minutes.

7. Twenty minutes before sauce is ready, bring a large pan of salted water to the boil. Add noodles and boil until tender but still *al dente*, 10 to 12 minutes depending on their quality. Drain thoroughly.

8. Heap noodles in a deep, heated serving dish and pour sauce over. Serve with a large bowl of Parmesan.

Serves 4

Macaroni Cheese

IMPERIAL	METRIC
8 oz. short macaroni	225 g. short macaroni
salt	salt
1 lb. ripe tomatoes, peeled and sliced	450 g. ripe tomatoes, peeled and sliced
2 tablespoons fresh white breadcrumbs	2 tablespoons fresh white breadcrumbs
Sauce:	*Sauce:*
1 oz. butter	25 g. butter
1 tablespoon finely chopped onion	1 tablespoon finely chopped onion
1 oz. plain flour	25 g. plain flour
$\frac{3}{4}$ pint hot milk	4 dl. hot milk
$\frac{1}{4}$ pint single cream	$1\frac{1}{2}$ dl. single cream
4–6 whole peppercorns	4–6 whole peppercorns
1 bay leaf	1 bay leaf
4–6 oz. strong Cheddar, grated	100–175 g. strong Cheddar, grated
salt and freshly ground black pepper	salt and freshly ground black pepper

1. Preheat oven to fairly hot (425°F., 220°C., Gas Mark 7).

2. Butter a 3-pint ($1\frac{3}{4}$-litre) baking dish.

3. To make the sauce, in a medium-sized pan, melt butter and sauté onion gently until soft but not coloured. Blend in flour over a low heat and cook for 2 minutes longer, stirring constantly, to make a pale roux.

4. Gradually add hot milk, stirring vigorously to prevent lumps forming. Stir in cream, peppercorns and bay leaf and bring to the boil over a moderately low heat, stirring constantly. Simmer gently for 10 to 15 minutes, stirring occasionally.

5. While sauce is simmering, cook macaroni in boiling salted water until just tender.

6. Reserve 2 to 3 tablespoons grated Cheddar for topping. Remove sauce from heat; add remaining Cheddar and beat vigorously until melted. Season generously with salt and pepper. Strain sauce through a sieve into a large bowl.

7. Drain macaroni well; add to sauce and mix. Season with more salt or freshly ground black pepper if necessary.

8. Spread half of macaroni mixture in baking dish. Reserve 12 tomato slices and arrange remainder on top of macaroni in a single layer. Sprinkle with salt and freshly ground black pepper and cover with remaining macaroni mixture. Arrange reserved tomato slices in an overlapping row down centre of dish.

9. Combine breadcrumbs with reserved Cheddar. Sprinkle over top of dish. Bake macaroni cheese for about 20 minutes, or until bubbly and golden brown on top. Serve hot.

Serves 4

Basic Rice Pilaff

IMPERIAL	METRIC
butter	butter
1 medium-sized Spanish onion, finely chopped	1 medium-sized Spanish onion, finely chopped
12 oz. long-grain rice	350 g. long-grain rice
1–1¼ pints boiling chicken stock	6–7 dl. boiling chicken stock
salt and freshly ground black pepper	salt and freshly ground black pepper
4 oz. button mushrooms, sliced and sautéed in butter (optional)	100 g. button mushrooms, sliced and sautéed in butter (optional)
chopped parsley, to garnish	chopped parsley, to garnish

1. Preheat oven to moderate (375°F., 190°C., Gas Mark 5).

2. Melt 4 tablespoons butter in a heavy, heatproof casserole and simmer finely chopped Spanish onion until golden brown.

3. Add rice and stir over a moderate heat for 2 or 3 minutes until grains are thoroughly coated with butter.

4. Pour in 1 pint (6 dl.) boiling stock (take care, as stock will sizzle up fiercely when it comes into contact with hot butter); season to taste with salt and freshly ground black pepper, and quickly cover casserole to prevent too much stock evaporating.

5. Bake casserole for 25 to 30 minutes, or until rice grains are fluffy and separate, and liquid has been absorbed, stirring once or twice and adding a little more boiling stock if it has all been absorbed before rice is tender.

6. To serve, *either* transfer rice to a serving dish, add sliced sautéed mushrooms and 2 tablespoons butter, and toss with a fork to mix them in lightly; *or* mix in 2 tablespoons butter with a fork and return casserole to the oven, uncovered, so that top layer of rice becomes nutty and slightly crisp. Sprinkle with parsley.

Serves 6

Portuguese Rice

IMPERIAL	METRIC
1 Spanish onion, chopped	1 Spanish onion, chopped
1 clove garlic, finely chopped	1 clove garlic, finely chopped
3 tablespoons olive oil	3 tablespoons olive oil
12 oz. long-grain rice	350 g. long-grain rice
1 tablespoon tomato paste	1 tablespoon tomato paste
1¼ pints hot beef stock	7 dl. hot beef stock
1 tablespoon paprika	1 tablespoon paprika
salt and freshly ground black pepper	salt and freshly ground black pepper

1. In a heavy saucepan, sauté chopped onion and garlic in olive oil until soft and golden.

2. Add rice and stir with a wooden spoon over a moderate heat for a minute or two so that each grain is coated with a film of golden oil.

3. Dissolve tomato paste in hot stock. Add to rice and bring to the boil, stirring and scraping bottom of pan to dislodge any grains stuck there.

4. When stock boils, clamp on a lid tightly; lower heat to the barest simmer and leave rice to cook undisturbed for 15 to 18 minutes, or until stock has been absorbed and rice is fluffy and separate.

5. Using a large fork to avoid crushing grains, carefully toss rice with paprika, adding salt and freshly ground black pepper, to taste.

6. Serve immediately.

Serves 4–6

Chef's tip:
Cooked in a tightly covered pan, rice will absorb its own volume in liquid, water, stock or whatever. Some people prefer to add up to twice the volume. This certainly makes the rice more tender, but it also makes the rice more liable to overcook and disintegrate.

Chef's tip:
To keep rice hot, butter a bowl and spoon in hot rice. Lay a folded cloth over bowl and cover tightly with a piece of foil (or lid, if you have one the right size) and set bowl over simmering water. Rice can safely be kept hot for several hours in this manner.

Avocado Pilaff

IMPERIAL	METRIC
4 oz. butter	100 g. butter
4 tablespoons finely chopped onion	4 tablespoons finely chopped onion
1 stalk celery, finely chopped	1 stalk celery, finely chopped
8 oz. long-grain rice	225 g. long-grain rice
2 oz. pine nuts	50 g. pine nuts
4 tablespoons dry white wine	4 tablespoons dry white wine
1¼ pints hot beef stock	7 dl. hot beef stock
salt	salt
4 oz. button mushrooms, sliced	100 g. button mushrooms, sliced
½ teaspoon finely chopped garlic	½ teaspoon finely chopped garlic
4 oz. fresh tomatoes, peeled, seeded and diced	100 g. fresh tomatoes, peeled, seeded and diced
¼ teaspoon dried marjoram	¼ teaspoon dried marjoram
freshly ground black pepper	freshly ground black pepper
1 avocado pear	1 avocado pear
lemon juice	lemon juice

1. Preheat oven to moderately hot (400°F., 200°C., Gas Mark 6).

2. Melt half the butter in a heavy casserole; add finely chopped onion and celery; sauté for 1 minute. Add rice and pine nuts; stir over a moderate heat for another minute, or until rice grains are thoroughly coated with fat.

3. Pour white wine and hot beef stock over rice. Stir well; season to taste with salt and bring to the boil.

4. Cover casserole tightly and transfer to oven. Bake rice for 15 to 20 minutes, stirring it once only with a fork halfway through cooking time.

5. In the meantime, sauté mushrooms in 2 tablespoons butter for 3 minutes; add finely chopped garlic, diced tomatoes and marjoram, and season to taste with salt and freshly ground black pepper. Simmer for 5 minutes longer.

6. Peel and dice avocado and brush pieces with lemon juice to preserve colour. Add them to the simmering vegetables, stir once and remove pan from heat.

7. Just before serving, add sautéed vegetable mixture to the casserole, together with remaining butter, and toss gently with a fork until well mixed.

Serves 6

Green Rice

IMPERIAL	METRIC
salt	salt
12 oz. long-grain rice	350 g. long-grain rice
8 tablespoons finely chopped celery	8 tablespoons finely chopped celery
8 tablespoons finely chopped parsley	8 tablespoons finely chopped parsley
6 tablespoons finely chopped spring onions	6 tablespoons finely chopped spring onions
1 clove garlic, finely chopped	1 clove garlic, finely chopped
4 oz. butter, diced	100 g. butter, diced
2 oz. freshly grated Parmesan	50 g. freshly grated Parmesan
freshly ground black pepper	freshly ground black pepper

1. Pour 2 pints (generous litre) boiling water into a large, heavy pan. Add 1½ teaspoons salt and bring to the boil again.

2. When water is bubbling briskly, shower in rice, stirring with a large fork to prevent grains sticking together.

3. Lower heat and simmer, uncovered, stirring occasionally with the fork, for 10 to 15 minutes, or until rice is almost cooked. It should still be wet enough for the whole mixture to find its own level when the pan is tilted slightly.

4. Remove pan from heat and, using the fork, carefully fold in finely chopped celery, parsley, spring onions and garlic.

5. Cover pan tightly and continue to simmer over a very low heat for 5 to 10 minutes longer, or until remaining water has been absorbed, leaving rice tender but not disintegrating and still on the creamy side.

6. Fold in diced butter and freshly grated Parmesan with the fork. Taste for seasoning, adding fresh ground black pepper and more salt if necessary, and serve immediately, mounded up on a heated serving dish.

Serves 4–6 as a first course, 6 as an accompaniment for chicken, veal or grilled lamb chops

Chef's tip:
There is no need to wash and rinse rice. This practice, which was originally intended to rid the grains of floury starch and impurities, has been rendered obsolete by modern milling and marketing methods.

Rice with Courgettes

Carrot Rice

IMPERIAL	METRIC
2 lb. courgettes	900 g. courgettes
salt	salt
5 tablespoons butter	5 tablespoons butter
1 Spanish onion, finely chopped	1 Spanish onion, finely chopped
1 clove garlic, finely chopped	1 clove garlic, finely chopped
1 lb. tomatoes, peeled and chopped	450 g. tomatoes, peeled and chopped
1 tablespoon tomato paste	1 tablespoon tomato paste
freshly ground black pepper	freshly ground black pepper
4 oz. long-grain rice	100 g. long-grain rice

1. Wash courgettes and trim ends. Cut courgettes into $\frac{1}{4}$-inch ($\frac{1}{2}$-cm.) cubes. Sprinkle cubes liberally with salt; place them in a colander and leave to drain for 1 hour.

2. In a large, heavy saucepan which has a tight-fitting lid, melt butter; add chopped onion, garlic and tomatoes, and simmer gently for 5 minutes, uncovered, stirring frequently.

3. Rinse courgettes with cold water. Drain well and combine with tomato and onion mixture in the saucepan. Stir in tomato paste and season generously with salt and freshly ground black pepper. Bring to simmering point; cover pan tightly and simmer gently for 30 minutes, stirring occasionally.

4. Add rice to pan. Mix well with other ingredients, taking care not to crush courgettes, which will be rather soft by now.

5. Cover pan tightly and simmer very gently until most of the liquid in the pan has been absorbed and rice is cooked but not mushy, 20 to 25 minutes.

6. Pile in a heated serving dish and serve immediately.

Serves 4

IMPERIAL	METRIC
2 tablespoons lemon juice	2 tablespoons lemon juice
salt	salt
8 oz. long-grain rice	225 g. long-grain rice
2 oz. coarsely grated raw carrot	50 g. coarsely grated raw carrot
chopped parsley, to garnish	chopped parsley, to garnish

1. Fill a large pan two-thirds full of water. Add lemon juice and a small handful of salt, and bring to the boil.

2. When water is boiling briskly, shower in rice. Stir well to dislodge any grains that have attached themselves to the bottom of the pan and boil, uncovered, for 10 to 12 minutes. Rice should be cooked but still very firm.

3. Drain rice thoroughly in a colander.

4. Cut a large square of double-thickness muslin. Heap rice in the centre and wrap up in a loose bundle.

5. Place bundle of rice in a steamer over boiling water. Cover steamer tightly and steam for 20 to 25 minutes, or until rice grains are fluffy, tender, and quite separate.

6. Gently fold grated carrot into steamed rice with a fork and garnish with chopped parsley.

Serves 4

Chef's tip:
Whichever method of cooking rice you prefer, the cooked rice should be fluffy, each grain separate and cooked tender but still with 'bite' to it. Test by pressing a grain between thumb and finger—it should have no hard 'core' to it.

Chef's tip:
The rice can be wrapped in a clean tea towel instead of muslin, but make sure that any washing soap or detergent has been thoroughly rinsed out of it to avoid tainting the rice. The grated carrot should not be folded in until, at most, 30 minutes before serving.

Saffron Rice

IMPERIAL	METRIC
½ teaspoon saffron strands	½ teaspoon saffron strands
1¼–1½ pints hot chicken stock	7–9 dl. hot chicken stock
2 tablespoons butter	2 tablespoons butter
1 Spanish onion, finely chopped	1 Spanish onion, finely chopped
1 bay leaf	1 bay leaf
2 cloves	2 cloves
12 oz. long-grain rice	350 g. long-grain rice
6 tablespoons dry white wine (optional)	6 tablespoons dry white wine (optional)
salt and freshly ground black pepper	salt and freshly ground black pepper

1. Pound saffron strands; then dissolve them in ¼ pint (1½ dl.) of the hot chicken stock.

2. Meanwhile, melt butter in a heavy pan and sauté finely chopped onion until transparent.

3. Stir in bay leaf, cloves and rice, together with dissolved saffron, remaining stock, and wine, if used. Mix well and season to taste with salt and freshly ground black pepper.

4. Bring to the boil; cover pan and simmer very gently for 15 minutes, or until rice is tender and stock has been absorbed, leaving rice quite moist.

5. Turn into a heated serving dish, picking out bay leaf and cloves as you come across them, and serve immediately.

Serves 4

Chef's tip:
You can vary the above dish by adding 12 oz. (350 g.) frozen peas with the raw rice. Use the full amount of chicken stock specified and leave out the wine. Buy a recognised spice company's saffron; poorer quality saffron will give little flavour or colour, but is just as expensive.

Spiced Oriental Rice

IMPERIAL	METRIC
2 Spanish onions, finely chopped	2 Spanish onions, finely chopped
4 tablespoons butter	4 tablespoons butter
4 whole cardamom pods	4 whole cardamom pods
4 whole cloves	4 whole cloves
4 black peppercorns	4 black peppercorns
½ teaspoon ground cinnamon	½ teaspoon ground cinnamon
2 teaspoons castor sugar	2 teaspoons castor sugar
salt	salt
12 oz. long-grain rice	350 g. long-grain rice
1¼ pints hot beef stock	7 dl. hot beef stock

1. In a wide, heavy casserole or sauté pan with a tight-fitting lid, sauté finely chopped onions in butter for 4 to 5 minutes until soft and golden.

2. Meanwhile, crush cardamom pods, cloves and peppercorns very finely in a mortar.

3. Stir pounded spices into sautéed onions, together with ground cinnamon, sugar and a good pinch or two of salt, to taste, and continue to stir over a moderate heat until onions are a rich brown colour, 3 to 4 minutes.

4. Add rice and fry for a further 4 or 5 minutes, stirring until grains are thoroughly coated with butter and spice.

5. Pour in hot stock; bring to the boil; stir well to dislodge any grains of rice stuck to the bottom, and cover tightly.

6. Reduce heat and leave to simmer gently without removing the lid for 15 to 20 minutes, or until rice is tender and stock has been absorbed.

7. Taste and add more salt if necessary before serving. The picture shows the rice served with brochettes.

Serves 4–6

Chef's tip:
When cooking rice by the covered method, as in the above recipe, avoid the temptation to lift off the lid every few minutes, otherwise the steamy vapour will escape instead of being forced into the grains to make them light and fluffy.

Thai Rice

IMPERIAL	METRIC
~~2 oz. seedless raisins~~	50 g. seedless raisins
…en stock cubes	
…poons butter	
…sh onion, sliced	
…garlic, chopped	
…ong-grain rice	
…aves	
…nom pods, lightly …ed	
…ce berries, lightly …ed	
…stick cinnamon	
…oon turmeric	
… freshly ground … pepper	
…olit blanched …nds	
…er with boiling water	

(text obscured by card)

…I 90 °C., Gas Mark 5).

…dl.) water in a sauce-
…to add to rice.

…ith a tight-fitting lid,
…y sauté thinly sliced
…oout 10 minutes until

…ntil grains are golden.

…n to taste with salt and
…d 1 pint (6 dl.) of the
… any grains stuck to
…d and quickly transfer
…es. Drain raisins well.

…Fold in raisins with a
…over and return to the

8. Meanwhile, melt remaining butter in a frying pan and sauté blanched almonds over a moderate heat until golden brown all over. Stir constantly as it is very easy to burn them.

9. Remove casserole from the oven. All the moisture in the rice should have been absorbed, leaving the grains tender but firm and separate. If rice is not quite cooked, add a few tablespoons more boiling stock and return to the oven for a further 5 minutes or so, covered.

10. Remove cinnamon stick and bay leaves. With a fork, fold in browned almonds. Taste; add more salt and freshly ground black pepper if necessary, and serve immediately.

Serves 4–6

Fried Rice

IMPERIAL	METRIC
2 eggs	2 eggs
salt and freshly ground black pepper	salt and freshly ground black pepper
1 teaspoon butter	1 teaspoon butter
4 tablespoons corn oil	4 tablespoons corn oil
½ Spanish onion, finely chopped	½ Spanish onion, finely chopped
about 1 lb. cold cooked long-grain rice (say 5 oz. uncooked weight)	about 450 g. cold cooked long-grain rice (say 150 g. uncooked weight)
2 oz. cooked pork, diced	50 g. cooked pork, diced
2 oz. cooked chicken meat, diced	50 g. cooked chicken meat, diced
2 oz. cooked Italian sausage, diced	50 g. cooked Italian sausage, diced
8 button mushrooms, diced	8 button mushrooms, diced
1 tablespoon soy sauce	1 tablespoon soy sauce

1. Break eggs into a small bowl. Season lightly with salt and freshly ground black pepper, and beat gently with a fork until well mixed.

2. Melt butter in a 6-inch (15-cm.) omelette pan. Make a thin flat omelette with the eggs, nicely coloured on both sides. Slip it out onto a plate to cool. Then roll it up and slice it vertically into strips ¼ inch (½ cm.) wide. Put aside.

3. Heat corn oil in a large, deep frying pan. Sauté finely chopped onion gently until soft and golden, about 10 minutes.

4. Add rice, diced pork, chicken, sausage and mushrooms, and continue to cook over a moderate heat, turning ingredients over and over with a wooden spoon to mix them thoroughly without crushing the rice. After 3 to 5 minutes, rice should be hot and show a tendency to stick to the base of the pan.

5. Stir in egg strips and sprinkle with soy sauce. Season to taste with salt and freshly ground black pepper. Continue to cook and stir for a further 2 minutes. Serve immediately.

Serves 4

Chef's tip:
Italian sausages are coarse-cut and spicy, with a lot more kick and a lot less cereal in them than English sausages. If you don't live near an Italian delicatessen which stocks them, use the best-quality English pork sausages you can find.

Arroz con Pollo

IMPERIAL	METRIC
1 2½-lb. frying chicken	1 1¼-kg. frying chicken
4–6 tablespoons olive oil	4–6 tablespoons olive oil
2 gloves garlic, chopped	2 gloves garlic, chopped
1 Spanish onion, finely chopped	1 Spanish onion, finely chopped
1 green sweet pepper, cored, seeded and finely chopped	1 green sweet pepper, cored, seeded and finely chopped
1 bay leaf	1 bay leaf
1 8-oz. can peeled tomatoes, drained	1 226-g. can peeled tomatoes, drained
¼ teaspoon dried thyme	¼ teaspoon dried thyme
¼ teaspoon dried oregano	¼ teaspoon dried oregano
6 oz. long-grain rice	175 g. long-grain rice
¼ teaspoon powdered saffron	¼ teaspoon powdered saffron
1¼ pints chicken stock	7 dl. chicken stock
2 tablespoons tomato paste	2 tablespoons tomato paste
2 teaspoons lemon juice	2 teaspoons lemon juice
salt and freshly ground black pepper	salt and freshly ground black pepper
Garnish:	*Garnish:*
2 canned red peppers, cut into strips	2 canned red peppers, cut into strips
6–8 tablespoons cooked green peas	6–8 tablespoons cooked green peas
4–6 cooked asparagus tips	4–6 cooked asparagus tips

1. Skin chicken and divide into eight pieces. Wipe dry.

2. Heat oil in a large, deep flameproof casserole and sauté chicken pieces until golden brown all over. Remove from casserole with a slotted spoon and keep hot.

3. Add finely chopped garlic, onion and green pepper to oil remaining in casserole, and sauté gently until soft and golden, about 10 minutes. Then stir in bay leaf, peeled tomatoes, thyme, oregano and rice, and continue to sauté for a further 4 to 5 minutes.

4. Preheat oven to moderate (350°F., 180°C., Gas Mark 4).

5. Return chicken pieces to casserole and mix well. Dissolve saffron in stock; add tomato paste and lemon juice, and pour over chicken joints. Bring to the boil and season with ½–1 teaspoon salt.

6. Cover casserole and bake for 20 minutes, or until rice is tender but not mushy. This dish should not be dry, but if it seems excessively liquid, remove the lid halfway through cooking time.

7. When rice and chicken are tender, taste for seasoning, adding salt and freshly ground black pepper, if necessary. Garnish with red pepper, green peas and asparagus tips.

Serves 4

Salade de Moules au Riz

IMPERIAL	METRIC
6 oz. long-grain rice	175 g. long-grain rice
salt	salt
3 pints mussels	1¾ litres mussels
½ pint dry white wine	3 dl. dry white wine
1 onion, finely chopped	1 onion, finely chopped
4 oz. shelled shrimps	100 g. shelled shrimps
2 firm tomatoes, peeled	2 firm tomatoes, peeled
1–2 tablespoons finely chopped parsley	1–2 tablespoons finely chopped parsley
Vinaigrette dressing:	*Vinaigrette dressing:*
1 shallot, finely chopped	1 shallot, finely chopped
2 tablespoons wine vinegar	2 tablespoons wine vinegar
5 tablespoons olive oil	5 tablespoons olive oil
salt and freshly ground black pepper	salt and freshly ground black pepper

1. Boil rice in plenty of salted water until tender but still firm. Drain thoroughly and allow to cool.

2. Scrub mussels clean and remove 'beards'. Place them in a heavy pan with dry white wine and finely chopped onion; cover tightly and cook over a high heat, shaking pan frequently, until mussels have all opened, 5 to 7 minutes.

3. Remove mussels from the pan, shaking back any liquor trapped in their shells. Filter liquor through a sieve lined with fine muslin and return to the rinsed-out pan; add shelled shrimps and simmer for 15 minutes.

4. Meanwhile, remove mussels from their shells.

5. Drain shrimps and combine with rice and mussels in a serving bowl. Slice tomatoes and add them to the bowl, together with finely chopped parsley.

6. Make a highly seasoned vinaigrette with ingredients listed, beating with a fork until they form an emulsion. Pour over salad; toss lightly and chill before serving.

Serves 4

Chef's tip:
Use long-grain rice and leave short-grain for puddings and Italian varieties for risottos. The above dish is excellent for an hors d'oeuvre salad or to serve in a selection of salads for a buffet. It is also extremely good dressed with a well-flavoured home-made mayonnaise.

Curried Chicken Rice Ring

IMPERIAL	METRIC
8 oz. long-grain rice	225 g. long-grain rice
salt	salt
2 tablespoons lemon juice	2 tablespoons lemon juice
6 oz. frozen peas	175 g. frozen peas
1 recipe basic vinaigrette (see page 99)	1 recipe basic vinaigrette (see page 99)
freshly ground black pepper	freshly ground black pepper
Filling:	*Filling:*
1 tablespoon butter	1 tablespoon butter
1 tablespoon olive oil	1 tablespoon olive oil
2 small onions, finely chopped	2 small onions, finely chopped
1 teaspoon curry paste	1 teaspoon curry paste
2 teaspoons curry powder	2 teaspoons curry powder
1 tablespoon flour	1 tablespoon flour
¾ pint chicken stock	4 dl. chicken stock
1 teaspoon tomato paste	1 teaspoon tomato paste
1 tablespoon redcurrant jelly	1 tablespoon redcurrant jelly
3 tablespoons single cream	3 tablespoons single cream
8 oz. cooked chicken meat	225 g. cooked chicken meat
parsley sprigs and twists of lemon, to garnish	parsley sprigs and twists of lemon, to garnish

1. Cook rice in boiling, salted, acidulated water, uncovered, for 10 to 12 minutes.

2. Whilst rice is cooking, cook peas as directed on the packet. Drain thoroughly.

3. Drain rice in a colander. Place rice in a basin and fold in peas and vinaigrette. Season to taste with salt and freshly ground black pepper, if necessary. Spoon the rice mixture into a plain, buttered 2-pint (1-litre) ring mould. Tap the mould once or twice to settle rice; do not press it into the mould. Cover mould tightly with foil.

4. Place mould in a roasting tin with hot water to come two-thirds of the way up the sides of the mould. Simmer very gently for 15 minutes; remove and allow to cool. Chill.

5. To make the filling, heat butter and oil together in a pan. Sauté onions until soft and golden. Add curry paste, curry powder and flour, stir and cook for a further 2 minutes.

6. Gradually stir in stock. Bring to the boil, stirring, then reduce heat and simmer very gently for 20 minutes, uncovered. Then stir in tomato paste and redcurrant jelly.

7. Strain sauce through a sieve into a bowl. Stir in cream; fold in diced chicken. Leave to cool. Chill.

8. When ready to serve, dip rice mould in hot water for a few seconds. Invert mould onto a plate. Place chicken mixture in centre of rice ring and garnish with parsley and lemon.

Serves 4–6

Gnocchi al Herbe

IMPERIAL	METRIC
2 lb. floury potatoes	900 g. floury potatoes
salt	salt
1 6-oz. packet frozen chopped spinach	1 170-g. packet frozen chopped spinach
4 tablespoons fresh parsley	4 tablespoons fresh parsley
1 tablespoon fresh chives	1 tablespoon fresh chives
1 tablespoon fresh basil leaves	1 tablespoon fresh basil leaves
1 tablespoon fresh marjoram leaves	1 tablespoon fresh marjoram leaves
2 egg yolks	2 egg yolks
3–4 tablespoons grated Parmesan	3–4 tablespoons grated Parmesan
about 3 oz. plain flour	about 75 g. plain flour
freshly grated nutmeg	freshly grated nutmeg
a few drops lemon juice	a few drops lemon juice
melted butter and grated Parmesan, to serve	melted butter and grated Parmesan, to serve

1. Peel potatoes and boil in salted water until cooked but not disintegrating. Drain well and shake in the dry pan over a moderate heat to evaporate remaining moisture.

2. Thaw spinach in a pan over a low heat; then simmer, stirring, to rid it of excess moisture.

3. Put potatoes, spinach and finely chopped herbs through the fine blade of a mincer into a large bowl.

4. Quickly blend potatoes, herbs and spinach together by hand (or work with a large wooden spoon), adding egg yolks, grated Parmesan, and enough flour to produce a dough which is quite soft but capable of being shaped into a roll with the aid of some flour. Season to taste with salt, a pinch of freshly grated nutmeg and a little lemon juice.

5. Wash and dry your hands if you have been working the dough by hand. Flour them generously and scoop out a portion of dough onto a floured board. Shape into a long roll about ½ inch (1 cm.) in diameter, and with a floured knife, cut at a slant into 1-inch (2½-cm.) lengths. Repeat with remaining dough.

6. Bring a large pan of salted water to the boil. Drop in a portion of gnocchi at a time—they should all be able to float in one layer when they come to the surface. Bring water back to the boil and simmer gnocchi for 1 minute, or until they have all surfaced. Skim off with a slotted spoon; drain in a colander and rinse briefly with very hot water. Cook remaining gnocchi in the same way, keeping them hot in a slow oven until they are all prepared.

7. Serve gnocchi hot, tossed with a little melted butter and a sprinkling of grated Parmesan.

Serves 6–8

Vegetables and Salads

Every main dish of meat demands some form of vegetable to accompany it. That old cliché, 'meat and two veg' still holds true—even if it is only a green leaf or two of salad and a sliced tomato.

But with very little extra effort, we can all go one better with a simply cooked vegetable or two. Of course, simplicity is no excuse for inferior ingredients or careless preparation. Vegetables, if they are boiled or steamed, must be cooked *à point* or until just tender and no more. (There's a world of difference though between an undercooked vegetable and one taken to the peak of crisp-textured perfection.)

In the English kitchen, more crimes are committed in the name of boiled vegetables than in any other branch of cooking I can think of. The most common mistake is to use too much water and the second to cook vegetables to within an inch of their lives.

Study our 'Boiled Basics' carefully before going any further. Discover for yourself a new world of flavours, unattainable in over-soft, waterlogged specimens. Then proceed to the recipes that follow.

* Find out what a stock cube can do for a simple vegetable dish.

* Marry vegetables with discreet pinches of chopped herbs, broad beans with savory, carrots with chervil, spinach with rosemary, and so on.

* Learn to be free with butter and cream when dressing hot vegetables.

* Above all, learn to look at our basic vegetables with an unjaundiced eye. Treat them with care and respect, and they will repay you a hundredfold.

The perfect green salad

How often have you racked your brain for an accompaniment to a simple dish of meat, poultry or fish, with the feeling that cooked vegetables would be out of place? In the majority of cases, the solution is as simple as the dish itself: a crisp green salad, tossed at the table with a classic dressing of olive oil and wine vinegar or fresh lemon juice.

Nor do you have to abandon the idea of a salad even when the main course includes a richly sauced dish. Just serve the salad on its own as a refreshing interlude between the main course and whatever you have planned to follow.

A separate salad course is also a good idea when you are serving wine with the main course, especially if it is a wine you want to show off, since it is generally recognised that the acidity of a salad dressing dulls the palate to the finer points of a wine.

There are two stages in perfect salad-making: the preparation of the salad itself, and, of course, the dressing.

Preparing the salad

Salad greens should be as fresh as possible—there is no kiss of life for a wilted lettuce, although you can keep one crisp as follows:

* Wash the leaves carefully under the cold tap; then gently pat each leaf dry between the folds of a clean cloth. Make sure they are perfectly dry. The dressing will not adhere to wet leaves, and any excess moisture, in its turn, will dilute the flavour of the dressing.

* Lay leaves out on a fresh cloth. Roll the cloth up loosely and chill in the vegetable compartment of the refrigerator for at least 1 hour, or until ready to serve.

Don't restrict your salad to just lettuce. Curly green endive, Belgian chicory, watercress and French *mâche*, even spinach leaves if they are baby young and tender, all give colour and texture variety. For 'crunch-appeal', add some diced celery, crisp green pepper or anise-flavoured Florence fennel, and a little *very* finely chopped onion or shallot.

Fresh green herbs—parsley, of course, and mint, chervil, basil, tarragon or chives—can either be snipped over the salad or combined with the dressing before the two are tossed together. And have you ever tried adding a chopped nasturtium leaf from the garden?

Preparing the dressing

There is no mystery about a simple French dressing or vinaigrette. Olive oil and vinegar are combined in the proportion of roughly 3 parts oil to 1 part vinegar or lemon juice, seasoned to taste with salt, freshly ground black pepper and perhaps a little mustard, French or English, then beaten vigorously with a fork until the whole thickens into an emulsion. Finally, the dressing can be flavoured with a little finely chopped garlic, and/or herbs.

* Always use the finest olive oil and wine vinegar for a vinaigrette. If your olive oil lacks 'fruitiness', try soaking a few plump black olives (themselves preserved in olive oil) in the bottle. After a week or so, the oil will have acquired a totally new, exciting flavour, with plenty of 'body'. The olives can be left in the bottle and topped up with more oil as necessary—just as you would use a vanilla pod to flavour sugar.

* Freshly ground black pepper is a must, but you should also try substituting coarse salt for table salt. It gives a much 'saltier' flavour.

* Don't drown your salad with dressing: a small to medium lettuce (round or cos) will take 4–6 tablespoons of dressing, a large one, 6–8 tablespoons.

To assemble salad

If you own a salad bowl, you can make the dressing right in it. Then, just before serving, *break* crisp, chilled leaves into the bowl in large pieces—they should *never* be cut with a knife. Toss well and serve, giving the leaves a final tossing at the table to ensure each leaf is thoroughly coated.

* Need I remind you that a wooden salad bowl should never be washed, only wiped clean and dry with plenty of kitchen paper? Store the bowl with a fresh sheet of kitchen paper laid over the bottom to keep it free of dust until the next time it is needed.

Broad Beans with Herb Butter

IMPERIAL	METRIC
1 lb. broad beans	450 g. broad beans
salt	salt
2 tablespoons butter	2 tablespoons butter
1 teaspoon finely chopped chervil	1 teaspoon finely chopped chervil
2 teaspoons finely chopped parsley	2 teaspoons finely chopped parsley
freshly ground black pepper	freshly ground black pepper

1. Simmer beans until tender in just enough boiling salted water to cover, about 12 to 15 minutes if fresh, 5 minutes only if frozen.

2. Meanwhile, pound butter with finely chopped herbs.

3. When beans are cooked, drain them thoroughly and put them in a heated serving dish.

4. Season lightly with salt and freshly ground black pepper; toss with herb butter and serve immediately.

Serves 4

Green Beans à l'Ancienne

IMPERIAL	METRIC
2 lb. green beans	900 g. green beans
salt	salt
12 baby carrots or 6 large carrots	12 baby carrots or 6 large carrots
12 button onions	12 button onions
6 oz. smoked streaky bacon slices, rind removed	175 g. smoked streaky bacon slices, rind removed
2 oz. butter	50 g. butter
1 tablespoon castor sugar	1 tablespoon castor sugar
3 tablespoons cream	3 tablespoons cream
freshly ground black pepper	freshly ground black pepper
1 tablespoon finely chopped chervil	1 tablespoon finely chopped chervil
1 tablespoon finely chopped parsley	1 tablespoon finely chopped parsley

1. Trim and wash beans, and cut them into 2-inch (5-cm.) lengths. Boil in a large pan of salted water, uncovered, for 12 to 15 minutes, or until beans are tender but still firm.

2. Meanwhile, scrape carrots. If baby carrots are used, cut them into thirds; if using larger ones, slice them thickly. Peel button onions.

3. Cut bacon in strips; sauté in butter until crisp and golden; remove with a slotted spoon and keep hot.

4. In the same fat, sauté carrots and button onions together until golden brown all over. Sprinkle with sugar and moisten with ½ pint (3 dl.) water. Simmer until water has evaporated, then continue to cook until remaining juices have caramelised, turning carrots and onions gently to glaze them all over.

5. Drain beans thoroughly and turn them into a large sauté pan or deep frying pan. Add carrots and onions, bacon strips and cream; season to taste with salt and freshly ground black pepper, and toss lightly over a low heat for 3 to 4 minutes.

6. Arrange vegetables in a heated serving dish. Sprinkle with finely chopped chervil and parsley, and serve immediately.

Serves 4–6

Chef's tip:
Use young broad beans, fresh or frozen. If they are too large you will have to remove the outer skins which can be unpleasantly tough. At the height of the season allow double the quantity of beans per person and serve them as a course in themselves.

Chef's tip:
Chervil is one of the famous 'fines herbes'. It is more delicate than parsley and more ferny in appearance. It is one of those herbs that it pays to grow because when dried it is almost totally without flavour.

Lemon-glazed Carrots

IMPERIAL	METRIC
2 lb. carrots	900 g. carrots
2 lemons	2 lemons
2 tablespoons sugar	2 tablespoons sugar
1 chicken stock cube	1 chicken stock cube
4 tablespoons butter	4 tablespoons butter
freshly ground black pepper	freshly ground black pepper
finely chopped parsley and/or chervil, to garnish	finely chopped parsley and/or chervil, to garnish

1. Scrape or peel carrots and cut them lengthwise into $\frac{1}{4}$-inch ($\frac{1}{2}$-cm.) thick slices; then cut slices into sticks $\frac{1}{4}$ inch wide and $1\frac{1}{2}$ inches ($3\frac{1}{2}$ cm.) long. Put carrot sticks in a heavy pan.

2. Grate rind of both lemons and add to the carrots, together with 2 tablespoons lemon juice, the sugar, stock cube, butter and freshly ground black pepper, to taste.

3. Pour in just enough water to cover; lay a buttered paper on top and bring to the boil. Simmer gently until carrots are tender and the liquid has almost completely evaporated, leaving carrots glazed with a light, lemony syrup. This will take about 30 minutes.

4. Give carrots a light toss and turn them out onto a heated serving dish. Garnish with a little finely chopped parsley or chervil, and serve immediately.

Serves 6

Broccoli with Quick Hollandaise Sauce

IMPERIAL	METRIC
$1\frac{1}{2}$ lb. frozen broccoli	675 g. frozen broccoli
salt	salt
8 oz. butter	225 g. butter
6 egg yolks	6 egg yolks
3–4 tablespoons lemon juice	3–4 tablespoons lemon juice
cayenne pepper	cayenne pepper

1. Cook frozen broccoli in salted water according to directions on packet until tender but still firm. Drain and arrange neatly in a heated serving dish.

2. Meanwhile, slowly melt butter in a heavy pan, removing it from the heat as soon as it begins to bubble.

3. Rinse goblet of an electric blender with very hot water and shake dry.

4. Put egg yolks, lemon juice and a pinch of salt into the goblet, and start blending at speed 1. When egg yolks are well mixed, trickle in hot melted butter as you would for mayonnaise, leaving behind the white sediment which will have settled at the bottom. Stop blending as soon as sauce is thick and velvety.

5. Have ready a double saucepan, or a bowl fitted *over* (not resting *in*) simmering water.

6. Pour in sauce, stirring as you do so, and continue to stir until sauce is hot.

7. Season to taste with more salt if necessary and a pinch of cayenne. Spoon over broccoli and serve immediately.

Serves 6

Chef's tip:
If the carrots are old ones, be prepared to cook them longer than the 30 minutes given in the recipe. In this case add a little more water if it has all evaporated before they are quite tender.

Chef's tip:
Ideally one needs a mixer with a glass goblet attachment rather than plastic, as plastic does not retain the heat quite as much. If, when you are heating the sauce in a double saucepan it becomes too thick, you can thin it down again by beating in a little boiling water.

Broccoli with Cheese and Slivered Almonds

IMPERIAL	METRIC
2 9-oz. packets frozen broccoli, thawed	2 255-g. packets frozen broccoli, thawed
salt	salt
Cheese sauce:	*Cheese sauce:*
3 oz. butter	75 g. butter
2 teaspoons Dijon mustard	2 teaspoons Dijon mustard
3 oz. plain flour	75 g. plain flour
1½ pints milk	scant litre milk
4 oz. Emmenthal, freshly grated	100 g. Emmenthal, freshly grated
2 oz. Parmesan, freshly grated	50 g. Parmesan, freshly grated
salt and white pepper	salt and white pepper
Garnish:	*Garnish:*
olive oil	olive oil
2 oz. blanched almonds, slivered	50 g. blanched almonds slivered
salt	salt

1. Start by preparing cheese sauce. Melt butter in a heavy, medium-sized pan; stir in mustard and flour and cook over a moderate heat for 2 to 3 minutes, stirring constantly to make a pale roux. Add milk gradually, stirring constantly to avoid lumps; bring to the boil, lower heat and simmer for 5 minutes, or until sauce has thickened.

2. Remove pan from heat and beat in grated cheeses. Season to taste with salt and white pepper; return to the heat and simmer gently for 2 or 3 minutes longer, stirring occasionally, until sauce is smooth and thick, and cheeses have completely melted. Keep hot.

3. Cook broccoli spears in boiling salted water until tender.

4. While broccoli is cooking, prepare garnish. Heat olive oil in a heavy pan until very hot. Add slivered almonds and toss over a high heat until golden brown, watching carefully to see that they do not burn. Drain thoroughly on absorbent paper and sprinkle with salt, tossing almond slivers about on the paper to coat them evenly.

5. When broccoli is cooked, drain thoroughly and lay in a flameproof dish. Pour over cheese sauce and sprinkle with salted almonds.

6. The broccoli can be served as it is, or browned lightly under a hot grill.

Serves 4–6

Chef's tip:
To sliver almonds successfully, place almonds (skinned or blanched) in a small saucepan with just enough water to cover; bring to the boil and remove from heat; skin and halve if necessary. Use a small sharp knife to cut almonds into long thin sticks.

Brussels Sprouts with Chestnuts and Bacon

IMPERIAL	METRIC
4 oz. streaky bacon, diced	100 g. streaky bacon, diced
3–4 tablespoons butter	3–4 tablespoons butter
8 oz. chestnuts, cooked and peeled	225 g. chestnuts, cooked and peeled
1 lb. Brussels sprouts, cooked	450 g. Brussels sprouts, cooked
salt and freshly ground black pepper	salt and freshly ground black pepper
freshly grated nutmeg	freshly grated nutmeg
4 tablespoons chicken stock	4 tablespoons chicken stock
1 oz. dry white breadcrumbs	25 g. dry white breadcrumbs

1. Preheat oven to moderate (350°F., 180°C., Gas Mark 4).

2. Sauté bacon in 1 tablespoon butter until crisp and golden. Add chestnuts and toss together for 2 minutes over a low heat.

3. Lay half the Brussels sprouts in a baking dish and cover with bacon and chestnut mixture. Top with remaining Brussels sprouts and season lightly with salt (remember bacon may already be rather salty), freshly ground black pepper and a generous pinch of freshly grated nutmeg.

4. Dot dish with half the remaining butter. Moisten with chicken stock and sprinkle with breadcrumbs. Dot with remaining butter and bake for about 15 minutes, or until thoroughly hot.

5. Finish dish by browning breadcrumbs under a hot grill and serve immediately.

Serves 4

Chef's tip:
To shell chestnuts, make two cross-cut gashes on their flat sides; place in a frying pan and fry over a high heat sprinkling with oil and shaking the nuts so they coat evenly; then place in a moderate oven until the shells and the inner skins can be removed easily.

Brussels Sprouts with Almonds

IMPERIAL	METRIC
1 lb. small Brussels sprouts	450 g. small Brussels sprouts
salt	salt
2 tablespoons butter	2 tablespoons butter
1 tablespoon olive oil	1 tablespoon olive oil
1 oz. flaked almonds	25 g. flaked almonds
freshly ground black pepper	freshly ground black pepper

1. Cut off stem ends and remove any wilted or damaged outer leaves from small Brussels sprouts. (If Brussels sprouts are older, remove tough outer leaves entirely.) Nick a small cross in their stems to help them cook evenly.

2. Soak sprouts in cold water with a little salt for 15 minutes.

3. Drop sprouts into a large pan of boiling salted water and simmer, uncovered, for 5 minutes. Cover pan and continue to cook for 7 (if very young) to 15 minutes longer, or until sprouts are just tender.

4. Meanwhile, heat butter and oil in a small heavy pan; add flaked almonds and sauté until golden.

5. Drain sprouts thoroughly and put them in a well-heated serving dish.

6. Pour over buttery almond sauce; season to taste with salt and freshly ground black pepper, and toss lightly. Serve immediately.

Serves 4

Sautéed Courgettes and Tomatoes

IMPERIAL	METRIC
12 courgettes	12 courgettes
salt	salt
6 tablespoons flour	6 tablespoons flour
6 tablespoons freshly grated Parmesan	6 tablespoons freshly grated Parmesan
freshly ground black pepper	freshly ground black pepper
4 tablespoons olive oil	4 tablespoons olive oil
4 tablespoons butter	4 tablespoons butter
1 Spanish onion, coarsely chopped	1 Spanish onion, coarsely chopped
8 tomatoes, peeled, seeded and chopped	8 tomatoes, peeled, seeded and chopped
4 coriander seeds, crushed	4 coriander seeds, crushed

1. Slice courgettes thickly and poach in boiling salted water until just tender, about 5 minutes. Drain thoroughly then dry slices on absorbent kitchen paper.

2. Combine flour with freshly grated Parmesan, and salt and freshly ground black pepper to taste. Toss courgette slices in this mixture until lightly coated.

3. Heat oil in a heavy sauté pan and sauté courgettes over a moderate heat until golden brown on all sides. Remove from pan with a slotted spoon; drain thoroughly on absorbent paper. Pile in centre of a suitable serving dish and keep hot.

4. Melt butter in sauté pan and sauté coarsely chopped onion until soft and transparent. Add chopped tomatoes and crushed coriander seeds and simmer for 2 to 3 minutes longer.

5. Surround courgettes with sautéed onion and tomato mixture. Serve hot.

Serves 6

Chef's tip:
The more stark and unadorned a vegetable is, the more it needs to be perfectly cooked, i.e., it must be cooked until *just* done and no more. The most common mistakes are to use too much water or to cook the vegetables to within an inch of their lives.

Chef's tip:
Now that courgettes are more readily available in this country try the most straightforward way of cooking them; slice them and put in a heavy pan with plenty of melted butter—no liquid. Cover and cook over a low heat, shaking pan occasionally. Serve sprinkled with salt and freshly ground black pepper.

Cabbage au Gratin

IMPERIAL	METRIC
1 head cabbage, about 2½ lb.	1 head cabbage, about 1¼ kg.
¾ pint chicken (cube) stock	4 dl. chicken (cube) stock
½ oz. butter	15 g. butter
½ oz. flour	15 g. flour
½ pint milk	3 dl. milk
1 egg yolk	1 egg yolk
1 oz. Parmesan, freshly grated	25 g. Parmesan, freshly grated
salt and freshly ground black pepper	salt and freshly ground black pepper

1. With a very sharp knife, slice cabbage in half and cut each half into three wedges. Trim away cores.

2. Bring chicken stock to the boil in a large pan; add cabbage wedges and poach for 10 minutes, or until cooked but still slightly crisp. Drain; transfer to a heatproof dish and keep hot.

3. Prepare a sauce by melting butter in a heavy pan; add flour and stir over a low heat for 2 or 3 minutes to make a pale roux. Add milk gradually, stirring constantly to avoid lumps; bring to the boil and simmer, stirring occasionally, until sauce thickens and no longer tastes of raw flour.

4. Remove pan from heat and beat in egg yolk vigorously; then return to the heat and cook for 2 minutes longer, stirring constantly and taking great care not to let sauce boil again, or egg yolk may curdle.

5. Remove pan from heat again. Beat in freshly grated Parmesan and season generously with salt and freshly ground black pepper.

6. Pour sauce over cabbage wedges and brown under a hot grill until golden and bubbling.

Serves 6

Pommes Fifine

IMPERIAL	METRIC
3 large new potatoes (1 lb.)	3 large new potatoes (450 g.)
salt	salt
1 medium-sized onion, finely chopped	1 medium-sized onion, finely chopped
4 teaspoons butter	4 teaspoons butter
3 tablespoons olive oil	3 tablespoons olive oil
freshly ground black pepper	freshly ground black pepper
3 slices streaky bacon, to garnish	3 slices streaky bacon, to garnish
2 tablespoons finely chopped parsley	2 tablespoons finely chopped parsley

1. Scrub potatoes clean and boil them in their jackets in salted water for 15 minutes only so that they remain under-cooked. Cool potatoes by plunging them into cold water.

2. Meanwhile, sauté finely chopped onion in 3 teaspoons (1 tablespoon) butter until golden, 4 to 5 minutes. Put aside.

3. Peel potatoes and cut them into ¼-inch (½-cm.) dice.

4. In a large, heavy frying pan, heat oil with remaining butter. Add diced potatoes and sauté over a high heat for 5 to 6 minutes until crisp and golden on all sides.

5. Season to taste with salt and freshly ground black pepper. Return sautéed onion to the pan; toss lightly to mix it thoroughly with the potatoes and sauté for 1 minute longer. Fry bacon slices until crisp.

6. Drain potato mixture well and serve immediately, garnished with finely chopped parsley and crumbled bacon.

Serves 3–4

Chef's tip:
You need not throw away the hard cores to any cabbages you are preparing as a vegetable for a meal. Use the coarsest side of your grater to shred them up and add to the saucepan of boiling cabbage.

Chef's tip:
When making mashed potatoes try adding a small onion or a cut clove of garlic, a piece of bay leaf and a stalk of celery with leaves, for additional flavouring. Remove the flavourings before mashing potatoes.

Casey's Potatoes

IMPERIAL	METRIC
2–2½ lb. potatoes	1–1¼ kg. potatoes
1 large green sweet pepper	1 large green sweet pepper
1 large Spanish onion	1 large Spanish onion
1 tablespoon flour	1 tablespoon flour
4 tablespoons finely chopped parsley	4 tablespoons finely chopped parsley
4 oz. cheese, freshly grated	100 g. cheese, freshly grated
pinch paprika	pinch paprika
pinch freshly grated nutmeg	pinch freshly grated nutmeg
salt and freshly ground black pepper	salt and freshly ground black pepper
¼ pint hot milk	1½ dl. hot milk
¼ pint double cream	1½ dl. double cream
2 tablespoons butter	2 tablespoons butter

1. Preheat oven to moderately hot (400°F., 200°C., Gas Mark 6).

2. Peel potatoes and cut them into ¼-inch (½-cm.) dice. Place them in a bowl. Slice pepper in half; remove core and seeds, and chop flesh finely. Add to potatoes. Peel onion and chop finely; toss lightly with diced potatoes and pepper.

3. Sprinkle with flour, chopped parsley and grated cheese, and toss again. Then season to taste with a pinch of paprika, freshly grated nutmeg, salt and a little freshly ground black pepper.

4. Spread potato mixture evenly in a 3-pint (1¾-litre) oven-proof dish; pour over milk and cream; dot with butter and bake for 1 hour, or until potatoes are soft, with a crisp, golden brown topping.

Serves 6

Vegetables in Cream Sauce

IMPERIAL	METRIC
1 lb. cooked mixed vegetables	450 g. cooked mixed vegetables
1 chicken stock cube	1 chicken stock cube
2 tablespoons butter	2 tablespoons butter
3 tablespoons flour	3 tablespoons flour
5 tablespoons single cream	5 tablespoons single cream
1 egg yolk	1 egg yolk
1 teaspoon lemon juice	1 teaspoon lemon juice
salt and freshly ground black pepper	salt and freshly ground black pepper

1. Prepare vegetables, cutting large pieces—carrots, turnips, etc.—into ¼-inch (½-cm.) dice.

2. Dissolve stock cube in ½ pint (3 dl.) boiling water.

3. In a heavy, medium-sized saucepan, melt butter. Blend in flour and cook over a low heat for 2 minutes, stirring constantly, to make a pale roux.

4. Gradually add chicken stock, beating vigorously to prevent lumps forming. Bring to the boil, stirring, and simmer for 2 to 3 minutes longer.

5. Remove pan from heat. Stir in cream and the egg yolk; return pan to a low heat and stir sauce until it thickens again. Take care not to let it boil, however, or egg yolk may curdle.

6. Fold in cooked vegetables. Add lemon juice and season to taste with salt and freshly ground black pepper.

7. Continue to cook just long enough to heat the vegetables through, stirring frequently. Serve immediately.

Serves 4–6

Chef's tip:
It's easy to keep old potatoes firm for potato salad if you boil them in their jackets until just done and allow them to cool completely in their cooking water. This way, the skin peels off easily, leaving potatoes smooth and firm enough to dice without crumbling.

Chef's tip:
You can use leftover cooked vegetables for this dish—any combination you have on hand, e.g., equal quantities of diced carrots and peas, diced carrots and turnips, or carrots, turnips *and* peas. Also cooked celery, sweet-corn, broad beans, green beans cut into 1-inch (2½-cm.) lengths, etc.

Corn Fritters

IMPERIAL	METRIC
1 10-oz. can creamed sweetcorn	1 283-g. can creamed sweetcorn
4 oz. plain flour	100 g. plain flour
2 teaspoons baking powder	2 teaspoons baking powder
¾ teaspoon salt	¾ teaspoon salt
¼ teaspoon paprika	¼ teaspoon paprika
2 teaspoons castor sugar	2 teaspoons castor sugar
2 eggs, separated	2 eggs, separated
6 tablespoons milk	5½ tablespoons milk
oil for deep-frying	oil for deep-frying
paprika or castor sugar, to serve	paprika or castor sugar, to serve

1. Place contents of can of sweetcorn in a sieve and leave over a bowl to drain of its own accord, i.e., without pushing or pressing with a spoon.

2. Sift the next five ingredients into a bowl. Make a well in the centre.

3. Add egg yolks and 3 tablespoons milk, and mix vigorously with a wooden spoon or a wire whisk, gradually incorporating flour from sides of well and adding remaining milk to make a thick, smooth batter.

4. Weigh out 6 oz. (175 g.) of the drained sweetcorn and stir it into the batter (you will have some left to use in another recipe).

5. Whisk egg whites until stiff but not dry. Fold into batter with a metal spoon or spatula.

6. Heat a pan of oil for deep-frying to 375°F. (190°C.).

7. Drop tablespoons of batter into oil, holding the spoon close to the surface so that fritters keep a neat, rounded shape. Allow them to puff up and brown on one side, then flip them over and continue to fry until crisp and golden brown all over. Drain on absorbent paper.

8. Serve fritters immediately, before they lose their crispness, either lightly dusted with a pinch of paprika, or tossed with castor sugar.

Serves 4–6

Chef's tip:
It is a wise precaution to have either a large lid or a baking sheet handy when deep-frying to drop over the pan should it go up in flames. After frying off one batch let the oil come up to temperature again before proceeding with the next.

Cauliflower Beignets

IMPERIAL	METRIC
1 large firm cauliflower	1 large firm cauliflower
coarse salt	coarse salt
salt and freshly ground black pepper	salt and freshly ground black pepper
oil for deep-frying	oil for deep-frying
Beer batter:	*Beer batter:*
5 oz. plain flour	150 g. plain flour
pinch salt	pinch salt
2 tablespoons olive oil	2 tablespoons olive oil
¼ pint beer, preferably lager	1½ dl. beer, preferably lager
1 egg white	1 egg white

1. To make the beer batter, sift flour and salt into a bowl and make a well in the centre.

2. Pour in olive oil and gradually add beer, stirring with a wooden spoon to incorporate flour from sides of well. Batter should be completely smooth and slightly thicker than a crêpe batter. Leave to rest for 2 hours.

3. Divide cauliflower into flowerets; wash carefully and throw into a large pan of boiling water to which you have added a tablespoon of coarse salt. Boil until tender but still very firm, about 10 minutes.

4. Drain thoroughly and leave to become quite cold; then season generously with salt and freshly ground black pepper.

5. Heat a pan of oil for deep-frying to 375°F. (190°C.).

6. When ready to use batter, whisk egg white until stiff but not dry and fold in lightly but thoroughly.

7. Immediately dip cauliflowerets into batter, a few at a time; shake off excess batter and deep-fry for 4 to 5 minutes, or until a rich golden colour. Drain thoroughly on absorbent paper and serve immediately.

Serves 4–6

Chef's tip:
Please use a thermometer when deep-frying, especially if you always use oil. Thermometers which are marked off with recommended temperatures from junket to chips and upwards can be bought. They are also an important piece of equipment when boiling sugar to a specific point.

Basic Vinaigrette (French Dressing)

Salade Verte (Green Appetizer Salad)

IMPERIAL	METRIC
2 tablespoons wine vinegar or lemon juice	2 tablespoons wine vinegar or lemon juice
coarse salt and freshly ground black pepper	coarse salt and freshly ground black pepper
dry or French mustard (optional)	dry or French mustard (optional)
6–8 tablespoons olive oil	6–8 tablespoons olive oil

1. In a bowl, stir wine vinegar or lemon juice with a generous pinch of coarse salt and freshly ground black pepper to taste, and a little mustard, if liked.

2. Beat in olive oil with a fork until dressing thickens and emulsifies.

Note: For a creamier dressing, stir an ice cube with it for a minute or two. Remove cube and serve dressing immediately.

Variations

Herb dressing Flavour basic vinaigrette with 1 clove garlic, finely chopped, and 1 teaspoon each finely chopped fresh parsley or chervil, marjoram, basil and chives.

Tarragon dressing Flavour basic vinaigrette with a teaspoon of chopped fresh tarragon leaves.

Mint dressing Flavour basic vinaigrette with 2 tablespoons finely chopped fresh mint, 1 tablespoon finely chopped fresh parsley and $\frac{1}{4}$ teaspoon French mustard.

Caper dressing Flavour basic vinaigrette with 1 teaspoon chopped capers, $\frac{1}{2}$ clove garlic, finely chopped, and a little anchovy paste.

Curry dressing Flavour basic vinaigrette with $\frac{1}{2}$ teaspoon curry paste or powder, and 1 teaspoon very finely chopped shallot.

IMPERIAL	METRIC
1 green sweet pepper	1 green sweet pepper
1 small bulb Florence fennel	1 small bulb Florence fennel
$\frac{1}{2}$ cucumber	$\frac{1}{2}$ cucumber
6 spring onions	6 spring onions
1 tablespoon finely chopped parsley, chives and tarragon	1 tablespoon finely chopped parsley, chives and tarragon
juice of 1 small lemon	juice of 1 small lemon
coarse salt and freshly ground black pepper	coarse salt and freshly ground black pepper

1. Seed and core green pepper and slice into strips about $\frac{1}{4}$ inch ($\frac{1}{2}$ cm.) thick.

2. Slice the bulb of fennel in half. Wash it thoroughly and cut into thick strips about $\frac{1}{2}$ inch (1 cm.) thick.

3. Halve cucumber lengthwise; then cut across into slices about $\frac{1}{4}$ inch thick.

4. Trim spring onions and chop them coarsely.

5. Toss prepared vegetables together in a large salad bowl.

6. Stir herbs into lemon juice and pour over vegetables. Toss again, adding coarse salt and freshly ground black pepper to taste, and serve immediately.

Serves 4

Chef's tip:
Always use olive oil for vinaigrette, never salad oil. Find an olive oil that you like the flavour of and stick to it. I find the medium priced oils are the best—the more expensive ones seem to have the flavour refined out of them.

Chef's tip:
The leaves and the seeds of fennel can be used in cooking. The slightly anise flavour goes well with fish—especially if the fish is grilled on a bed of dried fennel twigs. The seeds can be used in apple pie which makes a welcome change from the usual cloves.

Lettuce with Roquefort Dressing

IMPERIAL	METRIC
2 heads lettuce	2 heads lettuce
6–8 tablespoons olive oil	6–8 tablespoons olive oil
2 tablespoons wine vinegar	2 tablespoons wine vinegar
2 tablespoons double cream	2 tablespoons double cream
2 tablespoons Roquefort cheese	2 tablespoons Roquefort cheese
1 hard-boiled egg, finely chopped	1 hard-boiled egg, finely chopped
1 slice bacon, grilled and crumbled	1 slice bacon, grilled and crumbled
freshly ground black pepper	freshly ground black pepper
dash Tabasco	dash Tabasco

1. Wash lettuce leaves carefully. Shake them dry in a salad basket or pat each leaf dry individually. Wrap in a clean cloth and leave to crisp in the bottom of the refrigerator until ready to use.

2. To make dressing, combine olive oil, vinegar, cream and Roquefort in a small bowl and whisk until smooth. Stir in finely chopped hard-boiled egg and crumbled bacon, and season to taste with freshly ground black pepper and Tabasco.

3. Just before serving, tear lettuce leaves coarsely into a salad bowl. Pour over dressing; toss thoroughly and serve.

Serves 4–6

Lettuce with Green Goddess Dressing

IMPERIAL	METRIC
1 large cos lettuce, or 2 small ones	1 large cos lettuce, or 2 small ones
Green goddess dressing:	*Green goddess dressing:*
½ pint thick, home-made mayonnaise	3 dl. thick, home-made mayonnaise
3–4 anchovy fillets, pounded	3–4 anchovy fillets, pounded
4 tablespoons finely chopped parsley	4 tablespoons finely chopped parsley
4 tablespoons finely chopped spring onion tops or chives	4 tablespoons finely chopped spring onion tops or chives
1 clove garlic, very finely chopped or crushed	1 clove garlic, very finely chopped or crushed
1 tablespoon lemon juice	1 tablespoon lemon juice
1 tablespoon tarragon vinegar	1 tablespoon tarragon vinegar
4 tablespoons double cream, whipped, or thick sour cream	4 tablespoons double cream, whipped, or thick sour cream
salt and freshly ground black pepper	salt and freshly ground black pepper

1. Wash lettuce leaves carefully; pat them dry individually and roll them up in a clean cloth. Leave to crisp in the vegetable compartment of your refrigerator until ready to use.

2. Prepare green goddess dressing. Combine first seven ingredients in a bowl or jug, and beat with a spoon until well mixed. Fold in cream and season to taste with salt and freshly ground black pepper. Cover bowl or jug tightly with foil and chill in the refrigerator until ready to serve.

3. Just before serving, tear lettuce leaves coarsely into a salad bowl. Spoon over some of the dressing and toss until leaves are thoroughly but lightly coated. Serve remaining dressing in a separate bowl for guests to help themselves to more if they like.

Serves 6

Chef's tip:
Always use your common sense and good taste in the matter of salad dressings. Don't go overboard in experimenting: a heavy dressing will make any lettuce collapse just when you want it to stay crisp.

Chef's tip:
The dressing for this salad, which comes from America, keeps well in the refrigerator for at least 48 hours. The herbs should be chopped so finely that they are practically powdered.

Tossed Green Salad with Cheddar Dressing

IMPERIAL	METRIC
1 small cos lettuce	1 small cos lettuce
1 small round lettuce	1 small round lettuce
1 small head curly green endive (optional)	1 small head curly green endive (optional)
2 bulbs white chicory	2 bulbs white chicory
1 small clove garlic	1 small clove garlic
8 tablespoons olive oil	8 tablespoons olive oil
4 tablespoons finely chopped parsley	4 tablespoons finely chopped parsley
2 tablespoon finely chopped chives or spring onion tops	2 tablespoons finely chopped chives or spring onion tops
$\frac{1}{2}$ teaspoon dry mustard	$\frac{1}{2}$ teaspoon dry mustard
1 tablespoon wine vinegar	1 tablespoon wine vinegar
2 tablespoons lemon juice	2 tablespoons lemon juice
salt and freshly ground black pepper	salt and freshly ground black pepper
4 tablespoons grated Cheddar cheese	4 tablespoons grated Cheddar cheese

1. Wash lettuces, green endive (if used), and white chicory, separating out leaves and discarding any bruised or discoloured ones. Dry leaves individually; wrap them in a damp cloth and leave to crisp in the vegetable compartment of the refrigerator.

2. Peel and crush garlic clove. Put it in a small bowl; pour over olive oil and leave at room temperature for about 1 hour. Then strain garlic-flavoured oil and discard garlic.

3. Break salad greens into a salad bowl in fairly large pieces. Sprinkle with finely chopped parsley and chives or spring onion tops, and toss well.

4. Blend dry mustard smoothly with wine vinegar. Add to garlic oil, together with lemon juice, and beat with a fork until ingredients form an emulsion. Season to taste with salt and freshly ground black pepper.

5. Pour dressing over salad and toss thoroughly.

6. Finally, sprinkle salad with grated Cheddar. Toss again and serve immediately.

Serves 4–6

Chef's tip:
You either like or hate garlic. If you dislike it, then leave it out. Do not use garlic powder or garlic salt—use the real thing. Either finely chop the peeled cloves or mash them up finely together with a little salt, using a broad-bladed knife.

Beetroot in Orange Butter

IMPERIAL	METRIC
2 medium-sized cooked beetroot	2 medium-sized cooked beetroot
3 tablespoons butter	3 tablespoons butter
4 tablespoons orange juice	4 tablespoons orange juice
1 teaspoon grated orange rind	1 teaspoon grated orange rind
salt	salt
sugar (optional)	sugar (optional)

1. Peel cooked beetroot and cut into small dice. Put it in a small, heavy pan together with butter, orange juice, orange rind, and salt to taste. Add a pinch of sugar if orange juice is very sour.

2. Heat through, shaking pan, until butter has melted; then cover pan and cook over a very low heat for 12 to 15 minutes, or until piping hot.

Serves 4

Chef's tip:
Beetroot are more satisfactory baked than boiled. Remove leaves leaving a 1-inch (2½-cm.) length of stem, scrub well and place in a casserole. Half cover with boiling water, add a little salt; cover and cook in a moderately hot oven (400°F., 200°C., Gas Mark 6). Allow 1 hour for young beets; 1 to 2 hours for old ones.

Orange and Chicory Salad

IMPERIAL
4 oranges
12 oz. white chicory
generous pinch cayenne
3 tablespoons olive oil
1 tablespoon wine vinegar
salt and freshly ground
    black pepper
2 tablespoons finely
    chopped parsley
1 head crisp round lettuce
black olives, halved and
    stoned, to garnish

METRIC
4 oranges
350 g. white chicory
generous pinch cayenne
3 tablespoons olive oil
1 tablespoon wine vinegar
salt and freshly ground
    black pepper
2 tablespoons finely
    chopped parsley
1 head crisp round lettuce
black olives, halved and
    stoned, to garnish

1. Peel oranges and cut them into segments over a bowl to catch their juices. Squeeze remaining juice from orange scraps into the bowl as well.

2. Separate each head of chicory into leaves; wash and dry them thoroughly.

3. Put a generous pinch of cayenne into a small bowl and whisk in olive oil slowly. Then beat in vinegar and juice drained off from orange segments; season to taste with salt and freshly ground black pepper and stir in finely chopped parsley.

4. Wash lettuce carefully; pat each leaf dry with a cloth and use leaves to line six individual serving plates.

5. Arrange chicory leaves in a fan shape on top and place an orange segment in the hollow of each leaf. Spoon over vinaigrette dressing and decorate each plate with pieces of black olive. Serve immediately.

Serves 6

Chef's tip:
Pitting black olives is a tedious job but there are several types of olive (and cherry) pitters on the market and they do save a lot of time and energy with this otherwise fiddly job.

Chinese Vegetable Salad

IMPERIAL
8 radishes
2 large carrots
4 stalks celery
8 spring onions
lettuce leaves
Dressing:
3 tablespoons olive oil
2 teaspoons lemon juice
1 teaspoon soy sauce
1 teaspoon sugar
pinch monosodium
    glutamate
freshly ground black pepper

METRIC
8 radishes
2 large carrots
4 stalks celery
8 spring onions
lettuce leaves
Dressing:
3 tablespoons olive oil
2 teaspoons lemon juice
1 teaspoon soy sauce
1 teaspoon sugar
pinch monosodium
    glutamate
freshly ground black pepper

1. Have ready a large bowl of water with ice cubes.

2. With a small, sharp knife, trim radishes and pare down red skins into petals. Then pare in white centres to produce a rose-like shape. Drop into iced water.

3. Slice carrots thinly lengthwise and cut into thin, 2-inch (5-cm.) strips. Add to bowl.

4. Cut celery stalks into thin strips lengthwise, then into $1\frac{1}{2}$-inch (4-cm.) lengths. Add to the bowl.

5. Trim roots of spring onions and cut off green parts to make them about $2\frac{1}{2}$ inches (6 cm.) long, with white bulbs included. Then make three or four 1-inch ($2\frac{1}{2}$-cm.) cuts at either end, taking care not to separate onion strips completely. Add them to the bowl.

6. Leave the bowl of vegetables to soak in the refrigerator for at least 1 hour, during which time they will all curl up most attractively.

7. Prepare dressing. Beat ingredients together until they form an emulsion.

8. Just before serving, drain chilled vegetables thoroughly and arrange them in a bowl lined with lettuce leaves. Pour over dressing; toss and serve.

Serves 4

Chef's tip:
Monosodium glutamate (known as M.S.G.) is a crystalline salt occurring naturally in many foods. It has the ability to bring out the natural flavours of foods although the salt itself has no distinctive flavour. It can be bought under the name of Ac'cent in this country.

Chef's Salad

IMPERIAL	METRIC
1 crisp lettuce	1 crisp lettuce
1 bunch watercress	1 bunch watercress
4 oz. cooked chicken	100 g. cooked chicken
4 oz. smoked cooked ox tongue	100 g. smoked cooked ox tongue
4 oz. cooked ham	100 g. cooked ham
4 oz. Gruyère	100 g. Gruyère
2 eggs, hard-boiled	2 eggs, hard-boiled
4 tomatoes	4 tomatoes
$\frac{1}{4}$ pint well-flavoured French dressing (see page 99)	1$\frac{1}{2}$ dl. well-flavoured French dressing (see page 99)

1. Wash lettuce and watercress.

2. Dry lettuce carefully, leaf by leaf. Tear leaves up coarsely and arrange them at the bottom of a salad bowl.

3. Cut chicken, tongue, ham and cheese into thin strips.

4. Shell and quarter hard-boiled eggs.

5. Cut tomatoes into wedges.

6. Arrange meats, cheese, eggs and tomatoes on the bed of lettuce, grouping them according to colour. Place a cluster of watercress in the centre.

7. Serve immediately with a well-flavoured French dressing.

Serves 4

Chef's tip:
If you cannot get Gruyère substitute Emmenthal. These are easy to distinguish when buying. Gruyère is usually full of small holes and is more expensive, Emmenthal has large holes and is considered the poor relation; Gruyère is made in France, Emmenthal comes from Switzerland.

Celeriac, Ham and Apple Salad

IMPERIAL	METRIC
1 head celeriac, about 1 lb.	1 head celeriac, about 450 g.
salt	salt
6–8 oz. cooked ham, in one piece	175–225 g. cooked ham, in one piece
2 large tart dessert apples	2 large tart dessert apples
juice of 1 lemon	juice of 1 lemon
4 tablespoons double cream	4 tablespoons double cream
freshly ground black pepper	freshly ground black pepper
$\frac{1}{2}$ small Spanish onion, finely chopped	$\frac{1}{2}$ small Spanish onion, finely chopped
2 tablespoons finely chopped chives	2 tablespoons finely chopped chives
a few quartered walnuts (optional)	a few quartered walnuts (optional)

1. Peel celeriac and cut into $\frac{1}{3}$-inch ($\frac{3}{4}$-cm.) thick slices. Drop them into a large pan of boiling salted water and simmer until cooked but still firm, about 15 minutes. Drain well and allow to cool.

2. Cut ham into rectangles $\frac{1}{2}$ inch (1 cm.) wide, 1 inch (2$\frac{1}{2}$ cm.) long and about $\frac{1}{3}$ inch thick.

3. Peel and core apples and dice neatly. Toss with lemon juice to prevent discolouration.

4. Season cream generously with salt and freshly ground black pepper.

5. Dice celeriac and combine with ham, apples and finely chopped onion in a large serving bowl.

6. Dress with seasoned cream and toss carefully until well mixed. Correct seasoning, adding more salt, freshly ground black pepper or lemon juice, to taste, and chill lightly before serving.

7. When ready to serve, give salad a final toss and garnish with chopped chives, and walnuts, if liked. Serve very cold.

Serves 6

Chef's tip:
Celeriac is a variety of celery available during the winter months which is cultivated for its turnip-like base; the stalks of this particular plant are not eaten. Do not buy too large a root as they tend to be hollow and woody in the centre.

Cakes, Sweets and Desserts

Successful cake-making is a science demanding a greater degree of accuracy and self-discipline than most other branches of cooking. Some people seem to be able to turn out light cakes right from the word go. For others, the knack only comes with practice. I suspect it's a question of temperament.

Although it is perfectly true that our grandmothers baked good cakes without accurate weights and measures or thermostatically controlled ovens to go by, that is no reason for us to deprive ourselves of these modern aids. You may remember Granny's marvellous fruit cakes with nostalgic longings, but doesn't it strike you now that her repertoire was pretty limited after all? And have you ever wondered why

it is so difficult to reproduce successfully a cake recipe that has been written down in teacups and Victorian tablespoons—the answer is that only Granny knows the size of the cup and spoon she used, as well as the vagaries of her temperamental old stove. So, if you want to be a successful cake-maker, I urge you to start by investing in reliable measuring equipment.

Next, check your oven thermostat and find out about its peculiarities. You can use an oven thermometer, or the following method. Make up a portion of Victoria sandwich batter (see recipe below). Divide it between two 7-inch (18-cm.) sandwich tins and place them, side by side, in the centre of a moderate

oven (350°F., 180°C., Gas Mark 4) that has been pre-heated for at least 20 minutes. Exactly 25 minutes later, the cakes should be perfectly risen and cooked, the top a rich, even golden brown.

Oven too hot:

1. Cake rises in a cone in the centre—the sides harden with a crust before the batter has finished rising. Sometimes the top cracks badly into the bargain.

2. Cake browns too fast.

3. Hard crust forms on top—delicate sponge-type cakes are prone to this.

Oven too cool:

1. Cake shrinks in the middle.

2. Fruit drops to the bottom.

3. Coarse and/or close and/or dry, crumbly texture.

Oven uneven:

1. Cracked or overbrowned top indicates oven is much hotter towards the top. In future, bake on a lower shelf.

2. Bottom of cake too brown—next time, place the tin on an asbestos mat, as your oven seems to be hotter towards the bottom. (It might also indicate that your baking tins are too thin.)

3. Cake rises lopsidedly. If you are *sure* that you levelled off the top before putting the cake into the oven, then the likelihood is that the oven is hotter on the side that rose higher. Correct this by gently turning the cake tin from time to time while baking.

Victoria Sandwich Cake   — 1½ or Double !

IMPERIAL	METRIC
melted butter	melted butter
4 oz. plain flour	110 g. plain flour
1 teaspoon baking powder	1 teaspoon baking powder
4 oz. butter	110 g. butter
4 oz. castor sugar	110 g. castor sugar
few drops vanilla essence or finely grated lemon rind, to taste	few drops vanilla essence or finely grated lemon rind, to taste
2 eggs	2 eggs
red jam	red jam
icing sugar	icing sugar

1. Preheat oven to moderate (375°F., 190°C., Gas Mark 5).

2. Brush two 7-inch sandwich tins with melted butter. Line bases with circles of greaseproof paper and brush these with melted butter as well.

3. Sift flour with baking powder.

4. In a large bowl, cream butter, sugar and flavouring together until light and fluffy.

5. In another, small bowl, whisk eggs until frothy. Add to creamed mixture a few tablespoons at a time, beating well between each addition.

6. Resift flour mixture over creamed mixture. Fold in lightly but thoroughly with a large metal spoon or spatula.

7. Divide batter evenly between prepared tins and level off tops with the back of your spoon.

8. Bake layers (on the same shelf if possible) for 25 minutes, or until they are a rich golden colour on top, have shrunk slightly from sides of tins and spring back when pressed lightly with a finger.

9. Turn layers out onto a folded cloth and carefully peel off base papers. Then turn right side up again and place on wire rack to cool.

10. When layers are quite cold, sandwich with good red jam, warmed to make it spread more easily, and dust with sifted icing sugar.

Makes 6 portions

Cinnamon Coffee Cake

IMPERIAL	METRIC
6 oz. plain flour	175 g. plain flour
1½ teaspoons baking powder	1½ teaspoons baking powder
pinch salt	pinch salt
4 oz. softened butter	110 g. softened butter
3 oz. castor sugar	85 g. castor sugar
2 eggs	2 eggs
2–3 tablespoons milk	2–3 tablespoons milk
Topping:	*Topping:*
3 oz. castor sugar	85 g. castor sugar
1½ tablespoons ground cinnamon	1½ tablespoons ground cinnamon
1 oz. unsalted butter	25 g. unsalted butter

1. Butter a 7½-inch (19-cm.) square cake tin and line base with buttered greaseproof paper.

2. Preheat oven to moderate (350°F., 180°C., Gas Mark 4).

3. Sift flour with baking powder and salt.

4. In a large bowl, beat the softened butter and castor sugar with a wooden spoon until pale and fluffy.

5. Whisk eggs lightly in a small bowl and add to the butter and sugar mixture a little at a time, beating vigorously.

6. Finally, beat in dry ingredients a little at a time, alternately with milk.

7. Spread batter evenly in prepared tin.

8. To make topping, mix together castor sugar and cinnamon and sprinkle evenly over top of raw cake mixture. Dot entire surface with small flakes of unsalted butter.

9. Bake for 50 to 55 minutes, or until cake is firm and well risen, and topping crisp.

10. Turn out and serve lukewarm, cut into squares.

Serves 8

Almond Fruit Cake

IMPERIAL	METRIC
6 oz. softened butter	175 g. softened butter
6 oz. granulated sugar	175 g. granulated sugar
2 eggs	2 eggs
8 oz. self-raising flour	225 g. self-raising flour
8 oz. mixed dried fruit	225 g. mixed dried fruit
2 oz. glacé cherries, quartered	50 g. glacé cherries, quartered
2 tablespoons orange marmalade	2 tablespoons orange marmalade
¼–½ teaspoon almond essence	¼–½ teaspoon almond essence
2 tablespoons milk	2 tablespoons milk
1½ oz. flaked almonds	40 g. flaked almonds

1. Preheat oven to moderate (350°F., 180°C., Gas Mark 4).

2. Line a deep, round cake tin 7 or 8 inches (18 or 20 cm.) in diameter with buttered greaseproof paper.

3. Put all the ingredients, except flaked almonds, in a large bowl and beat vigorously with a wooden spoon for about 3 minutes, or until well mixed. (If using an electric mixer, run it for only about 1 minute.) Batter should be of dropping consistency.

4. Spoon batter into prepared cake tin; smooth top with back of spoon and cover thickly with flaked almonds.

5. Bake cake for 1¾–2¼ hours. Halfway through baking time, cover top of tin with foil to prevent almonds browning too much.

6. Test cake with a skewer. When it comes out clean and dry, remove cake from oven and let it cool for about 5 minutes in the tin. Then turn out of tin and peel off lining paper. Leave cake on a wire rack to become quite cold before cutting.

Makes 8–10 portions

Chef's tip:
It is important when making creamed cakes to have the fat and eggs at room temperature; sit the eggs on top of the stove whilst you preheat the oven. If you do this you will find the cake mixture is less likely to curdle and the baked cake will be lighter.

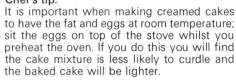

Chef's tip:
If a cake seems reluctant to come out of the tin (which it shouldn't, unless you didn't line it for some reason), stand the cake in the tin on a damp cloth for a minute or two and the cake should turn out with no further trouble.

Fudge Cake

IMPERIAL	METRIC
4 oz. dark bitter chocolate	110 g. dark bitter chocolate
4 oz. butter	110 g. butter
4 eggs, separated	4 eggs, separated
$\frac{1}{2}$ teaspoon salt	$\frac{1}{2}$ teaspoon salt
1 teaspoon vanilla essence	1 teaspoon vanilla essence
6 oz. castor sugar	175 g. castor sugar
4 oz. plain flour, sifted	110 g. plain flour, sifted
$\frac{1}{4}$ pint double cream	$1\frac{1}{2}$ dl. double cream
1 oz. flaked almonds, toasted	25 g. flaked almonds, toasted

1. Preheat oven to moderate (350°F., 180°C., Gas Mark 4).

2. Lightly butter two 7-inch (18-cm.) sandwich tins and line bases with circles of buttered greaseproof paper.

3. Break chocolate into the top of a double saucepan; add the butter and cook over hot water, stirring occasionally, until melted and smoothly blended. Remove from heat and allow to cool.

4. Beat egg yolks with salt and vanilla; gradually add sugar, beating vigorously, and continue to beat until light and fluffy.

5. With a few rapid strokes, combine chocolate mixture with eggs and sugar; then, with the mixture still streaky, carefully fold in flour.

6. Whisk egg whites until stiff but not dry. Fold them lightly into the cake batter.

7. Divide batter equally between prepared cake tins, and bake for 20 to 25 minutes, or until layers are well risen and springy to the touch.

8. Turn layers out onto wire cooling racks and allow to become quite cold.

9. When ready to serve, whip cream until it holds its shape in soft peaks. Spread half over one layer of cake; cover with remaining cake layer and spread remaining cream on top, swirling it lightly with the tines of a fork. Sprinkle with flaked toasted almonds and serve.

Makes 8 portions

Chef's tip:
To cool chocolate mixture more quickly after melting it, place saucepan in a bowl of cold water until mixture is cool enough. Use a pair of balance scales if you can, and balance one sandwich tin against the other to divide cake mixture *exactly* between the two tins.

Prune and Walnut Loaf

IMPERIAL	METRIC
6 oz. plump dried prunes	175 g. plump dried prunes
$\frac{1}{2}$ pint strong tea	3 dl. strong tea
4 oz. butter	110 g. butter
6 oz. castor sugar	175 g. castor sugar
2 eggs, lightly beaten	2 eggs, lightly beaten
8 oz. stone-ground wheatmeal flour (85%)	225 g. stone-ground wheatmeal flour (85%)
pinch salt	pinch salt
1 teaspoon baking powder	1 teaspoon baking powder
4 oz. walnuts, coarsely chopped	110 g. walnuts, coarsely chopped
3 tablespoons milk	3 tablespoons milk
demerara sugar, to decorate (optional)	demerara sugar, to decorate (optional)

1. The day before you plan to make the cake, put prunes in a bowl; cover with hot tea and leave to soak overnight.

2. The following day, preheat oven to moderate (350°F., 180°C., Gas Mark 4).

3. Butter a 9- by 5-inch (23- by 13-cm.) loaf tin.

4. Drain prunes; remove stones and chop prunes roughly.

5. In a large bowl, cream butter thoroughly; add sugar and continue to beat vigorously until mixture is white and fluffy. Add lightly beaten eggs a little at a time, beating well between each addition.

6. Sift flour with salt and baking powder. Blend into creamed mixture gently but thoroughly.

7. Add prunes, walnuts and milk; mix well and immediately pour into prepared loaf tin.

8. Bake loaf for 45 to 50 minutes, or until well risen and firm to the touch.

9. Remove loaf from the oven and turn out onto a wire rack to cool. Sprinkle top with demerara sugar if you like, and serve cut in thick slices.

Makes 6–8 portions

Chef's tip:
Allow the prunes to soak in strong tea for at least 24 hours before making the cake to allow them to swell as much as possible. Instead of throwing away the cold tea, try using it to cook prunes and other dried fruits; it improves their flavour tremendously.

Banana Bread

IMPERIAL	METRIC
1½ oz. butter	40 g. butter
1½ oz. lard	40 g. lard
4 oz. castor sugar	110 g. castor sugar
1 egg	1 egg
finely grated rinds of 1 orange and 1 lemon	finely grated rinds of 1 orange and 1 lemon
8 oz. plain flour	225 g. plain flour
2 teaspoons baking powder	2 teaspoons baking powder
4 bananas, peeled and mashed to pulp	4 bananas, peeled and mashed to pulp
2 oz. shelled walnuts, coarsely chopped	50 g. shelled walnuts, coarsely chopped

1. Preheat oven to moderate (350°F., 180°C., Gas Mark 4).

2. Butter a 9- by 5-inch (23- by 13-cm.) loaf tin.

3. Cream butter with lard; add sugar and beat until fluffy; then beat in egg, followed by grated orange and lemon rinds.

4. Sift flour with baking powder and add to creamed mixture alternately with mashed banana. Stir in coarsely chopped walnuts.

5. Spoon batter into prepared tin and level off the top. Bake for 50 minutes, or until a skewer pushed through the thickest part comes out clean.

6. Turn out onto a cake rack and cool before serving.

Makes 6–8 portions

Chef's tip:
If you use really ripe bananas for this cake you can place the peeled bananas in a basin, chop them roughly and then quickly mash them down using either an electric hand beater or a rotary whisk. This loaf keeps very well stored in an airtight tin.

Summer Strawberry Cake

IMPERIAL	METRIC
melted butter, for cake tin	melted butter, for cake tin
2 oz. butter, softened	55 g. butter, softened
4 oz. castor sugar	110 g. castor sugar
½ teaspoon vanilla essence	½ teaspoon vanilla essence
4 egg yolks	4 egg yolks
4 oz. plain flour	110 g. plain flour
1 teaspoon baking powder	1 teaspoon baking powder
3 tablespoons milk	3 tablespoons milk
Meringue:	*Meringue:*
4 egg whites	4 egg whites
8 oz. castor sugar	225 g. castor sugar
2 tablespoons flaked almonds	2 tablespoons flaked almonds
Filling:	*Filling:*
½ pint double cream	3 dl. double cream
1 tablespoon castor sugar	1 tablespoon castor sugar
8–10 oz. fresh strawberries	225–275 g. fresh strawberries

1. Preheat oven to moderate (350°F., 180°C., Gas Mark 4).

2. Brush two 8½-inch (21-cm.) round sandwich tins with melted butter. Line base and sides with greaseproof paper; brush paper with melted butter.

3. Cream butter and sugar together with vanilla essence in a bowl until light and fluffy. Add egg yolks one by one, beating well between each addition.

4. Sift flour and baking powder. Fold in lightly but thoroughly with a large metal spoon, alternately with milk. Divide mixture evenly between tins and level surfaces with back of spoon.

5. To make meringue, beat egg whites until stiff, and gradually add sugar.

6. Divide meringue between tins; spread evenly. Sprinkle surface of one with flaked almonds.

7. Bake for 45 to 50 minutes or until cakes have shrunk away from sides of tins.

8. Turn out carefully onto a wire rack and leave to cool, meringue side down.

9. For the filling, whisk cream with sugar until it holds its shape. Spread half cream over each cake round. Cover base cake with sliced strawberries; place almond-sprinkled cake round on top. Chill until ready to serve.

Serves 12

Brandy Snap Gâteau

IMPERIAL	METRIC
melted butter, for cake tin	melted butter, for cake tin
5 oz. unsalted butter	150 g. unsalted butter
4 eggs	4 eggs
4 oz. castor sugar	110 g. castor sugar
3 oz. plain flour	85 g. plain flour
1 oz. cornflour	25 g. cornflour
¾ pint double cream	4 dl. double cream
¼ pint single cream	1½ dl. single cream
about 1 lb. fresh raspberries	about 450 g. fresh raspberries
16 brandy snaps, bought or home-made	16 brandy snaps, bought or home-made

1. Preheat oven to moderate (350°F., 180°C., Gas Mark 4).

2. Brush three 7½- to 8-inch (19- to 20-cm.) sandwich tins with melted butter. Line bases with greaseproof paper; brush paper.

3. In a small saucepan, melt butter over a low heat, without allowing it to sizzle; remove from heat.

4. Combine eggs and sugar in a large bowl. Place over a pan of simmering water and whisk until light and thick.

5. Remove bowl from heat and whisk until cool. Sift flour and cornflour over surface, folding it in lightly but thoroughly with a large metal spoon.

6. Gradually spoon in the melted butter and fold in gently until thoroughly combined. Pour into prepared tins.

7. Bake for 40 minutes or until cake is well risen and springy to the touch. Turn out onto a wire rack, remove lining paper and leave to cool.

8. Beat creams until soft peaks form.

9. Use some of cream to spread on two of rounds; cover these with raspberries, reserving nine for decoration. Re-form cake; cover with some of remaining cream.

10. Pipe a blob of cream into one end of each of eight brandy snaps. Arrange brandy snaps on top of cake, decorated ends pointing out, and put a raspberry between each. Crush remaining brandy snaps and use to coat sides of cake. Finally, pipe a swirl of cream in centre and top with a raspberry. Serve chilled and eat on the same day.

Serves 8

Chef's tip:
Serious cake-makers should equip themselves with vanilla sugar which will give a much more subtle flavour than essence. Just plunge one or two whole vanilla pods into a jar of castor sugar. The pods will go on flavouring fresh sugar for years.

Hazelnut Roll

IMPERIAL	METRIC
melted butter, for tin	melted butter, for tin
3 oz. hazelnuts, finely ground	85 g. hazelnuts, finely ground
2 tablespoons cornflour	2 tablespoons cornflour
1 teaspoon baking powder	1 teaspoon baking powder
3 eggs	3 eggs
4 oz. castor sugar	110 g. castor sugar
½ pint double cream	3 dl. double cream
¼ pint single cream	1½ dl. single cream
2–3 bananas	2–3 bananas
plain dark chocolate, grated, to decorate	plain dark chocolate, grated, to decorate
12 hazelnuts, to decorate	12 hazelnuts, to decorate

1. Preheat oven to moderately hot (400°F., 200°C., Gas Mark 6).

2. Brush a 9- by 14-inch (23- by 35-cm.) swiss roll tin with melted butter. Line with greaseproof paper, brushing this also with melted butter.

3. Mix ground hazelnuts with sifted cornflour and baking powder.

4. Combine eggs and castor sugar in a bowl. Whisk until thick and fluffy.

5. Fold hazelnut mixture gently but thoroughly into creamed eggs with a large metal spoon. Spread batter evenly in prepared tin.

6. Bake for 10 to 15 minutes or until cake is just firm to the touch and has shrunk away from sides of tin.

7. While cake is in the oven, prepare a large sheet of grease-proof paper, sprinkled with more castor sugar. Turn cake out onto sugared paper and carefully peel off lining paper.

8. Beat double cream with single cream until it holds its shape.

9. When cake is cool, spread with just over half the cream and cover with thinly sliced bananas.

10. Roll up cake from the long side and place carefully on a serving plate, trimming ends at an angle.

11. Spread roll with some of remaining cream. Mark 12 serving slices, following angle of trimming cuts. Decorate each slice with grated chocolate and use remaining cream to pipe swirls, topping each swirl with a hazelnut. Serve chilled and eat the same day.

Makes 12 slices

Madeleines de Commercy

IMPERIAL	METRIC
4½ oz. butter	125 g. butter
4 oz. castor sugar	110 g. castor sugar
2 eggs	2 eggs
4 oz. plain flour	110 g. plain flour
1 teaspoon baking powder	1 teaspoon baking powder
1 teaspoon finely grated orange rind	1 teaspoon finely grated orange rind
1 tablespoon orange juice	1 tablespoon orange juice

1. Preheat oven to moderately hot (400°F., 200°C., Gas Mark 6).

2. Grease eighteen madeleine moulds, using ½ oz. (15 g.) of the butter.

3. Cream remaining butter; add sugar and beat with a wooden spoon until light and fluffy.

4. Beat eggs lightly and add to butter mixture gradually, beating vigorously between each addition.

5. Sift flour with baking powder and fold lightly into butter mixture.

6. When batter is smooth and well blended, add grated orange rind and juice and mix well.

7. Fill prepared moulds three-quarters full with batter.

8. Bake for 8 to 10 minutes, or until madeleines are well risen, golden brown on top and springy to the touch.

9. Turn madeleines out onto a wire rack and allow to cool before serving.

Makes 18 madeleines

Butter Scones

IMPERIAL	METRIC
12 oz. plain flour	350 g. plain flour
2 teaspoons baking powder	2 teaspoons baking powder
salt	salt
5 oz. butter	150 g. butter
2 eggs, well beaten	2 eggs, well beaten
7 tablespoons very cold milk	7 tablespoons very cold milk

1. Preheat oven to very hot (475°F., 240°C., Gas Mark 9).

2. Sift flour, baking powder and ½ teaspoon salt into a bowl. Rub in butter with your fingertips until mixture resembles very coarse breadcrumbs.

3. Make a well in the centre and pour in beaten eggs and cold milk. Combine lightly and quickly with a fork until dough holds together.

4. Turn dough out onto a lightly floured board and roll lightly and rapidly into a rectangle about ½ inch (1 cm.) thick. Fold in three as you would puff pastry and roll out again. Repeat procedure twice more, handling dough as little as possible and working as quickly as you can.

5. After folding dough for the third time, roll it out just under ½ inch thick and cut into 2½-inch (6-cm.) rounds with a floured biscuit cutter.

6. Arrange scones on an ungreased baking sheet and bake for 10 to 15 minutes, or until well risen and a rich golden colour. Serve warm with jam or cream.

Makes 12–14

Chef's tip:
You can buy special baking sheets for madeleines, each stamped with a dozen of these characteristic little boat shapes, lightly ribbed underneath. Madeleines are at their best eaten very fresh, lightly dusted with icing sugar.

Chef's tip:
To make cheese scones, add 3 oz. (75 g.) finely grated strong Cheddar after rubbing in the butter. To make savoury scones add 2 tablespoons chopped parsley or ½–1 teaspoon dried herbs; sprinkle tops with a little onion or celery salt before baking.

Bread and Butter Pudding à l'Orange

IMPERIAL	METRIC
4–6 oz. softened butter	100–175 g. softened butter
10–12 slices thick-cut white bread	10–12 slices thick-cut white bread
4 tablespoons marmalade	4 tablespoons marmalade
juice and finely grated rind of 2 large oranges	juice and finely grated rind of 2 large oranges
juice and finely grated rind of 1 lemon	juice and finely grated rind of 1 lemon
3 oz. castor sugar	75 g. castor sugar
Custard:	*Custard:*
¾ pint milk	4 dl. milk
2 eggs	2 eggs
2 tablespoons castor sugar	2 tablespoons castor sugar
4 tablespoons lightly whipped cream	4 tablespoons lightly whipped cream

1. Preheat oven to moderately hot (400°F., 200°C., Gas Mark 6).

2. Grease a shallow, 3-pint (1¾-litre) baking dish generously with some of the butter.

3. Remove crusts from bread. Spread slices with butter and marmalade and cut into triangles (four to each slice).

4. Combine juice and finely grated rinds of oranges and lemon in a bowl. Add castor sugar and stir until dissolved.

5. Line bottom and sides of baking dish completely with bread triangles, dipping them in orange syrup as you use them and arranging them buttered side up. Fill lined dish with some of remaining bread triangles, reserving a few to decorate top of pudding.

6. Make custard by heating milk to just below boiling point. Beat eggs lightly and pour hot milk onto them gradually, beating constantly. Return mixture to pan; add sugar and stir over a low heat until custard thickens enough to coat back of spoon.

7. Remove custard from heat; cool slightly and stir in cream.

8. Pour custard over bread in baking dish. Cut remaining bread triangles in half; soak in remaining orange syrup and arrange on top of the pudding. Sprinkle top with any left-over orange syrup.

9. Bake pudding for 30 minutes, or until crisp and golden on the outside, with a soft, creamy centre.

Serves 6

Chef's tip:
If you wish, you can add 1 oz. seedless raisins to custard just before returning egg mixture to heat. Take great care not to let custard boil, or eggs will curdle. Use a double saucepan for this operation if you have one.

Queen of Puddings

IMPERIAL	METRIC
4 oz. fresh white breadcrumbs	100 g. fresh white breadcrumbs
5 tablespoons castor sugar	5 tablespoons castor sugar
¾ pint milk	4 dl. milk
butter	butter
3 eggs, separated	3 eggs, separated
few drops vanilla essence	few drops vanilla essence
finely grated rind of 1 lemon	finely grated rind of 1 lemon
3 tablespoons raspberry jam or other sharp-flavoured jam	3 tablespoons raspberry jam or other sharp-flavoured jam

1. Preheat oven to moderate (375°F., 190°C., Gas Mark 5).

2. In a bowl, mix breadcrumbs with 2 tablespoons castor sugar.

3. Combine milk and 2 tablespoons butter in a pan. Bring to the boil, stirring until butter has melted, and pour over breadcrumbs.

4. Beat in egg yolks, vanilla essence and finely grated lemon rind until thoroughly blended.

5. Grease a 2-pint (1-litre) pie dish lightly with butter. Pour in breadcrumb mixture; level it off and bake for 30 to 35 minutes, or until pudding is set and a rich golden colour on top.

6. Remove pudding from the oven and allow to cool slightly. Reduce oven temperature to slow (325°F., 170°C., Gas Mark 3).

7. Whisk egg whites until soft peaks form. Then gradually whisk in remaining 3 tablespoons castor sugar and continue to whisk until very stiff and glossy.

8. Spread surface of pudding evenly with raspberry or other jam and pile meringue over the top, drawing it up in swirls and peaks.

9. Return pudding to the oven for 10 to 12 minutes, or until meringue is set on the surface and well coloured. Serve immediately.

Serves 4

Chef's tip:
When beating egg whites for a meringue it is most important to use a scrupulously clean, grease-free bowl and beater. A good way to ensure this is to moisten a wad of kitchen paper with vinegar and thoroughly wipe bowl and beater before starting.

Chocolate Kirsch Mould

IMPERIAL	METRIC
4 oz. bitter chocolate	110 g. bitter chocolate
8 oz. butter, softened	225 g. butter, softened
4 egg yolks	4 egg yolks
4 oz. castor sugar	110 g. castor sugar
finely grated rind of	finely grated rind of
1 orange	1 orange
8 tablespoons Kirsch	8 tablespoons Kirsch
about 3 dozen sponge	about 3 dozen sponge
finger biscuits	finger biscuits
whipped cream, to serve	whipped cream, to serve

1. Combine chocolate with half the butter in a small saucepan. Melt over a low heat, stirring occasionally; then beat until smooth and well blended. Remove from heat.

2. Whisk egg yolks with sugar in a bowl over hot water until thick, creamy and pale. Whisk in chocolate mixture; then add remaining butter in small pieces and beat vigorously until smooth. (If mixture is lumpy, strain it through a fine sieve.) Beat in grated orange rind and half the Kirsch.

3. Butter a 2-pint (1-litre) charlotte mould.

4. Dilute remaining Kirsch with 4 tablespoons water in a shallow dish.

5. Line bottom of mould with a layer of sponge biscuits, dipping each one quickly in diluted Kirsch before using it. Spoon a layer of chocolate cream over biscuits. Continue to alternate layers of biscuits soaked in Kirsch and chocolate cream until mould is full, ending with a layer of biscuits.

6. Cover mould with foil and chill in the refrigerator overnight, or until firmly set.

7. When ready to serve, dip mould into very hot water for about 10 seconds only to loosen it, and carefully turn out onto a serving dish. Decorate with swirls of piped whipped cream and serve.

Serves 6–8

Orange Water Ice

IMPERIAL	METRIC
12 oz. sugar	350 g. sugar
$\frac{3}{4}$ pint fresh orange juice	4 dl. fresh orange juice
$\frac{1}{4}$ pint fresh lemon juice	$1\frac{1}{2}$ dl. fresh lemon juice
finely grated rind of	finely grated rind of
1 orange and 1 lemon	1 orange and 1 lemon
orange segments, to	orange segments, to
decorate (optional)	decorate (optional)
coarsely grated orange rind,	coarsely grated orange rind,
to decorate (optional)	to decorate (optional)

1. Turn refrigerator down to its lowest temperature, i.e., highest setting.

2. In a heavy saucepan, combine sugar with $1\frac{1}{2}$ pints (scant litre) water. Bring to the boil, stirring until sugar has dissolved, and boil for 5 minutes.

3. Remove pan from heat. Cool syrup slightly.

4. Stir in orange juice, lemon juice, and the finely grated rinds of 1 orange and 1 lemon. Leave to cool.

5. Strain mixture through a fine sieve into freezing trays or into a $2\frac{1}{2}$-pint ($1\frac{1}{2}$-litre) container shallow enough to fit into your freezing compartment.

6. Freeze mixture for 4 hours, or until firm.

7. Transfer water ice to the main cabinet of the refrigerator at least 1 hour before serving to allow it to soften slightly.

8. Serve water ice in individual dishes. If you like, you can decorate each portion with fresh orange segments or a sprinkling of coarsely grated orange rind.

Serves 6

Chef's tip:
This dish will make an ideal sweet for your next dinner party—it is extremely rich and fragrant with Kirsch. However, it must be chilled overnight so that the chocolate cream sets firmly enough to turn out.

Chef's tip:
If you do not possess a fine sieve, simply line a colander or steamer with a square of kitchen paper and pour the mixture to be strained through this. I find this is even more effective than the fine sieve.

Blender Strawberry Sorbet

IMPERIAL	METRIC
2 8-oz. packets frozen strawberries	2 226-g. packets frozen strawberries
4 oz. icing sugar	100 g. icing sugar
juice of 1½ lemons	juice of 1½ lemons
whipped cream, to decorate	whipped cream, to decorate

1. Turn blender to low speed (No. 2). Gradually drop frozen strawberries onto turning blades in a steady stream. When completely blended, spoon in icing sugar and lemon juice. Blend for a further half minute.

2. Pour into four individual glasses and freeze until firm.

3. Serve each glass decorated with a whirl of whipped cream.

Serves 4

Chef's tip:
This recipe takes care of the only disadvantage of frozen strawberries which is their appearance when they are defrosted. Some packs of deep-frozen strawberries already contain a little sugar, so check this and if necessary adjust the amount you add to taste.

Biscuit Tortoni

IMPERIAL	METRIC
½ pint double cream	3 dl. double cream
½ pint single cream	3 dl. single cream
2 oz. icing sugar, sifted	50 g. icing sugar, sifted
3 oz. macaroons, crumbled	75 g. macaroons, crumbled
3 oz. toasted almonds, finely chopped	75 g. toasted almonds, finely chopped
3 tablespoons Marsala or sweet sherry	3 tablespoons Marsala or sweet sherry
2 egg whites	2 egg whites

1. Turn refrigerator down to its lowest temperature, i.e., highest setting.

2. Beat creams with sifted icing sugar until soft peaks form. Freeze until firm but not hard, about 1 hour.

3. Toss macaroon crumbs with finely toasted almonds.

4. Remove whipped cream from refrigerator and beat in two-thirds of the macaroon mixture, together with Marsala, or sweet sherry.

5. Whisk egg whites until stiff but not dry and fold into cream mixture gently but thoroughly, using a metal spoon.

6. Pour mixture into a plain rectangular mould (a 2-lb. (900-g.) loaf tin is ideal) and freeze until very firm.

7. When ready to serve, wring a cloth out in hot water and wrap it around bottom and sides of mould to loosen ice cream; then turn out carefully onto a flat serving dish.

8. Sprinkle top evenly with remaining macaroon mixture and serve immediately, cut in thick slices.

Serves 6–8

Chef's tip:
To toast almonds, either place them on a baking sheet and bake in a moderate oven (350°F., 180°C., Gas Mark 4) for 10 minutes, or place them under a grill for a few minutes until browned. To crush macaroons place in a strong bag and roll with a rolling pin until biscuits are crushed finely enough.

113

Vanilla Ice Cream

IMPERIAL	METRIC
4 egg yolks	4 egg yolks
2 oz. castor sugar	50 g. castor sugar
pinch salt	pinch salt
$\frac{3}{4}$ pint single cream	4 dl. single cream
$\frac{1}{2}$ teaspoon vanilla essence, or to taste	$\frac{1}{2}$ teaspoon vanilla essence, or to taste

1. Turn refrigerator to its lowest temperature, i.e., highest setting.

2. Combine egg yolks, castor sugar and salt in a bowl, and whisk until light, fluffy and lemon-coloured.

3. Scald cream and pour over egg yolk mixture in a thin stream, whisking vigorously.

4. Pour mixture into the top of a double saucepan and stir over lightly simmering water until it thickens into a custard which coats back of spoon. Take great care not to let it boil, or egg yolks will curdle.

5. Strain custard through a fine sieve and leave to cool.

6. Flavour to taste with vanilla essence. Pour into a freezing tray and freeze, stirring the mixture up vigorously with a fork every half hour, until half-frozen, then leaving it for a further 2 or 3 hours until frozen hard.

7. Transfer ice cream to main cabinet of refrigerator about 1 hour before serving.

Serves 4

Syllabub

IMPERIAL	METRIC
very finely grated rind of 2 lemons	very finely grated rind of 2 lemons
$\frac{1}{2}$ pint sweet cream sherry	3 dl. sweet cream sherry
2 tablespoons brandy	2 tablespoons brandy
1 pint double cream	6 dl. double cream
2 egg whites	2 egg whites
6 tablespoons castor sugar	6 tablespoons castor sugar

1. In a porcelain bowl, cover grated lemon rind with sherry and leave to soak overnight.

2. The following day, strain sherry into a bowl through a fine sieve lined with muslin.

3. Add remaining ingredients and beat with a whisk until thick and frothy.

4. Pour into six tall glasses and chill for at least 4 hours before serving. Serve with small, plain sponge fingers or crisp biscuits.

Serves 6

Chef's tip:
It is most important to remember when making ice cream to *over*-flavour and *over*-sweeten the mixture prior to freezing. You will be surprised how much flavour is lost with freezing. Also do allow it that one hour to soften before serving, or it will taste like an icy nothing.

Chef's tip:
When serving this sweet I usually top each glass with two or three thin lengths of lemon zest as a decoration. To do this I use a gadget called a *zesteur*. It comes in useful for all sorts of garnishes and decorations and generally does a lighter job than a canelle knife.

Petits Pots de Vanille

IMPERIAL	METRIC
3 eggs	3 eggs
3 oz. castor sugar	85 g. castor sugar
½ teaspoon vanilla essence	½ teaspoon vanilla essence
finely grated rind of 1 orange	finely grated rind of 1 orange
6 fl. oz. double cream	1¾ dl. double cream
1–2 tablespoons coarsely grated dark chocolate	1–2 tablespoons coarsely grated dark chocolate

1. Separate eggs.

2. Combine egg yolks with castor sugar in the top of a double saucepan.

3. Set pan over lightly simmering water—make sure bottom is not touching water—and beat with a wire whisk for 5 minutes, until very thick and creamy.

4. Remove pan from heat. Beat in vanilla essence and finely grated orange rind, and allow to cool.

5. Whip cream.

6. Whisk egg whites until stiff but not dry.

7. With a metal spoon or spatula, fold whipped cream into cool egg mixture, followed by stiffly beaten egg whites, using short, light strokes and working just long enough to blend ingredients thoroughly.

8. Spoon into individual custard cups or soufflé dishes of about 4-fl. oz. (1-dl.) capacity, and chill for 2 or 3 hours.

9. Serve chilled, each little cream sprinkled with a little coarsely grated chocolate.

Serves 6

Chef's tip:

When grating orange and lemon rind be careful to remove only the zest (the coloured part of the fruit). The oil and flavour are near the surface of any citrus fruit and this is the part to remove. The white pith underneath gives a bitter flavour, so go carefully.

Crème Brûlée (Burnt Cream)

IMPERIAL	METRIC
8 egg yolks	8 egg yolks
7 tablespoons castor sugar	7 tablespoons castor sugar
1 pint single cream	6 dl. single cream
½–¾ teaspoon finely grated lemon rind	½–¾ teaspoon finely grated lemon rind
½–1 teaspoon vanilla essence	½–1 teaspoon vanilla essence

1. Beat egg yolks lightly in a bowl.

2. Add 4 tablespoons castor sugar to single cream in the top of a double saucepan, and bring to the boil over a low heat, stirring constantly.

3. Pour boiling cream over egg yolks in a thin stream, beating vigorously with a wire whisk.

4. Return mixture to top of a double saucepan. Add finely grated lemon rind, to taste, and stir over lightly simmering water for 5 to 7 minutes until custard coats back of spoon. Do not allow it to boil, or egg will curdle.

5. Remove pan from heat. Cool custard slightly and flavour to taste with vanilla essence.

6. Pour custard into six individual heatproof ramekins of about 4-fl. oz. (1-dl.) capacity, or into a 1½-pint (1-litre) soufflé dish. Allow to cool; then chill for 2 to 3 hours until quite set.

7. When little moulds are firm, preheat your grill turned up to maximum for about 20 minutes.

8. Sprinkle each individual mould evenly with ½ tablespoon castor sugar (or sprinkle all of the remaining sugar over the top of the large mould).

9. Place mould(s) under the preheated grill 2 to 3 inches from source of heat and grill for 2 to 3 minutes until sugar has melted in a sheet of golden brown caramel. Keep a careful eye on it while it is grilling as sugar will burn at the slightest provocation.

10. Allow to cool; then return mould(s) to the refrigerator to chill before serving.

Serves 6

Chef's tip:

The critical point in this recipe is where the custard is cooked over simmering water. At this stage the egg yolks must be given every chance to thicken the custard, and it will thicken considerably. So, if necessary give it more time than stated in the recipe.

Pêche Cardinale
(Peaches in Raspberry Sauce)

IMPERIAL	METRIC
6 large ripe peaches	6 large ripe peaches
8 oz. sugar	225 g. sugar
cinnamon	cinnamon
lemon juice	lemon juice
Raspberry sauce:	*Raspberry sauce:*
1 lb. fresh raspberries	450 g. fresh raspberries
2–3 tablespoons lemon juice	2–3 tablespoons lemon juice
2–3 tablespoons icing sugar	2–3 tablespoons icing sugar
To decorate:	*To decorate:*
¾ pint double cream, whipped	4 dl. double cream, whipped
slivered toasted almonds	slivered toasted almonds

1. Pour boiling water over peaches to loosen skins; then peel skin off each peach, taking care not to bruise or crush them.

2. Make a syrup with the sugar and ½ pint (3 dl.) water, flavoured to taste with cinnamon and lemon juice.

3. Add peaches and poach, uncovered, until they are tender but not so soft that they are in danger of losing their shape. Allow peaches to cool in the syrup; then chill until ready to serve.

4. To make raspberry sauce, wash raspberries if necessary, and whirl them until smooth in an electric blender with lemon juice and icing sugar—or purée through a fine sieve. Taste and add more lemon juice or sugar if necessary. If a blender has been used, rub purée through a fine sieve to eliminate seeds.

5. When ready to serve, place each poached peach in a sorbet cup or sundae dish. Spoon raspberry sauce over peaches and decorate with whipped cream and slivered toasted almonds. Serve accompanied by remaining cream in a small bowl.

Serves 6

Italian Baked Peaches

IMPERIAL	METRIC
4 large firm peaches	4 large firm peaches
2 tablespoons softened butter	2 tablespoons softened butter
4 teaspoons icing sugar	4 teaspoons icing sugar
5–6 tablespoons crushed macaroons	5–6 tablespoons crushed macaroons
3 tablespoons ground almonds	3 tablespoons ground almonds
2–3 teaspoons finely chopped candied orange peel	2–3 teaspoons finely chopped candied orange peel
1 egg white	1 egg white
6 tablespoons Marsala	6 tablespoons Marsala

1. Preheat oven to moderate (350°F., 180°C., Gas Mark 4).

2. To peel peaches, place them in a sieve over a bowl, one or two at a time, and pour over boiling water to loosen skins. Then, holding peach in a cloth, peel off skin with your fingers.

3. Cut peaches in half and remove stones. Arrange peach halves, cut sides up, side by side in a baking dish.

4. In a bowl, work butter with a wooden spoon until soft. Sift in icing sugar; beat until creamy; then stir in crushed macaroons, ground almonds and chopped candied orange peel.

5. Beat egg white until stiff but not dry and fold lightly into macaroon mixture with a metal spoon.

6. Pile macaroon mixture into the cavity of each peach, mounding it up attractively.

7. Spoon Marsala over peaches (and filling), and bake for 15 minutes, or until soft but not mushy.

8. Serve peaches hot, with some of the Marsala-flavoured juices poured over them, accompanied by chilled cream.

Serves 6

Chef's tip:
If you want only a small quantity of lemon juice at a time, instead of cutting lemon in half and squeezing it, merely dig a sharp knife or fork into fruit and squeeze out the few drops of lemon juice you require. The raspberry sauce is also delicious with ice cream.

Chef's tip:
If you find you have no icing sugar and you own a liquidiser, place castor sugar or granulated sugar in the liquidiser and blend until sugar is reduced to a powder. The sugary deposit which has to be removed before chopping candied peel is excellent for sweetening stewed apples.

Cherries Jubilee

IMPERIAL	METRIC
1 lb. ripe sweet black cherries	450 g. ripe sweet black cherries
1 oz. castor sugar	25 g. castor sugar
piece cinnamon stick	piece cinnamon stick
finely grated rind and juice of ½ orange	finely grated rind and juice of ½ orange
1 teaspoon cornflour	1 teaspoon cornflour
2–3 tablespoons cognac	2–3 tablespoons cognac
2–3 tablespoons cherry brandy	2–3 tablespoons cherry brandy
vanilla ice cream, to serve	vanilla ice cream, to serve

1. Stone cherries.

2. In a heavy pan, combine cherries with a generous ⅓ pint (2¼ dl.) water; simmer until soft but not disintegrating, about 10 minutes depending on ripeness. Then remove cherries to a bowl with a slotted spoon.

3. To juices remaining in the pan, add sugar, cinnamon stick, grated orange rind and orange juice.

4. Mix cornflour smoothly with a tablespoon or two of the liquid; stir into the pan and bring to the boil. Allow to bubble gently, stirring occasionally, for about 5 minutes, or until liquid is reduced to a light, syrupy consistency. The sauce should be rather sweet, so taste it while it is cooking, and add a little more sugar if necessary.

5. Add cherries and heat through gently. Turn into a wide shallow bowl.

6. Pour cognac and cherry brandy into a large metal ladle which you have first heated thoroughly with boiling water, or by holding it over an open flame. Swirl around to warm the alcohol; set a match to it, and as soon as the flames are well established, pour all over the hot cherries.

7. Serve immediately as soon as flames have died down, spooned over individual portions of ice cream.

Serves 3–4

Clafoutis

IMPERIAL	METRIC
1 lb. ripe black cherries	450 g. ripe black cherries
4 eggs plus 2 egg yolks	4 eggs plus 2 egg yolks
pinch salt	pinch salt
4½ oz. castor sugar	125 g. castor sugar
3½ oz. plain flour	100 g. plain flour
2 oz. butter	50 g. butter
1 pint milk	6 dl. milk
½ teaspoon vanilla essence	½ teaspoon vanilla essence

1. Preheat oven to moderate (350°F., 180°C., Gas Mark 4).

2. Butter a shallow ovenproof dish about 15 by 9 inches (38 by 24 cm.). (You can substitute a round dish if you prefer, but don't use a tin because it conducts the heat too fiercely and tends to make the bottom and sides of the pudding tough instead of creamy.)

3. Wash cherries and remove stems and stones.

4. Beat whole eggs and egg yolks together with a pinch of salt until well mixed. Add castor sugar and beat until light; then gradually sift in flour, beating vigorously until mixture is quite smooth and free of lumps.

5. Melt half the butter over a low heat, taking care not to let it bubble, and incorporate smoothly into egg batter, followed by milk and vanilla essence, beating vigorously until batter is smooth and well blended again.

6. Scatter prepared cherries evenly over prepared baking dish and cover with batter.

7. Dot with remaining butter and bake for 45 minutes, or until clafoutis is golden and set, but still creamy inside.

8. Serve hot or lukewarm.

Serves 6–8

Chef's tip:
When fresh cherries are not available, substitute a large (14-oz., 396-g.) can of stoned dark cherries and use ½ pint (3 dl.) of syrup from the can for the sauce. You will find it will need proportionately less sugar to allow for their extra sweetness.

Chef's tip:
This dish can either be spooned straight out of the dish, or carefully unmoulded. It is at its best lukewarm, dusted with a little icing sugar. Canned, pitted cherries can be used instead of fresh ones if it is more convenient, but drain them thoroughly before using.

Pies, Tarts, Flans and Pastry

If pastry-making hasn't been your strong point in the past, shortcrust pastry is the one to start with. Once you acquire the knack of handling a simple short-crust, trickier ones like flaky and puff will seem far less daunting.

Like most other pastries, shortcrust is just a combination of flour and fat, with a drop or two of liquid —iced water, milk or beaten egg yolk—to help it hold together.

The flour

* Use a good-quality plain flour. Never use self-raising flour unless a recipe specially calls for it.

* Make sure your flour is quite dry. If it is damp, the carefully balanced moisture content of the pastry will be put out, and your pastry will be tough.

* Always sift flour with any other dry ingredients before rubbing in fat. This not only ensures that they are thoroughly blended and free of lumps, but also helps to make the pastry lighter.

The fat

The ratio of fat to flour is the crucial factor that decides the richness and flavour of a shortcrust pastry. For me, there is nothing quite like the flavour of pure butter shortcrust, even though some of the other fats—lard and whipped vegetable fats especially—give a 'shorter' texture.

When making shortcrust pastry, use firm butter, straight from the refrigerator. Dice the butter, then toss the pieces in sifted flour so that each piece is thoroughly coated before you start combining the butter and the flour.

Binding the pastry

A pastry that is very rich in fat (like a shortbread, for example) can be kneaded together without the help of liquid, but most pastries will need a sprinkling of iced water or iced water and beaten egg yolk to bind them. Once you have added the amount specified in the recipe, however, make *quite* sure the pastry needs it before adding any more, and then keep it down to a miserly teaspoon at a time.

Using too much liquid is the most common cause of tough, badly shrunk pastry.

Handling a shortcrust pastry

The standard method of combining fat and flour for a shortcrust pastry is known as 'rubbing in'. The objective is to distribute the fat as finely as possible throughout the flour, coating each microscopic grain with a waterproof film of fat. When the starch is subjected to heat, it explodes and absorbs the fat around it.

Obviously, you will have to work very quickly and lightly if all this fat and flour are to be reduced to 'fine breadcrumbs' without turning oily—and this is precisely what we mean when we talk about so-and-so having a 'light hand' with pastry.

Using just your fingertips, first break the fat down to smaller pieces, making sure there is always a protective barrier of flour between you and the fat. Then start rubbing the flakes of floury fat between your fingers and thumbs to make a crumblike mixture. Don't attempt to deal with all the mixture at once. Cup your hands slightly; scoop a portion of the mixture up into the air and let it run through your fingers and thumbs, rubbing out the little lumps of fat with a quick, light movement as you feel them pass through your fingers.

When you come to add the liquid, sprinkle it over as large a surface as possible so that the actual *mixing* will be cut down to a minimum.

As soon as you see that the pastry is holding together in lumps, stop mixing. Cup your hand and gently coax the mixture into a ball. The bottom and sides of the bowl should be quite clean.

Chilling

All pastries behave better after a spell in the refrigerator, especially in hot weather.

Wrap pastry up in greaseproof paper, a damp tea towel or a piece of foil or plastic wrap to keep surface from drying out.

Rolling out

Remove pastry from refrigerator and leave it at room temperature for a little while to soften slightly. Then dust your working surface and a rolling pin *lightly* with flour. Flatten the ball of pastry with a few strokes of the rolling pin; then start rolling it out to the required size and thickness, using short, light strokes and trying to keep the pressure even at both sides.

Use only as much flour as you need to keep the pastry from sticking to the board or rolling pin, shaking it through a sifter if you have one, and when the rolling is completed, dust off loose flour with a soft pastry brush.

To cover a pie or tart

Roll out shortcrust pastry about $\frac{1}{4}$ inch ($\frac{1}{2}$ cm.) thick. If the filling comes up in a mound above the rim of the dish, you will have to allow for this by making your lid about half as large again as the top of the dish.

To make a pastry case

Roll out pastry between $\frac{1}{8}$ and $\frac{1}{16}$ inch (3 and 1 mm.) thick. Fold the rolled-out sheet of pastry loosely over your rolling pin and transfer it to the tart tin. Ease the pastry into the tin. *Don't* stretch it into shape, or it will just shrink back again when it is baked. Lightly press sides of pastry against tart tin with your fingers.

Prick base of shell all over with a sharp-pronged fork. *Then chill for 30 minutes* to allow the pastry to 'mature' and minimise the danger of shrinking or sagging when baking.

To bake an unfilled pastry shell

A pastry shell that is baked without any filling is liable to sag badly at the sides if it is not supported, and the base may bubble up. To prevent this, line the shell with greaseproof paper or foil and weight pastry down with dried beans, which incidentally can be re-used indefinitely.

Bake in a preheated, moderately hot oven (400°F., 200°C., Gas Mark 6) for 10 minutes. Remove from the oven and carefully lift out paper, foil and beans.

* If tart shell is to be rebaked after it has been filled, return it to the oven, minus beans and lining paper, for just 8 to 10 minutes longer to dry out out the base without colouring it.

* If tart shell is to be cooked completely at this stage, return it to the oven for 10 to 15 minutes, or until set and a rich golden colour.

Always cool pastry shell at room temperature.

Basic Sweet Shortcrust Pastry

IMPERIAL	METRIC
8 oz. plain flour	225 g. plain flour
1–2 tablespoons icing sugar	1–2 tablespoons icing sugar
pinch salt	pinch salt
4 oz. cold butter	110 g. cold butter
$\frac{1}{4}$ teaspoon lemon juice	$\frac{1}{4}$ teaspoon lemon juice
$\frac{1}{4}$–$\frac{1}{2}$ teaspoon vanilla essence	$\frac{1}{4}$–$\frac{1}{2}$ teaspoon vanilla essence
iced water	iced water

1. Sift flour, icing sugar and salt into a large bowl.

2. Dice butter coarsely and toss with flour. Then lightly rub butter into flour with your fingertips. Keep lifting your hands well above the bowl as you work so that the rubbed-in mixture is, as it were, aerated as it falls back into the bowl. This will keep the pastry light and prevent the butter becoming too soft.

3. When flour mixture resembles fine breadcrumbs, combine lemon juice and vanilla essence with 2 tablespoons iced water and sprinkle over the surface, mixing lightly with a fork or a broad-bladed knife until pastry starts holding together in lumps. In the final stages, use a cupped hand to press the pastry gently into a ball.

4. Pastry may be used immediately, but if you have time to chill it for 30 minutes, wrapped in greaseproof paper or foil, so much the better.

Basic Savoury Shortcrust Pastry

IMPERIAL	METRIC
8 oz. plain flour	225 g. plain flour
1 teaspoon castor sugar	1 teaspoon castor sugar
generous pinch salt	generous pinch salt
4 oz. cold butter	110 g. cold butter
$\frac{1}{4}$ teaspoon lemon juice	$\frac{1}{4}$ teaspoon lemon juice
iced water	iced water

1. Sift flour, sugar and salt into a large bowl.

2. Dice butter coarsely and toss with flour. Then lightly rub butter into flour with your fingertips. Keep lifting your hands well above the bowl as you work so that the rubbed-in mixture is, as it were, aerated as it falls back into the bowl. This will keep the pastry light and prevent the butter becoming too soft.

3. When flour mixture resembles fine breadcrumbs, combine lemon juice with 2 tablespoons iced water and sprinkle over the surface, mixing lightly with a fork or a broad-bladed knife until pastry starts holding together in lumps. In the final stages, use a cupped hand to press the pastry gently into a ball.

4. Pastry may be used immediately, but if you have time to chill it for 30 minutes, wrapped in greaseproof paper or foil, so much the better.

Chef's tip:
The most common cause of tough, badly shrunk pastry is using too much liquid. Follow the amount suggested in the above recipe, but only add a teaspoon of water at a time for any amount over the given quantity. You should leave the bottom and sides of the bowl quite clean.

Chef's tip:
An invaluable piece of equipment for any would-be serious pastry maker is a marble slab. If you can get a marble slab that will readily fit into your refrigerator so that you can really chill it before you start, that is all to the good.

Peach and Hazelnut Flan

IMPERIAL	METRIC
2 oz. hazelnuts, toasted and skinned	50 g. hazelnuts, toasted and skinned
1 recipe basic sweet shortcrust pastry (see previous page)	1 recipe basic sweet shortcrust pastry (see previous page)
1–1¼ lb. fresh peaches	450–550 g. fresh peaches
2 teaspoons cornflour	2 teaspoons cornflour
castor sugar	castor sugar
milk	milk

1. Preheat oven to moderate (375°F., 190°C., Gas Mark 5).

2. Grind the toasted and skinned hazelnuts to a uniform fineness.

3. Make a pastry according to recipe for basic sweet short-crust pastry, but substituting the ground hazelnuts for 2 oz. (50 g.) of the flour. You will only require a sprinkling of water to bind the pastry.

4. Form dough into a ball, place in a plastic bag and refrigerate until ready to use.

5. Place peaches in a bowl and pour over boiling water; leave for 1 minute. Remove skins, halve and slice peaches.

6. In a small bowl, mix cornflour with 3 tablespoons castor sugar.

7. Place an 8-inch (20-cm.) fluted flan ring on a baking sheet. Roll out two-thirds of the pastry and use to line flan ring.

8. Place sliced peaches in lined flan ring and sprinkle with cornflour and sugar mixture. Glaze edge of pastry with milk.

9. Roll out remaining pastry and cover top of flan; seal edges firmly and trim. Re-roll trimmings and use to decorate top of pie; glaze with a little milk and sprinkle with castor sugar.

10. Bake for 45 minutes. If pastry seems to be browning too fast before end of cooking time, cover with foil.

11. Serve warm with sweetened, whipped cream.

Serves 6

French Grape Tart

IMPERIAL	METRIC
1 deep 7-inch shortcrust pastry shell, prebaked	1 deep 18-cm. shortcrust pastry shell, prebaked
1½ lb. white grapes	675 g. white grapes
2 tablespoons Calvados	2 tablespoons Calvados
2 oz. castor sugar	50 g. castor sugar
2 teaspoons cornflour	2 teaspoons cornflour
4 tablespoons double cream	4 tablespoons double cream
1 egg	1 egg
1–2 teaspoons lemon juice	1–2 teaspoons lemon juice

1. Leave prebaked pastry shell in its tin on a baking sheet.

2. Rinse grapes. Peel and pip them over a bowl to catch juices. Drop grapes into the bowl as you prepare them.

3. Add Calvados and sugar; toss thoroughly, using a fork to avoid crushing grapes, and leave to macerate for 1 hour.

4. Preheat oven to slow (325°F., 170°C., Gas Mark 3).

5. In another bowl of the same size, blend cornflour smoothly with double cream. Beat in the egg. Add grapes, together with all their juices, and mix well, taking care as before not to mash grapes. Flavour with a little lemon juice, to taste.

6. Pour grape filling into pastry shell.

7. Bake tart for 40 minutes, or until set and lightly coloured on top.

8. Cool and chill before serving.

Serves 4–6

Chef's tip:
To toast and skin hazelnuts, place them on a baking sheet and toast in a moderate oven for 10 to 15 minutes until skins are papery and brittle. Put hazelnuts in a clean cloth and roll vigorously to remove outer skins.

Chef's tip:
It is sometimes a good ploy to place the filled, half-baked pastry shell onto a pre-heated baking sheet immediately before the tart goes into the oven. The heat from the baking sheet helps to keep the base pastry crisp.

Gooseberry Pie

IMPERIAL	METRIC
1 lb. hard green gooseberries	450 g. hard green gooseberries
3 tablespoons soft light brown sugar	3 tablespoons soft light brown sugar
4 tablespoons cornflour	4 tablespoons cornflour
8 oz. (bought) puff pastry	225 g. (bought) puff pastry
1 tablespoon castor sugar	1 tablespoon castor sugar
cream or custard sauce, to serve	cream or custard sauce, to serve

1. Preheat oven to fairly hot (425°F., 220°C., Gas Mark 7).

2. Top and tail gooseberries; wash them quickly in a colander under cold running water and put them in a 2-pint (1-litre) pie dish.

3. Toss gooseberries with brown sugar.

4. Blend cornflour smoothly with 1 tablespoon cold water. Sprinkle over gooseberries and toss again until well mixed.

5. On a floured board, roll out puff pastry about $\frac{1}{16}$ inch (1 to 2 mm.) thick. Cut a top for the pie slightly larger in size than the top of the dish. With the remaining pastry, cut strips $\frac{1}{2}$ inch (1 cm.) wide to line the rim of the dish.

6. Moisten rim of dish with cold water and press pastry strips onto it all the way round. Moisten underside rim of pastry lid with water as well, and carefully lay it in position on top of the pie, pressing edges lightly so that they stick to the rim.

7. With a sharp knife, flake edge of pastry and make $\frac{1}{4}$ inch ($\frac{1}{2}$-cm.) scallops all the way around. Cut a slit in the centre to allow steam to escape.

8. Bake pie for 15 minutes, then turn oven temperature down to 375°F., 190°C., Gas Mark 5 and continue to bake for a further 15 minutes, or until pastry is crisply puffed and golden, and gooseberries are soft.

9. Sprinkle top of pie with castor sugar and serve hot or lukewarm, with cream or custard sauce.

Serves 4

Chef's tip:
Pies containing an acid fruit are thickened with cornflour or arrowroot because the acidity of the fruit may neutralise the thickening power of flour. Test gooseberries to see if they are cooked by prodding them through the slit with a thin skewer.

French Cherry Tart

IMPERIAL	METRIC
Pastry:	*Pastry:*
6 oz. plain flour	175 g. plain flour
pinch salt	pinch salt
3 oz. butter	85 g. butter
1 egg	1 egg
1½ oz. castor sugar	40 g. castor sugar
Filling:	*Filling:*
4 oz. castor sugar	110 g. castor sugar
2 lb. fresh red cherries, washed and stoned	900 g. fresh red cherries, washed and stoned
2 tablespoons lemon juice	2 tablespoons lemon juice
few drops almond essence	few drops almond essence
4 tablespoons redcurrant (or raspberry) jelly	4 tablespoons redcurrant (or raspberry) jelly

1. To make pastry, sift flour and salt into a bowl and make a well in the centre. Cut butter into small dice and drop into well, together with egg and castor sugar. Incorporate these ingredients into the flour with your fingers or a pastry blender, working rapidly and handling dough as little as possible. Roll or pat into a ball; wrap in a damp cloth or greaseproof paper; chill lightly in the refrigerator for about 1 hour.

2. Preheat oven to moderate (350°F., 180°C., Gas Mark 4).

3. Press pastry evenly over base and sides of an 8½- or 9-inch (22- or 23-cm.) tart tin. Prick all over with a fork and bake 'blind' for 20 to 25 minutes, or until pastry is firm and golden, but not brown. Remove from oven and allow to cool.

4. Melt sugar in a small, heavy pan with 3 tablespoons water, stirring constantly. Bring to the boil and simmer for 5 minutes. Add cherries and poach over a very low heat for 15 to 20 minutes.

5. Drain and remove cherries; arrange them in prebaked pastry case.

6. Simmer cooking juices until very syrupy. Remove from heat and add lemon juice, almond essence and redcurrant jelly, stirring until jelly has melted.

7. Transfer tart to a flat serving dish; glaze with syrup and serve lukewarm or cold.

Serves 6—8

Chef's tip:
When rolling out dough to line a flan tin roll out a round to a diameter about 2 inches (5 cm.) larger than the flan tin. The flan tin can be buttered to help brown the base of the pastry shell but it is not absolutely necessary.

Basque Apple Tart

IMPERIAL	METRIC
1 recipe basic sweet shortcrust pastry (see page 120)	1 recipe basic sweet shortcrust pastry (see page 120)
8 large crisp apples	8 large crisp apples
juice of 1 lemon	juice of 1 lemon
2 teaspoons ground cinnamon	2 teaspoons ground cinnamon
4 oz. castor sugar	100 g. castor sugar
3 oz. butter	75 g. butter
chilled double cream, to serve	chilled double cream, to serve

1. Preheat oven to moderate (375°F., 190°C., Gas Mark 5).

2. Roll pastry out to line an 8½- or 9-inch (22- or 23-cm.) fluted tart tin with a removable base. Prick base all over with a fork; line with greaseproof paper and weight down with baking beans.

3. Bake tart case 'blind' for 10 minutes; then remove beans and paper, and return to the oven for a further 10 minutes.

4. Cool pastry shell in its tin.

5. Quarter apples; peel and core them, and slice them fairly thickly into a bowl. Toss lightly with lemon juice to prevent discolouration.

6. Mix cinnamon with 3 oz. (75 g.) castor sugar and add to the bowl, together with 2 oz. (50 g.) butter in flakes. Toss thoroughly.

7. Turn apple mixture into a 3-pint (1¾-litre) baking dish. Cover tightly with foil and bake for 30 to 40 minutes, or until apple slices are tender but not disintegrating.

8. Drain apple slices, reserving juices, and arrange them neatly in the pastry shell.

9. Pour juices into a small pan. Simmer until thick and syrupy, and reduced to almost half their original volume. Spoon over apples.

10. Sprinkle apples with remaining castor sugar and dot with remaining butter.

11. Finish tart under a moderate grill until top is golden and bubbling, 5 to 7 minutes, protecting pastry edges with a little crumpled foil if they brown too quickly.

12. Serve lukewarm, with chilled thick cream.

Serves 6–8

Chef's tip:
When lining flan cases with pastry always chill the pastry for 30 minutes to allow it time to relax after all the rolling and 'set' with the cold of the refrigerator. This will minimise the danger of shrinking.

Brandied Apple Tart

IMPERIAL	METRIC
1 8-inch shortcrust pastry case, prebaked	1 20-cm. shortcrust pastry case, prebaked
3 tablespoons apricot jam	3 tablespoons apricot jam
Filling:	*Filling:*
1 tablespoon butter	1 tablespoon butter
1 lb. dessert apples	450 g. dessert apples
1 tablespoon castor sugar	1 tablespoon castor sugar
1 egg yolk	1 egg yolk
1 tablespoon brandy	1 tablespoon brandy
Topping:	*Topping:*
2 teaspoons brandy	2 teaspoons brandy
1 teaspoon lemon juice	1 teaspoon lemon juice
3–4 dessert apples	3–4 dessert apples
1 tablespoon melted butter	1 tablespoon melted butter
1 tablespoon sugar	1 tablespoon sugar

1. Leave the prebaked pastry case in its tin.

2. Preheat oven to hot (450°F., 230°C., Gas Mark 8). Heat a baking sheet in the oven at the same time.

3. To make the filling, melt butter in a heavy pan which has a tight-fitting lid. Remove from heat.

4. Chop apples coarsely; add to buttery pan.

5. Cover pan tightly. Cook over a moderate heat until apples are soft, about 15 minutes, shaking pan occasionally to prevent apples burning.

6. Rub apple pulp through a sieve into a bowl, discarding skins and cores. Beat sugar into purée, then add egg yolk and brandy. Put aside.

7. In a small pan, heat apricot jam with 1 tablespoon water, stirring, until melted. Rub jam through a sieve onto base of pastry case and spread jam all over base with a brush. Then spread with apple purée.

8. For the topping, mix brandy and lemon juice together in a bowl. Quarter, core and peel each apple and cut into slices about ⅛ inch (3 mm.) thick. Toss the slices in the bowl and arrange on top of the purée in neat, overlapping, concentric circles, starting from outside edge.

9. Brush apple slices with melted butter and sprinkle with sugar.

10. Place tart on heated baking sheet and bake for 20 to 25 minutes, or until apple slices on top are tender and tinged with brown.

11. Unmould tart just before serving. Serve lukewarm with sweetened, whipped cream.

Serves 4–6

Chocolate Almond Pie

IMPERIAL	METRIC
1 8-inch shortcrust pastry shell, prebaked	1 20-cm. shortcrust pastry shell, prebaked
2 oz. blanched toasted almonds, chopped	50 g. blanched toasted almonds, chopped
whipped cream and toasted flaked almonds, to decorate	whipped cream and toasted flaked almonds, to decorate
Chocolate filling:	*Chocolate filling:*
3 oz. bitter chocolate	75 g. bitter chocolate
½ pint milk	3 dl. milk
2 eggs, separated	2 eggs, separated
2 oz. castor sugar	50 g. castor sugar
grated rind of ½ orange	grated rind of ½ orange
1 tablespoon rum (optional)	1 tablespoon rum (optional)
1 tablespoon powdered gelatine	1 tablespoon powdered gelatine
¼ pint double cream	1½ dl. double cream

1. Scatter prebaked pastry shell with coarsely chopped toasted almonds.

2. To make chocolate filling, break bitter chocolate into the top of a double saucepan and melt over simmering water. Add milk gradually, stirring until smoothly blended.

3. Beat egg yolks with sugar until pale and fluffy. Pour hot chocolate milk onto egg yolks, beating constantly; then return mixture to top of double saucepan and cook over simmering water, stirring, until custard coats the back of a spoon. Do not allow it to boil, or eggs will curdle.

4. As soon as custard thickens, plunge base of pan into cold water to halt the cooking process. Beat in grated orange rind, and rum, if used, and allow to cool.

5. Soften gelatine in 2 tablespoons cold water in a small cup or bowl. Put cup in a small pan of hot water and stir until gelatine has dissolved and liquid is quite clear.

6. Whisk egg whites until stiff but not dry. In a separate bowl, beat cream until thick.

7. Blend dissolved gelatine into cooled chocolate custard; then fold in cream, followed by beaten egg whites.

8. Pour mixture into pastry shell and chill until firm. Serve decorated with piped whipped cream and toasted almonds.

Serves 6

Chef's tip:
To beat cream, bowl, beater and cream should all be chilled. Never overwhip—aim for the point where the cream falls in large globs and will hold a soft peak and still carries a gloss; then serve immediately. If it is to be used decoratively, whip to one stage stiffer.

American Pumpkin Pie

IMPERIAL	METRIC
1 8½- to 9-inch shortcrust pastry shell, prebaked	1 22- to 23-cm. shortcrust pastry shell, prebaked
¼ pint double cream, whipped	1½ dl. double cream, whipped
Filling:	*Filling:*
8 oz. canned pumpkin pulp	225 g. canned pumpkin pulp
1 tablespoon melted butter	1 tablespoon melted butter
2 oz. soft light brown sugar	50 g. soft light brown sugar
¼ teaspoon salt	¼ teaspoon salt
¼ teaspoon each ground cinnamon, ginger and freshly grated nutmeg	¼ teaspoon each ground cinnamon, ginger and freshly grated nutmeg
pinch ground cloves	pinch ground cloves
generous pinch ground mace	generous pinch ground mace
¼ pint single cream	1½ dl. single cream
2 eggs	2 eggs

1. Preheat oven to hot (450°F., 230°C., Gas Mark 8).

2. Make the filling. If you have not been able to get strained pumpkin, rub the pulp through a sieve into a large bowl.

3. Beat in melted butter, sugar, salt, spices and the single cream.

4. Whisk eggs thoroughly. Blend them with pumpkin mixture.

5. Pour filling into prebaked pastry shell.

6. Bake for 10 minutes; then reduce temperature to 350°F., 180°C., Gas Mark 4 and continue to bake for 30 minutes longer, or until filling has set. Leave pie to cool.

7. When ready to serve, decorate pie with piped whipped cream.

Serves 4–6

Chef's tip:
When buying canned pumpkin, make sure you get the unsweetened, unseasoned variety. If it is the first time you have used pumpkin, don't taste the pulp—it might put you off the resulting pie which is delicious.

Linzertorte

IMPERIAL	METRIC
Pastry:	*Pastry:*
6 oz. plain flour	175 g. plain flour
pinch ground cinnamon	pinch ground cinnamon
3 oz. ground hazelnuts	85 g. ground hazelnuts
1 oz. castor sugar	25 g. castor sugar
4 oz. softened butter	110 g. softened butter
1 tablespoon rum	1 tablespoon rum
(optional)	(optional)
1 teaspoon vanilla essence	1 teaspoon vanilla essence
1 teaspoon grated lemon	1 teaspoon grated lemon
rind	rind
Filling:	*Filling:*
1 lb. raspberry jam, sieved	450 g. raspberry jam, sieved
¼ teaspoon ground cloves	¼ teaspoon ground cloves
lemon juice	lemon juice
1 egg, lightly beaten, to	1 egg, lightly beaten, to
glaze	glaze

1. To make pastry, in a bowl, mix flour, cinnamon, ground hazelnuts and castor sugar, and rub in butter until completely blended. Add rum, if used, vanilla essence and grated lemon rind, and knead lightly to a smooth paste.

2. Roll pastry into a ball; wrap in a cloth and chill in the refrigerator for about 1 hour.

3. Preheat oven to moderate (375 °F., 190 °C., Gas Mark 5).

4. Meanwhile, melt sieved jam in a small saucepan. Add ground cloves and flavour to taste with lemon juice. Bring to the boil and simmer gently, stirring, until jam is reduced to about one third. Put aside until ready to use.

5. Press about three-quarters of the pastry into the base of a loose-bottomed, plain-edged tart tin 9 inches (23 cm.) in diameter, pushing some of the pastry up sides of the tin to make a neat border about 1 inch (2½ cm.) deep.

6. Decorate pastry border with a fork; brush with beaten egg and bake for 30 to 35 minutes, or until pastry is cooked through and golden brown.

7. Spread jam evenly into baked pastry case.

8. Roll remaining pastry into strips and use to decorate top of tart in a lattice pattern. Brush strips with remaining beaten egg.

9. Return tart to the oven for 10 to 15 minutes or until lattice is golden brown. Cool before serving.

Serves 6–8

Chef's tip:
This famous tart is a speciality of the town of Linz. It is also often made with a cranberry filling, made by melting cranberry jelly or sieved cranberry preserve and reducing it by about one third, as above.

Sultana Meringue Pie

IMPERIAL	METRIC
1 7-inch shortcrust pastry	1 18-cm. shortcrust pastry
shell, prebaked	shell, prebaked
Filling:	*Filling:*
2 oz. sultanas	50 g. sultanas
1 tablespoon rum	1 tablespoon rum
2 teaspoons castor sugar	2 teaspoons castor sugar
1 tablespoon cornflour	1 tablespoon cornflour
¼ teaspoon ground	¼ teaspoon ground
cinnamon	cinnamon
¼ teaspoon freshly grated	¼ teaspoon freshly grated
nutmeg	nutmeg
pinch salt	pinch salt
¼ pint sour cream	1½ dl. sour cream
3 tablespoons double	3 tablespoons double
cream	cream
3 egg yolks	3 egg yolks
Meringue:	*Meringue:*
2 egg whites	2 egg whites
4 oz. castor sugar	110 g. castor sugar

1. For the filling, macerate sultanas in rum for 30 minutes.

2. Stir sugar, cornflour, spices and salt together in top of a double saucepan. Add sour cream and double cream, stirring smoothly until blended.

3. Cook over simmering water, stirring, for 15 minutes, or until mixture is smooth and thick. Remove from heat.

4. Beat egg yolks. Add them to cream mixture in a thin stream, beating vigorously.

5. Replace pan over simmering water and continue to cook, stirring, for a further 7 to 10 minutes, or until mixture is thick again. Do not boil, or egg yolks will curdle.

6. Remove from heat. Stir in soaked sultanas together with any remaining rum, and leave to cool, stirring occasionally to prevent a skin forming on top.

7. Meanwhile, preheat oven to moderate (350 °F., 180 °C., Gas Mark 4).

8. To make meringue, with a spotlessly clean whisk, beat egg whites until soft peaks form. Add half the castor sugar and continue to beat to a stiff, glossy meringue. Fold in remaining sugar with a metal spoon.

9. Spoon sultana filling into pastry shell. Pile meringue on top, bringing it right up to rim of pastry. Swirl surface attractively with the blade of a knife.

10. Bake pie for 15 minutes, or until meringue is crisp and golden on top. Serve lukewarm or cold.

Serves 4–6

Butterscotch Cream Pie

Coconut Cream Pie

IMPERIAL	METRIC
1 9-inch shortcrust pastry shell, prebaked	1 23-cm. shortcrust pastry shell, prebaked
¼ pint double cream, whipped	1½ dl. double cream, whipped
1 oz. flaked almonds, lightly toasted	25 g. flaked almonds, lightly toasted
Butterscotch filling:	*Butterscotch filling:*
6 oz. soft dark brown sugar	175 g. soft dark brown sugar
3 tablespoons cornflour	3 tablespoons cornflour
½–¾ teaspoon salt	½–¾ teaspoon salt
1 pint milk	6 dl. milk
2 large eggs	2 large eggs
4 tablespoons butter	4 tablespoons butter
½ teaspoon vanilla essence	½ teaspoon vanilla essence

1. To make butterscotch filling, combine sugar, cornflour and salt in the top of a double saucepan. Stir in milk gradually to make a smooth mixture; bring to the boil over direct heat and simmer, stirring occasionally, for 4 minutes.

2. Beat eggs lightly in a bowl. Add a little of the hot mixture; mix well and blend with remaining hot milk mixture. Cook over lightly simmering water for a further 3 minutes, or until thick and smooth, stirring constantly.

3. Remove pan from heat and beat in butter. Allow to cool.

4. Flavour filling to taste with vanilla essence; strain through a fine sieve.

5. Fill prebaked pastry shell with butterscotch filling and leave until set.

6. When ready to serve, decorate pie with piped whipped cream and sprinkle with toasted flaked almonds.

Serves 6

IMPERIAL	METRIC
5 oz. castor sugar	150 g. castor sugar
½ pint single cream	3 dl. single cream
¼ pint milk	1½ dl. milk
1 tablespoon cornflour	1 tablespoon cornflour
2 eggs	2 eggs
½ teaspoon vanilla essence	½ teaspoon vanilla essence
pinch salt	pinch salt
pinch freshly grated nutmeg	pinch freshly grated nutmeg
7 tablespoons toasted coconut	7 tablespoons toasted coconut
1 8-inch shortcrust pastry shell, prebaked	1 20-cm. shortcrust pastry shell, prebaked
1 tablespoon untoasted coconut, to decorate	1 tablespoon untoasted coconut, to decorate

1. Combine sugar, cream and milk in the top of a double saucepan, and stir over direct heat until sugar has dissolved.

2. Mix cornflour to a smooth paste with a little of the heated milk mixture.

3. Beat eggs lightly; blend in cornflour mixture and combine with contents of double saucepan. Cook over simmering water, stirring constantly, until custard thickens.

4. Remove pan from heat; stir in vanilla essence, salt and freshly grated nutmeg, to taste. Cool.

5. Beat in toasted coconut. Pour coconut filling into baked pastry shell. Sprinkle with untoasted coconut to decorate and chill until set.

Serves 6–8

Chef's tip:
The pastry shell is less likely to bubble up at any time during baking if the base of the shell has been pricked all over with a sharp pronged fork, held vertically so that you make tiny holes, not gashes.

Chef's tip:
To toast coconut just place the coconut on a baking sheet and toast under a moderate grill, shaking the coconut frequently so it browns evenly. Always leave a pastry shell to cool at room temperature. If cooled too quickly it is liable to become tough.

Lemon Meringue Pie

IMPERIAL	METRIC
4 tablespoons cornflour	4 tablespoons cornflour
salt	salt
12 oz. castor sugar	350 g. castor sugar
1 tablespoon butter	1 tablespoon butter
6 tablespoons lemon juice	6 tablespoons lemon juice
finely grated rind of ½ lemon	finely grated rind of ½ lemon
4 eggs, separated	4 eggs, separated
1 8-inch shortcust pastry shell, prebaked	1 20-cm. shortcrust pastry shell, prebaked

1. In the top of a double saucepan, blend cornflour with ½ teaspoon salt and 4 oz. (110 g.) castor sugar. Gradually add ¾ pint (4 dl.) boiling water, stirring vigorously with a wooden spoon to prevent cornflour lumping. Bring to the boil over direct heat and simmer, stirring from time to time, until sauce is thick and smooth, and no longer tastes of cornflour, 7 to 10 minutes.

2. Remove pan from heat; beat in butter, lemon juice and grated lemon rind.

3. Beat egg yolks lightly; add them to the hot mixture, beating vigorously, and continue to cook over hot water until mixture thickens, stirring constantly and taking great care not to let it boil, or egg yolks may curdle. Cool, stirring occasionally to prevent a skin forming on top.

4. Meanwhile, preheat oven to moderate (350°F., 180°C., Gas Mark 4).

5. Prepare meringue. Whisk egg whites with a pinch of salt until soft peaks form; add 4 oz. (110 g.) castor sugar and continue to whisk until stiff and glossy again. Fold in remaining sugar lightly with a metal spoon.

6. Pour cooled lemon filling into prebaked pastry case. Pile meringue on top, making sure that filling is completely covered. Use a knife blade to flick surface of meringue up in peaks.

7. Bake pie for about 15 minutes, or until meringue is firm on top and peaks are tinged with golden brown.

Serves 4–6

Chef's tip:
You might prefer the rind more coarsely grated. If you like a very lemony flavour, add more rind rather than more juice. Additional acid liquid may thin the filling too much. This pie is best if eaten straight after it comes out of the oven.

Almond Puffs

IMPERIAL	METRIC
melted butter	melted butter
1 7½-oz. packet frozen puff pastry, thawed	1 212-g. packet frozen puff pastry, thawed
raspberry jam	raspberry jam
1 oz. butter	25 g. butter
1 oz. castor sugar	25 g. castor sugar
1 egg	1 egg
1 oz. ground almonds	25 g. ground almonds
a little almond essence	a little almond essence
2–3 oz. icing sugar	50–75 g. icing sugar
½ teaspoon flour	½ teaspoon flour

1. Brush a 12-hole patty tin with melted butter.

2. Preheat oven to moderately hot (400°F., 200°C., Gas Mark 6).

3. Roll out puff pastry to the thickness of a one- (new) penny piece.

4. Using a plain cutter of slightly larger diameter than that of the patty tin holes, cut out twenty circles; use half to line ten of the holes. Reserve pastry trimmings.

5. Place ½ teaspoon of raspberry jam in the base of each case.

6. Cream butter and sugar in a basin until light and fluffy.

7. Separate egg, reserving white; beat egg yolk into creamed mixture and add ground almonds and a few drops of almond essence.

8. Divide mixture evenly between patty cases. Dampen edges of remaining pastry circles and cover each tartlet.

9. Beat reserved egg white until stiff; gradually work in sifted icing sugar and flour to give a stiffish coating consistency. Spread top of each tartlet with icing.

10. Re-roll pastry trimmings into a strip the length of the patty tin. Lay down the length of the patty tin, two strips, slightly apart, over each line of tartlets. Repeat procedure with strips across, and snip pastry strips between each tartlet.

11. Bake for 20 minutes or until well-risen and golden.

Makes 10

Chef's tip:
Make sure each tartlet lid is on firmly before baking. Do this with a cutter that fits just inside the diameter of the top of the tartlet; using the *reverse* end press the lid onto the base. Remember, one piece of pastry sticks better to another if only one piece is dampened.

Leftovers Pie

IMPERIAL	METRIC
5 tablespoons butter	5 tablespoons butter
1 small onion, chopped	1 small onion, chopped
1 stalk celery, chopped	1 stalk celery, chopped
4 tablespoons flour	4 tablespoons flour
1 pint thin gravy or stock	6 dl. thin gravy or stock
12 oz. cooked, cold lamb or beef	350 g. cooked, cold lamb or beef
12 oz. mixed cooked vegetables	350 g. mixed cooked vegetables
2–3 tablespoons dry red wine	2–3 tablespoons dry red wine
2 teaspoons Worcestershire sauce	2 teaspoons Worcestershire sauce
1 teaspoon soy sauce	1 teaspoon soy sauce
salt and freshly ground black pepper	salt and freshly ground black pepper
6 oz. basic savoury shortcrust pastry (see page 120)	175 g. basic savoury shortcrust pastry (see page 120)

1. Preheat oven to moderately hot (400°F., 200°C., Gas Mark 6).

2. Melt butter in a medium-sized saucepan. Sauté onion and celery over a moderate heat for 5 minutes. Stir in flour and continue to cook roux for a further 10 to 15 minutes or until it has turned a deep golden colour.

3. Gradually add gravy or stock, stirring quickly. Simmer for a further 10 minutes, uncovered, then add meat and vegetables. Stir in wine, Worcestershire sauce and soy sauce, and season to taste with salt and freshly ground black pepper.

4. Pour mixture into a 1¾-pint (1-litre) pie dish. Cover and leave on one side to cool, whilst preparing pastry.

5. Roll out pastry to an oblong, 2 inches (5 cm.) larger than the top of the pie. Cut off a ½-inch (1-cm.) wide strip from around edge of pastry.

6. Brush rim of pie dish with water and press pastry strip around rim of pie dish; brush with water.

7. Lift remaining pastry over rolling pin; place in position over top of pie. Lightly press edges together and trim off excess pastry around edge of pie. Pinch edges of pie to seal well, and decorate. Brush all over with beaten egg to glaze.

8. Re-roll pastry trimmings and cut out 'leaves' to decorate top of pie. Make a steam hole in centre of lid. Glaze decoration. Place pie on a baking sheet.

9. Bake for 30 to 40 minutes or until pie is golden brown on top. Serve immediately.

Serves 5–6

Bacon and Apple Pie

IMPERIAL	METRIC
1 lb. boned forehock, trimmed and cut into small pieces	450 g. boned forehock, trimmed and cut into small pieces
1 Spanish onion	1 Spanish onion
1 large cooking apple	1 large cooking apple
2 medium-sized potatoes	2 medium-sized potatoes
freshly ground black pepper	freshly ground black pepper
1 teaspoon sugar	1 teaspoon sugar
2–3 tablespoons dry white wine	2–3 tablespoons dry white wine
chicken or ham stock	chicken or ham stock
6 oz. basic savoury shortcrust pastry (see page 120)	175 g. basic savoury shortcrust pastry (see page 120)
beaten egg, to glaze	beaten egg, to glaze
sprig of parsley, to garnish	sprig of parsley, to garnish

1. Preheat oven to moderate (375°F., 190°C., Gas Mark 5).

2. Place bacon in a bowl. Add thinly sliced onion.

3. Peel, quarter and core apple. Cut into thin slices; peel and slice potatoes thinly. Add to bowl with freshly ground black pepper and sugar; toss well to mix.

4. Press mixture firmly into a 1½-pint (1-litre) pie dish. Pour over white wine and add 4–6 tablespoons stock. Cover and leave on one side whilst preparing the pastry.

5. Roll out pastry to cover top of pie (see preceding recipe, steps 5 to 8).

6. Bake for 1½ hours. Cover top of pie with foil if the pastry seems to be browning too much before the end of the cooking time. Garnish with parsley, and serve hot.

Serves 4

Chef's tip:
Press the mixture as firmly as possible into the pie dish before covering with the pastry lid. The apples, potatoes and onions all tend to collapse on cooking and unless the pie is firmly filled you will be faced with a cavernous space between pie crust and pie filling.

Country-style Pie

Fish Pie

Country-style Pie

IMPERIAL	METRIC
1 lb. pie veal	450 g. pie veal
1 lb. belly of pork	450 g. belly of pork
5 slices streaky bacon, diced	5 slices streaky bacon, diced
1 medium-sized potato, peeled and chopped	1 medium-sized potato, peeled and chopped
1 onion, chopped	1 onion, chopped
1 clove garlic, crushed	1 clove garlic, crushed
good pinch dried thyme	good pinch dried thyme
generous pinch powdered allspice	generous pinch powdered allspice
1 teaspoon salt	1 teaspoon salt
freshly ground black pepper	freshly ground black pepper
1 tablespoon dry white wine	1 tablespoon dry white wine
1 tablespoon brandy	1 tablespoon brandy
1 13-oz. packet frozen puff pastry, thawed	1 368-g. packet frozen puff pastry, thawed
beaten egg, to glaze	beaten egg, to glaze
sprig of watercress, to garnish	sprig of watercress, to garnish

1. Preheat oven to moderately hot (400°F., 200°C., Gas Mark 6).

2. Trim excess fat from meat and cut meat into small pieces.

3. Place meat in a large bowl and mix thoroughly with chopped bacon, potato and onion, garlic, thyme, allspice, salt and freshly ground black pepper, dry white wine and brandy. Put on one side whilst preparing pastry.

4. Cut off one third of pastry. Roll out on a floured working surface. Using a plate or saucepan lid as a guide, cut out a round, 9½ to 10 inches (24 to 25 cm.) in diameter; place on a baking sheet. Reserve trimmings.

5. Roll out remaining, larger piece of pastry and cut out a round, about 11 to 11½ inches (28 to 29 cm.) in diameter, again using a suitably-sized plate or saucepan lid as a guide.

6. Pile prepared meat mixture onto smaller pastry round on baking sheet, leaving a clear 1-inch (2½-cm.) border around edge; brush edge with beaten egg.

7. Cover meat with larger round of pastry, lifting pastry over rolling pin, to prevent pastry stretching. Pinch edges together firmly to seal well and decorate.

8. Re-roll pastry trimmings and cut out 'leaf' shapes to decorate top of pie. Make a steam hole in centre. Glaze decorations.

9. Bake pie for 10 minutes, then reduce heat to 350°F., 180°C., Gas Mark 4 and bake for a further 65 minutes or until pie is a deep golden brown on top. Serve hot or cold.

Serves 6–8

Fish Pie

IMPERIAL	METRIC
4 tablespoons butter	4 tablespoons butter
1 small onion, chopped	1 small onion, chopped
2 stalks celery, chopped	2 stalks celery, chopped
4 tablespoons flour	4 tablespoons flour
½ teaspoon dry mustard	½ teaspoon dry mustard
freshly ground black pepper	freshly ground black pepper
2 teaspoons Worcestershire sauce	2 teaspoons Worcestershire sauce
1 3¼-oz. can crabmeat	1 92-g. can crabmeat
milk	milk
¼ pint double cream	1½ dl. double cream
1½ lb. cooked, smoked fish, flaked	675 g. cooked, smoked fish, flaked
4 oz. peeled shrimps or prawns	100 g. peeled shrimps or prawns
2 hard-boiled eggs	2 hard-boiled eggs
3 tablespoons chopped parsley	3 tablespoons chopped parsley
lemon juice	lemon juice
2–3 tablespoons dry white wine	2–3 tablespoons dry white wine
freshly grated nutmeg	freshly grated nutmeg
8 oz. basic savoury shortcrust pastry (see page 120)	225 g. basic savoury shortcrust pastry (see page 120)
beaten egg, to glaze	beaten egg, to glaze

1. Heat butter in a medium-sized saucepan until frothy.

2. Sauté onion and celery over a low heat until softened, but not browned, about 10 minutes.

3. Stir in flour, dry mustard, freshly ground black pepper and Worcestershire sauce. Drain juices from can of crabmeat into a measuring jug and make up to ½ pint (3 dl.) with milk; gradually add this, followed by the cream, to basic roux, stirring briskly to prevent lumps forming.

4. Bring sauce to the boil, then simmer gently for 2 to 3 minutes. Remove from heat.

5. Fold in flaked fish, shrimps or prawns, crabmeat (with white strips of cartilage removed), chopped hard-boiled eggs, parsley, lemon juice, dry white wine, and nutmeg.

6. Pour mixture into a 2- to 3-pint (1- to 1¾-litre) dish. Cover and cool.

7. Preheat oven to fairly hot (425°F., 220°C., Gas Mark 7).

8. Roll out pastry and proceed as directed in Leftovers pie, steps 5 to 6 (see previous page), glazing with beaten egg. Re-roll pastry trimmings, cut into strips, and make a decorative latticework on top of pie. Glaze with beaten egg. Place pie on a baking sheet. Bake for 35 to 40 minutes or until pastry is golden brown. Serve immediately.

Serves 6–8

Chicken Pie with Green Olives

IMPERIAL	METRIC
1 3- to 3½-lb. roasting chicken, cut into 8 joints	1 1¼- to 1½-kg. roasting chicken, cut into 8 joints
seasoned flour	seasoned flour
1 tablespoon butter	1 tablespoon butter
1 tablespoon olive oil	1 tablespoon olive oil
4 oz. unsmoked bacon, diced	100 g. unsmoked bacon, diced
2 small onions, thinly sliced	2 small onions, thinly sliced
8 large white button mushrooms	8 large white button mushrooms
¼ pint dry white wine	1½ dl. dry white wine
2 hard-boiled eggs, sliced	2 hard-boiled eggs, sliced
12 large green olives, stoned and sliced	12 large green olives, stoned and sliced
3–4 tablespoons chicken stock	3–4 tablespoons chicken stock
12 oz. puff pastry	350 g. puff pastry
a little milk, to glaze	a little milk, to glaze

1. Shape chicken joints into neat parcels; coat with seasoned flour. Reserve.

2. Heat butter and oil in a large frying pan, and sauté bacon gently for 15 minutes. Drain bacon and reserve.

3. In the same fat, sauté onions until soft and golden, about 5 minutes. Drain well and reserve onions with bacon bits, leaving behind as much fat as possible.

4. Fry chicken joints in remaining fat until well coloured on all sides. Reserve together with bacon and onion.

5. Finally, toss button mushrooms in remaining fat for 2 minutes until lightly coloured.

6. Return bacon, onions and chicken joints to pan. Pour over dry white wine. Cover pan tightly; simmer for 15 minutes.

7. Pack layers of chicken, bacon, onions, mushrooms, egg and olives into a 1¾- to 2-pint (about 1-litre) pie dish. Pour over pan juices and add enough chicken stock to bring liquid a third of the way up dish. Cover and cool.

8. Preheat oven to fairly hot (425°F., 220°C., Gas Mark 7).

9. Roll out pastry and cover pie. Use trimmings to decorate pie. Brush top of pie with milk.

10. Place pie on a baking sheet and bake for 30 to 35 minutes, or until cooked through and golden. Serve hot.

Serves 4

Quiche Lorraine

IMPERIAL	METRIC
1 8-inch shortcrust pastry case, prebaked	1 20-cm. shortcrust pastry case, prebaked
3 thick slices unsmoked fat bacon	3 thick slices unsmoked fat bacon
3 oz. Gruyère, in one piece	75 g. Gruyère, in one piece
3 egg yolks	3 egg yolks
¼ pint plus 2 tablespoons single cream	1½ dl. single cream
salt and freshly ground black pepper	salt and freshly ground black pepper
freshly grated nutmeg	freshly grated nutmeg

1. Leave the prebaked pastry case in its tin on a baking sheet.

2. Preheat oven to moderate (350°F., 180°C., Gas Mark 4).

3. If bacon slices are very salty, blanch them in boiling water for 3 minutes. Drain slices; cut them into thin strips, and place them in a cold frying pan. Heat gently until fat begins to run; then sauté for about 5 minutes, or until golden. Drain strips on kitchen paper.

4. Cut Gruyère into very small dice.

5. Combine egg yolks and cream in a jug or bowl. Beat with a fork until thoroughly blended, adding salt, freshly ground black pepper and a pinch of freshly grated nutmeg, to taste.

6. Sprinkle bacon strips and diced Gruyère over base of pastry case. Three-quarters fill it with cream mixture, pouring it in gently over the back of a tablespoon to avoid disturbing bacon and cheese.

7. Transfer pastry case on its baking sheet to the oven and carefully pour in remaining cream mixture.

8. Bake quiche for 25 to 30 minutes until filling is puffed and set, and a rich golden colour on top. Serve immediately.

Serves 4

Chef's tip:
When tart shell is to be subjected to further baking after it has been filled, bake pastry case for 10 minutes in a moderately hot oven (400°F., 200°C., Gas Mark 6). Remove baking beans and paper then return to the oven for just 10 minutes longer to dry out the base without colouring it.

Tarte aux Asperges

IMPERIAL	METRIC
1 lb. puff pastry	450 g. puff pastry
lightly beaten egg white	lightly beaten egg white
Filling:	*Filling:*
12 oz. frozen asparagus stalks	350 g. frozen asparagus stalks
½ pint chicken (cube) stock	3 dl. chicken (cube) stock
3 oz. Cheddar, freshly grated	75 g. Cheddar, freshly grated
1 oz. Parmesan, freshly grated	25 g. Parmesan, freshly grated
2 eggs	2 eggs
8 tablespoons cream	8 tablespoons cream
salt and freshly ground black pepper	salt and freshly ground black pepper
freshly grated nutmeg	freshly grated nutmeg
extra asparagus spears, to garnish (optional)	extra asparagus spears, to garnish (optional)

1. Preheat oven to moderately hot (400°F., 200°C., Gas Mark 6).

2. Roll out pastry to fit a loose-bottomed, 9-inch (23-cm.) tart tin. Brush the surface with lightly beaten egg white; prick the base all over with a fork and place a piece of foil in the centre to prevent uneven rising.

3. Bake the pastry case 'blind' for 15 to 20 minutes, removing the foil for the last 5 minutes to allow the base to dry out. Remove from oven and reduce temperature to 375°F., 190°C., Gas Mark 5.

4. While the pastry is in the oven, trim asparagus stalks to fit the tin. Simmer them in chicken stock for 8 to 10 minutes, or until tender. Drain well and dry on absorbent paper. Keep warm.

5. Mix freshly grated Cheddar and Parmesan together, and sprinkle two-thirds over the base of the pastry case. Arrange asparagus attractively on top, halving the stalks lengthwise if they are not all of the same thickness.

6. Beat eggs lightly; add cream and beat again until well mixed. Season to taste with salt, freshly ground black pepper and a pinch of freshly grated nutmeg. Pour egg mixture over asparagus and sprinkle top with remaining cheese.

7. Bake tart for 15 to 20 minutes, or until egg mixture has set.

8. Remove tart from the oven and slip under a hot grill until top is golden brown and bubbling, shielding pastry rim with crumpled foil, if it looks like burning. Garnish with asparagus if you like, and serve.

Serves 6–8

Pizza al Tonno

IMPERIAL	METRIC
Pizza dough:	*Pizza dough:*
1 tablespoon dried yeast	1 tablespoon dried yeast
1 teaspoon castor sugar	1 teaspoon castor sugar
8 oz. plain flour	225 g. plain flour
¼ pint tepid milk and water	1½ dl. tepid milk and water
1 tablespoon olive oil	1 tablespoon olive oil
Filling:	*Filling:*
1 7-oz. can tuna in oil	1 198-g. can tuna in oil
1 small onion, chopped	1 small onion, chopped
1 8-oz. can tomatoes	1 225-g. can tomatoes
1 bay leaf	1 bay leaf
¼ teaspoon marjoram	¼ teaspoon marjoram
¼ teaspoon sugar	¼ teaspoon sugar
salt and black pepper	salt and black pepper
Garnish:	*Garnish:*
anchovy fillets, halved lengthwise	anchovy fillets, halved lengthwise
black olives, stoned and halved	black olives, stoned and halved
grated Parmesan	grated Parmesan

1. To make the dough, dissolve yeast in 3 tablespoons luke-warm water mixed with sugar, following directions on can.

2. Place flour in bowl; make a well in the centre and pour in frothy yeast mixture. Work into flour with your fingertips, adding enough milk and water to make a soft dough; then knead vigorously until dough is springy and leaves bowl and hands clean. Add oil and knead until smooth again.

3. Roll dough into a ball. Cover bowl and leave dough to rise in a warm place until doubled in bulk, 30 minutes.

4. For the filling, drain oil from tuna into a medium-sized saucepan. Add chopped onion and sauté until soft.

5. Stir in tuna, tomatoes, herbs and sugar; mix well and season to taste with salt and freshly ground black pepper.

6. Cook gently, uncovered, for 20 to 30 minutes or until mixture has thick, jam-like consistency. Remove from heat, discard bay leaf and leave mixture to cool slightly.

7. Preheat oven to fairly hot (425°F., 220°C., Gas Mark 7).

8. When dough has doubled in bulk, knead lightly, then push out with the palm of your hand to a round, about 10 inches (25 cm.) in diameter or to fit a rectangular baking tray 12 by 8 inches (30 by 20 cm.). Build up outside edge slightly to contain filling. Brush dough all over with oil.

9. Spread filling over top to within ½ inch (1 cm.) of edge. Arrange anchovy fillets in a lattice pattern on top and dot each lattice with half an olive. Sprinkle with Parmesan.

10. Bake for 15 to 20 minutes or until golden. Serve immediately.

Serves 6

Meals to Cook Ahead

I don't think that cooking will ever lose its fascination for me. How often have I sat back confidently, secure in the knowledge—or so I thought—that I had at last perfected a method of cooking a dish, only to have some exciting new possibility of making it even better reveal itself like a bolt from the blue, often by sheer accident. And so the search for perfection starts all over again.

In the last few years, I doubt if any branch of cooking has offered me a greater challenge than that mainstay of novice cooks—the casserole.

The casserole is the main stand-by of meals cooked in advance, so don't treat casseroling with contempt. On the face of it, making a casserole is derisively easy. You can cut up some meat—or fish or poultry—brown it or not (depending on whether you are making a brown stew or a white one), sauté some vegetables, add liquid, seasonings, etc., pop on a lid and let it go. But the secret lies in the care and patience with which you carry out these simple operations.

What cuts of meat can you casserole?

Casserole—or pot roast:

(*a*) anything that you wouldn't risk roasting (the long, slow cooking will tenderise the toughest of meat, and any bird past its prime);

(*b*) any meat that you prefer to serve really well done (you have the sauce and vegetables to keep the meat moist until it's ready).

It goes without saying that most roasting and grilling cuts will make superb pot-roasts and casseroles, although paradoxically some prime cuts are so fine that they will not take kindly to the long, slow cooking you need to blend flavours and produce a rich sauce, and most likely disintegrate.

Beef Rump, topside, brisket, flank, clod, shin (top part).

Veal Best end of neck, neck, shoulder, breast, knuckle, shin.

Lamb Leg, best end of neck, middle neck (scrag end), shoulder, breast.

Pork Any cut that is not too expensive, nor too fat.

Poultry Any farmyard bird, whole or jointed, especially one of doubtful age.

To prepare meat
Meat is cut into bite-sized cubes, or sliced or tied into shape with string and left in a piece. Poultry is usually jointed for a casserole. It pays to take time over this, making cubes the same size as far as possible and cutting slices of even thickness so that they will all cook evenly. Cut out gristle and excess fat as you go along, or you may find your guests doing it for you at the table, which is most embarrassing.

To sauté meat
The flavour and colour of any casserole other than a creamy blanquette are greatly improved if the meat and flavouring vegetables (onions, garlic, carrots, etc.) are first browned in fat.

Choose your fat according to the meat—fresh beef or pork dripping is safer, but lamb fat should never

be used with any meat other than lamb. Never use butter on its own, or it will burn. My favourite combination is a mixture of butter and olive oil, which gives the best of both worlds, a buttery flavour with no danger of burning.

The cooking pot
Give some thought to the pot you are going to use. Whether it is a casserole or a saucepan—or even a large deep frying pan—it should be large enough to protect the contents from scorching, have a tight-fitting lid to prevent the flavoursome sauce from cooking away, and be just large enough to be two-thirds full when all the ingredients are added.

If your casserole is to be cooked under a tight-fitting lid, it is highly improbable that much of the liquid added at the beginning will be lost by evaporation. Indeed, it will if anything be augmented by the juices from the onions and the meat itself.

The long, gentle cooking will develop flavours, blend them and transform the liquid into a rich sauce. However, you can't expect miracles. The quality and flavour of your sauce will inevitably be closely related to the quality of the liquid that you put into it at the start. If the stock you use is water, it will certainly have improved by the time the casserole is ready, but will still be watery.

One of the most exciting discoveries I have made in the past few years involves *reducing* the liquid—be it stock, wine or strained-off marinade—*before* adding it to the casserole. The results are quite dramatic. Instead of the liquid drawing flavour from the ingredients and at best giving only moisture in return, a veritable dialogue takes place, both sides contributing and both sides benefiting from it.

How to cook a casserole
More casseroles are ruined by excessive heat than through any other fault. If you want the meat to be tender without disintegrating into a bundle of dry, tasteless fibres, and the sauce to be rich in texture and flavour, the casserole cannot be hurried: throughout its cooking time it should be kept to a faint, barely perceptible simmer.

* When cooking on top of the stove, an asbestos or wire mat will certainly help, but you must still watch it like a hawk. Casseroles have a habit of starting to bubble the moment you turn your back. You can also try standing the pot on a trivet, out of direct contact with the heat.

* A far more convenient solution, if you have better things to do than stand guard over a casserole, is to use the oven, preheated to just 225°F., 110°C., Gas Mark $\frac{1}{4}$ or 250°F., 130°C., Gas Mark $\frac{1}{2}$. This will not be hot enough to bring the ingredients *up* to simmering point so, before putting the casserole into the oven, you will have to heat it gently on top of the stove until the first bubbles start to break on the surface of the sauce. As soon as these appear, remove the casserole from the heat, cover it tightly and transfer it to the oven, where the heat should be sufficient to keep it at this level and no more.

Carbonnade de Boeuf à la Flamande

IMPERIAL	METRIC
2–2½ lb. braising beef	about 1 kg. braising beef
4–6 tablespoons butter or lard	4–6 tablespoons butter or lard
3 large Spanish onions, thinly sliced	3 large Spanish onions, thinly sliced
1½ tablespoons flour	1½ tablespoons flour
salt and freshly ground black pepper	salt and freshly ground black pepper
1½ tablespoons wine vinegar	1½ tablespoons wine vinegar
1½ tablespoons light brown sugar	1½ tablespoons light brown sugar
bouquet garni	bouquet garni
⅓ pint beef stock	2 dl. beef stock
¾ pint pale ale	4 dl. pale ale
chopped parsley	chopped parsley

1. Cut beef across the grain into fairly thin slices.

2. In a heavy pan or casserole, brown beef slices on both sides in butter or lard. Remove from pan.

3. Add thinly sliced onions to fat remaining in pan and sauté over a steady, moderate heat until a rich golden colour. Sprinkle with flour and continue to cook, stirring, until flour is golden.

4. Return beef slices to the pan; turn onions over them, and season to taste with salt and freshly ground black pepper. Sprinkle with vinegar and brown sugar, stir for a minute or two longer, then add bouquet garni, stock and ale, and bring to the boil over a low heat, scraping bottom and sides of pan clean with a wooden spoon.

5. Cover pan and simmer over a very low heat for about 2½ hours, or until meat is very tender, adding a little more stock if sauce evaporates too quickly. Correct seasoning, sprinkle with parsley and serve very hot, accompanied by a bowl of plain boiled floury potatoes.

Serves 6

Quick Mexican Chili

IMPERIAL	METRIC
1 lb. red kidney beans	450 g. red kidney beans
2 tablespoons bacon fat or dripping	2 tablespoons bacon fat or dripping
1 lb. lean beef, minced	450 g. lean beef, minced
2 Spanish onions, finely chopped	2 Spanish onions, finely chopped
2 garlic cloves, finely chopped	2 garlic cloves, finely chopped
2 pints beef stock	generous litre beef stock
9 oz. tomato paste	250 g. tomato paste
4 teaspoons Mexican chili powder	4 teaspoons Mexican chili powder
1 tablespoon flour	1 tablespoon flour
2 bay leaves, crumbled	2 bay leaves, crumbled
¼ teaspoon powdered cumin	¼ teaspoon powdered cumin
½ teaspoon oregano	½ teaspoon oregano
1 teaspoon paprika	1 teaspoon paprika
salt and freshly ground black pepper	salt and freshly ground black pepper
chopped parsley	chopped parsley

1. Cover beans with cold water and bring to the boil; boil for 2 minutes, remove and allow to stand for 1 hour. Pour off water; cover with fresh cold water; bring to the boil again and simmer for 1 hour.

2. Melt bacon fat or dripping in a large, flameproof casserole. Add minced beef and chopped onions and garlic, and sauté until meat is crumbly and well browned. Stir in beef stock and tomato paste; bring to the boil and simmer gently.

3. Blend chili powder and flour with a little of the meat juices and stir into the casserole, together with crumbled bay leaves, cumin, oregano and paprika. Season to taste.

4. Add drained beans; mix lightly and continue to cook over a low heat for a further 1½ hours, or until both the beans and meat are done, and the sauce is rich and thick. Add a little more stock or water to the casserole if sauce dries out too quickly. Serve very hot, sprinkled with parsley.

Serves 4–6

Chef's tip:
You can use up stale or flat beer for this recipe—it will not affect the flavour. If using freshly opened beer, be sure that there is no head on it so the quantity used can be measured accurately. If it is too foamy to measure, stir rapidly then foam will subside.

Chef's tip:
Buy small quantities of paprika pepper as and when you need it, as this is a spice which quickly deteriorates. The Hungarian *edel-süss* paprika is the best, but as a general guide, the browner powder is thought to be the best.

Beer Pot Roast

IMPERIAL	METRIC
1 3- to 4-lb. joint beef topside	1 1½- to 1¾-kg. joint beef topside
well-seasoned flour	well-seasoned flour
2 oz. butter	50 g. butter
4 oz. unsmoked streaky bacon, sliced	100 g. unsmoked streaky bacon, sliced
½ pint dark beer	3 dl. dark beer
1 large onion, finely chopped	1 large onion, finely chopped
1 large carrot, diced	1 large carrot, diced
1 stalk celery, diced	1 stalk celery, diced
1 sprig parsley	1 sprig parsley
1 bay leaf	1 bay leaf
salt and freshly ground black pepper	salt and freshly ground black pepper

1. Preheat oven to cool (225°F., 110°C., Gas Mark ¼).

2. Wipe joint dry with a cloth or kitchen paper, and rub all over generously with well-seasoned flour.

3. Melt butter in a heavy, 5-pint (3-litre) casserole and sauté bacon slices until their fat runs.

4. Remove bacon; add beef and continue to sauté over a steady heat until well browned on all sides.

5. Remove meat from casserole; pour in beer, scraping bottom and sides of casserole to dislodge traces of browned flour that have stuck there.

6. Add vegetables, a sprig of parsley and a bay leaf; then replace beef and bacon in the casserole, spooning sauce over the joint to coat it. Season generously with salt and freshly ground black pepper, and cover casserole tightly.

7. Transfer casserole to the oven and bake for 2½ to 3 hours, or until meat is very tender, basting it frequently with its own juices and turning it occasionally.

8. Serve beef in thick slices, accompanied by pan juices and boiled or puréed potatoes or noodles.

Serves 6–8

Chef's tip:
A good heavy casserole with a well-fitting lid is very important for cooking stews and daubes, etc. It will heat more slowly and evenly and help to maintain that temperature just below a simmer which is so important for such dishes.

Italian Beef Stew

IMPERIAL	METRIC
2½–3 lb. lean beef	1¼–1½ kg lean beef
salt and freshly ground black pepper	salt and freshly ground black pepper
1 tablespoon lard	1 tablespoon lard
1 tablespoon olive oil	1 tablespoon olive oil
8 oz. fat salt pork, diced	225 g. fat salt pork, diced
1 onion, sliced	1 onion, sliced
2 cloves garlic, finely chopped	2 cloves garlic, finely chopped
generous pinch marjoram	generous pinch marjoram
generous pinch rosemary	generous pinch rosemary
¼ pint red wine	1½ dl red wine
4 tablespoons tomato paste	4 tablespoons tomato paste
12 button mushrooms	12 button mushrooms
12 button onions	12 button onions
chopped parsley	chopped parsley

1. Cut beef into bite-sized chunks, discarding fat and gristle. Sprinkle with salt and freshly ground black pepper.

2. Heat lard and olive oil in a heatproof casserole; when fat begins to bubble, add diced salt pork, sliced onion and chopped garlic, and sauté until golden.

3. Add beef chunks; sprinkle with herbs and cook, stirring frequently, until meat is well browned all over.

4. Pour red wine (one of the rougher Italian ones) into a small pan and boil until reduced to half the original quantity.

5. Dilute tomato paste with a few tablespoons cold water and pour over beef, together with reduced wine and boiling water to cover meat. Cover casserole and simmer slowly for about 2 hours, or until beef is tender and the sauce thick and richly coloured.

6. Half an hour before beef is ready, add button mushrooms and onions.

7. Correct seasoning with more salt or freshly ground black pepper, and serve straight from the casserole, sprinkled with parsley.

Serves 4–6

Chef's tip:
A tablespoon or two of red wine added just before serving will give an extra bouquet and flavour to this dish. If button onions cannot be had, substitute the canned variety of small, peeled onions.

Hungarian Veal Gulyas

IMPERIAL	METRIC
2½ lb. boned leg of veal	1¼ kg. boned leg of veal
2 red sweet peppers	2 red sweet peppers
2 green sweet peppers	2 green sweet peppers
8 oz. button mushrooms	225 g. button mushrooms
2 Spanish onions, finely chopped	2 Spanish onions, finely chopped
2 cloves garlic, finely chopped	2 cloves garlic, finely chopped
2 tablespoons lard	2 tablespoons lard
3 tablespoons paprika	3 tablespoons paprika
¼ teaspoon caraway seeds	¼ teaspoon caraway seeds
generous pinch each marjoram and thyme	generous pinch each marjoram and thyme
salt and freshly ground black pepper	salt and freshly ground black pepper
1 bay leaf	1 bay leaf
1 14-oz. can peeled tomatoes	1 396-g. can peeled tomatoes
parsley, to garnish	parsley, to garnish
about ½ pint sour cream, to serve	about 3 dl. sour cream, to serve

1. Preheat oven to cool (250°F., 130°C., Gas Mark ½).

2. Cut veal into neat, 2-inch (5-cm.) cubes, discarding fat or gristle.

3. Core and seed red and green peppers and cut them into ¼-inch (½-cm.) dice.

4. Clean mushrooms. Trim stems and slice mushrooms thinly.

5. In a heavy, flameproof casserole, sauté finely chopped onions and garlic in lard for 3 to 4 minutes, or until soft and transparent. Add the veal and cook for a further 2 to 3 minutes.

6. Sprinkle with paprika, caraway seeds, marjoram and thyme, and salt and freshly ground black pepper to taste. Add bay leaf; mix well and cook gently for 10 minutes, stirring occasionally.

7. Add diced peppers, thinly sliced mushrooms and canned tomatoes, together with their juices. Stir gently and bring to simmering point over a very low heat.

8. Cover casserole tightly; transfer to the oven and cook for 2 hours, or until veal is tender. Stir casserole occasionally, each time bringing it back to simmering point over a very low heat before returning it to the oven. Garnish with parsley. Serve with plenty of sour cream for each person to stir into his portion, and dumplings, noodles or rice.

Serves 6—8

Braised Pork with Cabbage

IMPERIAL	METRIC
4 tablespoons lard	4 tablespoons lard
4 oz. unsmoked bacon, diced	100 g. unsmoked bacon, diced
1 3-lb. joint leg of pork, tied	1 1⅓-kg. joint leg of pork, tied
salt and freshly ground black pepper	salt and freshly ground black pepper
1½–2 lb. new potatoes	675–900 g. new potatoes
1 large green cabbage	1 large green cabbage
4 tablespoons finely chopped parsley	4 tablespoons finely chopped parsley

1. Preheat oven to cool (225°F., 110°C., Gas Mark ¼).

2. Select a casserole large enough to hold pork, potatoes and cabbage comfortably. Melt lard in it and sauté diced green bacon for 2 to 3 minutes until golden.

3. Add joint of pork and brown it all over in the resulting mixture of fats over a steady heat.

4. Season meat. Cover casserole and bake in the oven for 2½ hours, turning meat occasionally.

5. Meanwhile, peel potatoes and leave in a bowl of cold water until required.

6. Trim and wash cabbage thoroughly. Put it in a large pan and cover with boiling water. Add salt; bring to the boil again and simmer for 15 minutes. Drain well; slice in half lengthwise; then cut each half into three wedges.

7. When pork has been cooking for 2½ hours, surround it with potatoes. Bring liquid in casserole to simmering point again over a low heat; cover and return to the oven.

8. After a further 45 minutes cooking, remove casserole from oven. Turn over meat and potatoes; add cabbage wedges, together with parsley and a few turns of the peppermill. Bring to simmering point over a low heat as before; cover tightly and return to the oven for a final 45 minutes, until contents of casserole are meltingly tender, turning and basting once or twice.

9. To serve, remove pork from casserole; untie it and place it in the centre of a large, heated serving platter. Arrange potatoes and cabbage round. Taste pan juices; correct seasoning and spoon over meat and vegetables. Serve hot.

Serves 6

Chef's tip:
To make pork skin really crackling, rub scored rind well with olive oil, salt and freshly ground black pepper. Give joint 15 minutes in a hot oven (450°F., 230°C., Gas Mark 8) then lower heat to very slow (300°F., 150°C., Gas Mark 2) for remaining cooking time.

Chili Pork Casserole

IMPERIAL	METRIC
4 tablespoons flour	4 tablespoons flour
2 teaspoons Mexican chili powder	2 teaspoons Mexican chili powder
2 cloves garlic, very finely chopped	2 cloves garlic, very finely chopped
salt	salt
2 lb. lean pork, cut into 1-inch cubes	900 g. lean pork, cut into 2½-cm. cubes
2 tablespoons butter	2 tablespoons butter
1 tablespoon olive oil	1 tablespoon olive oil
1 lb. ripe tomatoes, peeled and coarsely chopped	450 g. ripe tomatoes, peeled and coarsely chopped
freshly ground black pepper	freshly ground black pepper

1. Preheat oven to slow (325°F., 170°C., Gas Mark 3).

2. Combine flour, Mexican chili powder, very finely chopped garlic and a good pinch of salt together and mix well.

3. Toss cubed pork in seasoned flour.

4. Heat butter and oil in a 3-pint (1¾-litre) flameproof casserole and brown floured pork thoroughly over a steady moderate heat.

5. Cover with peeled and chopped tomatoes, and season with more salt if necessary, and freshly ground black pepper. Put on the lid.

6. Bake casserole for about 1½ hours, or until pork is tender and sauce rich and thick. Serve very hot.

Serves 4

Casserole of Lentils with Pork

IMPERIAL	METRIC
1½ lb. lean pork belly	675 g. lean pork belly
salt	salt
olive oil	olive oil
2 tablespoons lard	2 tablespoons lard
4 oz. smoked streaky bacon, diced	100 g. smoked streaky bacon, diced
2 leeks, white parts only, thinly sliced	2 leeks, white parts only, thinly sliced
2 carrots, thinly sliced	2 carrots, thinly sliced
2 pints chicken stock	generous litre chicken stock
1 Spanish onion, stuck with a clove	1 Spanish onion, stuck with a clove
bouquet garni (parsley, thyme, bay leaf)	bouquet garni (parsley, thyme, bay leaf)
freshly ground black pepper	freshly ground black pepper
12 oz. large brown lentils, soaked overnight	350 g. large brown lentils, soaked overnight
2 cloves garlic, crushed	2 cloves garlic, crushed

1. Preheat oven to hot (450°F., 230°C., Gas Mark 8).

2. With a sharp knife score pork skin. Rub all over with salt and olive oil. Roast pork for 15 minutes, or until crackling is crisp. Then reduce temperature to 325°F., 170°C., Gas Mark 3 and continue to roast until pork is cooked through, about 40 minutes longer.

3. Melt lard in a large, heavy casserole; add diced smoked bacon, thinly sliced leeks and carrots and sauté until golden. Cover with chicken stock; add onion stuck with a clove, bouquet garni and a good sprinkling of freshly ground black pepper (no salt at this stage) and bring to the boil.

4. Drain soaked lentils. Add them to casserole, together with crushed garlic. Simmer, covered, over a low heat for 15 to 20 minutes. Season with salt and more freshly ground black pepper, if necessary.

5. Place roast pork on top of lentils, making sure that the crackling remains uncovered, and continue to simmer with the lid off for a further 15 to 20 minutes, or until lentils are soft but not disintegrating.

6. Serve very hot from the casserole, with the pork cut into thick slices.

Serves 4

Chef's tip:
Be sure to use Mexican chili powder (a blend of spices) and not powdered chillis, which would made the dish inedibly hot. The Spice Island brand is very good. If the sauce seems too thick, it can be diluted with a little stock or water. Garnish with onion rings if you like.

Chef's tip:
Salt pork can be used instead of pork belly, but soak it first in several changes of water; cover sautéed diced pork and vegetables with water; add salt pork; boil until tender, then add lentils and garlic. Simmer until soft but not disintegrating.

Baked Beans with Bacon

IMPERIAL	METRIC
1 bacon hock, about 3 lb.	1 bacon hock, about 1⅓ kg.
1 lb. dried haricot beans	450 g. dried haricot beans
2 Spanish onions, thinly sliced	2 Spanish onions, thinly sliced
2 teaspoons salt	2 teaspoons salt
6 tablespoons tomato ketchup	6 tablespoons tomato ketchup
6 tablespoons golden syrup	6 tablespoons golden syrup
2 tablespoons cider vinegar	2 tablespoons cider vinegar
dash Tabasco	dash Tabasco
1 teaspoon dry mustard	1 teaspoon dry mustard

1. Soak bacon in a large bowl of cold water for at least 4 hours. Drain; place it in a large saucepan and cover with fresh cold water. Bring to the boil and simmer for 15 to 20 minutes. Drain thoroughly. This will rid the bacon of excess salt.

2. Cover the beans with water; bring to the boil and boil for 2 minutes. Remove pan from heat; cover and leave beans to soften and swell for 1 hour.

3. Add sliced onions to beans and season to taste with salt. Return pan to the heat, bring to the boil and simmer until beans are tender, 1 to 1½ hours, depending on quality, adding more liquid if necessary.

4. Preheat oven to slow (325°F., 170°C., Gas Mark 3).

5. When beans are tender, drain them, reserving ¾ pint (4 dl.) of their liquor. Combine the latter with ketchup, syrup, cider vinegar, a dash of Tabasco and the dry mustard.

6. Place bacon joint in a large, heatproof casserole. Surround with beans and pour liquid over the top. Cover and bake for 1½ hours.

7. Remove casserole from oven. Take out bacon and cut it into neat, bite-sized pieces. Return them to the casserole and continue to bake, uncovered, for a further hour. Check seasoning—you will probably find that the bacon has salted the beans sufficiently—and serve very hot.

Serves 6

Chef's tip:
This is a hearty casserole for an informal party, guaranteed to satisfy the most ravenous teenage appetites at very little cost in time or money. If the bacon seems very salty, leave to soak overnight, changing the water several times.

Swedish Lamb with Coffee Sauce

IMPERIAL	METRIC
3 lb. boned lamb shoulder or leg	1⅓ kg. boned lamb shoulder or leg
2 tablespoons butter	2 tablespoons butter
1 tablespoon olive oil	1 tablespoon olive oil
1 large Spanish onion, finely chopped	1 large Spanish onion, finely chopped
3–4 large carrots, thickly sliced	3–4 large carrots, thickly sliced
salt and freshly ground black pepper	salt and freshly ground black pepper
1–2 teaspoons sugar	1–2 teaspoons sugar
¼ pint beef stock	1½ dl. beef stock
½ pint freshly made strong coffee	3 dl. freshly made strong coffee
6–8 tablespoons double cream	6–8 tablespoons double cream
cornflour (optional)	cornflour (optional)

1. Cut lamb into 1½-inch (4-cm.) cubes, discarding fat and gristle.

2. Heat butter and olive oil in a heavy, heatproof casserole. Add finely chopped onion and sauté until soft and richly browned. Remove onion with a slotted spoon and reserve.

3. In the same fat, sauté lamb cubes until golden brown. Return sautéed onions to the casserole, together with carrots. Season with salt and freshly ground black pepper; sprinkle with sugar and sauté gently over a moderate heat for 5 minutes longer, stirring frequently to caramelise vegetables slightly.

4. Stir in stock, coffee and cream; cover and simmer gently for 1½ hours, or until lamb and carrots are tender. Stir from time to time to prevent meat sticking to bottom of casserole.

5. With a slotted spoon, transfer lamb and carrots to a heated serving dish. Keep hot.

6. Reduce sauce by half over a high heat, scraping bottom and sides of casserole with a wooden spoon. If sauce still remains thin after reduction, thicken it with a little cornflour blended with cold water and simmer for a final 2 or 3 minutes. Pour over meat and serve immediately.

Serves 6

Chef's tip:
To make stock in a pressure cooker, use raw or cooked bones and root vegetables to flavour. Add water to cover, some salt and a few peppercorns. Bring to boil then cover and bring slowly to 15-lb. (7-kg.) pressure; cook for 40 minutes then strain and cool at room temperature.

Breton Bean Casserole

IMPERIAL	METRIC
10 oz. dried haricot beans	275 g. dried haricot beans
1 breast of lamb, about 3 lb.	1 breast of lamb, about 1⅓ kg.
½ pint chicken stock	3 dl. chicken stock
1½ pint strained canned tomatoes	3 dl. strained canned tomatoes
1 Spanish onion, grated	1 Spanish onion, grated
1 clove garlic, crushed	1 clove garlic, crushed
2 tablespoons melted butter	2 tablespoons melted butter
salt and freshly ground black pepper	salt and freshly ground black pepper
4 canned pimentos, very finely chopped	4 canned pimentos, very finely chopped

1. Put beans in a saucepan and cover with about 3 pints (1¾ litres) water. Bring to the boil and simmer for 2 minutes. Remove pan from the heat; cover and allow to stand for 1 hour.

2. Replace pan on heat; bring to the boil and simmer beans in the same water until tender, 1 to 1½ hours, depending on quality. Add more water during cooking if liquid is absorbed too quickly.

3. Preheat oven to moderate (350°F., 180°C., Gas Mark 4).

4. Cut breast of lamb into 1½-inch (4-cm.) pieces, discarding excess fat.

5. Drain beans and place them in a 4-pint (2¼-litre) heatproof casserole. Stir in remaining ingredients. Cover tightly.

6. Bake casserole for 1 to 1½ hours, then uncover and continue to bake for a further 30 minutes.

7. Skim off excess fat; correct seasoning and serve very hot straight from casserole.

Serves 4–6

Chef's tip:
Use a lean breast of lamb for this recipe otherwise the dish can be heavy. A good way of telling when beans are cooked is to lift a few from the saucepan in a spoon and blow on them. The skins will curl back if the beans are done.

Pot-roasted Shoulder of Lamb Provençal

IMPERIAL	METRIC
2 cloves garlic	2 cloves garlic
1 shoulder of young lamb (3–4 lb.)	1 shoulder of young lamb (1½–1¾ kg.)
salt and freshly ground black pepper	salt and freshly ground black pepper
4 tablespoons olive oil	4 tablespoons olive oil
2 Spanish onions, finely chopped	2 Spanish onions, finely chopped
1 carrot, finely chopped	1 carrot, finely chopped
½ pint stock, made with cube if necessary	3 dl. stock, made with cube if necessary
3 large ripe tomatoes, peeled, seeded and finely chopped	3 large ripe tomatoes, peeled, seeded and finely chopped
2 tablespoons tomato paste	2 tablespoons tomato paste
½ teaspoon powdered thyme	½ teaspoon powdered thyme
3–4 oz. black olives, stoned	75–100 g. black olives, stoned
olives and watercress, to garnish	olives and watercress, to garnish

1. Peel garlic cloves and cut them into thin slivers. With the point of a sharp knife make slits all over shoulder of lamb and push in garlic slivers as deeply as possible. Season joint generously with salt and freshly ground black pepper.

2. Heat olive oil in a large, flameproof casserole and brown shoulder of lamb on all sides. Add chopped onions and carrot, and sauté until golden.

3. Moisten lamb with stock; add chopped tomatoes and tomato paste, and season vegetables to taste with salt and freshly ground black pepper. Sprinkle meat and vegetables with thyme.

4. Cover casserole and simmer gently until lamb is tender, 40 minutes for medium rare, and about 1 hour for a well-done joint, basting occasionally with the sauce.

5. Ten minutes before the end of cooking time, add stoned olives to casserole.

6. When lamb is tender, transfer to a heated serving dish. Skim fat from sauce if necessary and spoon vegetables and sauce around lamb. Serve very hot.

Serves 6

Chef's tip:
To remove a surface layer of fat from a liquid lay a sheet of absorbent kitchen paper gently down on the surface of the liquid. Give it time to absorb the fat, then gather up the corners of the paper and discard. Continue until no fat remains.

Daube of Lamb

Haricot Bean and Lamb Casserole

IMPERIAL	METRIC
4 lb. shoulder of lamb (on the bone)	1¾ kg. shoulder of lamb (on the bone)
4 tablespoons flour	4 tablespoons flour
1 lb. unsmoked bacon, in one piece	450 g. unsmoked bacon, in one piece
3 Spanish onions, thinly sliced	3 Spanish onions, thinly sliced
3 tablespoons butter	3 tablespoons butter
3 tablespoons olive oil	3 tablespoons olive oil
coarse salt and freshly ground black pepper	coarse salt and freshly ground black pepper
2 cloves garlic, peeled	2 cloves garlic, peeled
1 strip dried orange peel	1 strip dried orange peel
bouquet garni	bouquet garni
coarsely grated orange rind, to garnish	coarsely grated orange rind, to garnish

1. Have your butcher bone the shoulder of lamb for you. Cut meat into 1-inch (2½-cm.) cubes, discarding fat and gristle, and toss with flour until evenly coated.

2. Preheat oven to cool (225°F., 110°C., Gas Mark ¼).

3. Cut unsmoked bacon into ½-inch (1-cm.) dice.

4. In a large frying pan, sauté thinly sliced onions and diced bacon in butter and olive oil until golden and transparent, 8 to 10 minutes. Transfer to a large ovenproof casserole with a slotted spoon.

5. In the resulting fat, sauté floured lamb cubes over a steady heat until richly browned on all sides. Transfer to the casserole.

6. Toss contents of casserole until well mixed. Season to taste with coarse salt and freshly ground black pepper, and add garlic, a strip of dried orange peel and a bouquet garni.

7. Cover casserole tightly and bake for about 2½ hours, or until meat is meltingly tender and sauce is rich and thick. Remove casserole from the oven occasionally to give it a thorough stir, each time bringing it back to simmering point over a low heat before returning it to the oven.

8. Just before serving, remove bouquet garni and garlic cloves. Garnish with orange rind.

Serves 6–8

Chef's tip:
To dry orange (or lemon) peel, pare off thin strips of zest (the coloured part of the rind) with a potato peeler to avoid any of the bitter white pith. Then leave to dry overnight in a warm place on a piece of absorbent paper.

IMPERIAL	METRIC
12 oz. haricot beans, soaked in water overnight	350 g. haricot beans, soaked in water overnight
1 Spanish onion, peeled and stuck with 3 cloves	1 Spanish onion, peeled and stuck with 3 cloves
1 bay leaf	1 bay leaf
8 oz. streaky bacon slices, rind removed, diced	225 g. streaky bacon slices, rind removed, diced
2 lb. boned shoulder of of lamb, cut into 1-inch cubes	900 g. boned shoulder of of lamb, cut into 2½-cm. cubes
2 large Spanish onions, sliced	2 large Spanish onions, sliced
2 tablespoons tomato paste	2 tablespoons tomato paste
1 14-oz. can Italian tomatoes	1 396-g. can Italian tomatoes
2 cloves garlic, crushed	2 cloves garlic, crushed
½ teaspoon dried thyme	½ teaspoon dried thyme
1 large green sweet pepper, seeded and diced	1 large green sweet pepper, seeded and diced
salt and freshly ground black pepper	salt and freshly ground black pepper

1. In a medium-sized saucepan, place beans and their soaking liquor, with plenty of water to cover. Add onion, stuck with cloves, and the bay leaf. Bring to the boil and simmer gently, uncovered, for 30 minutes.

2. Meanwhile, sauté diced bacon in a large, heavy casserole until fat runs and bacon begins to crisp. Remove with a slotted spoon and reserve.

3. Over a high heat, sauté lamb cubes, a small amount at a time, until nicely browned. Drain meat with a slotted spoon; remove to a plate.

4. When meat has been fried, turn heat down to moderate and add sliced onion to fat remaining in pan and sauté until soft and transparent.

5. Return sautéed bacon and lamb cubes to casserole.

6. Drain haricot beans, reserving 1 pint (6 dl.) of poaching liquor. Discard onion stuck with cloves.

7. Add beans and measured poaching liquor to casserole together with tomato paste, canned tomatoes, crushed garlic cloves and thyme. Bring to the boil and simmer very gently for 1½ hours or until meat is tender.

8. Thirty minutes before end of cooking time, add diced green pepper. Correct seasoning with a pinch of salt and a few turns of your peppermill.

9. Serve casserole very hot.

Serves 6–8

Lamb Korma

IMPERIAL	METRIC
½ pint plain yoghurt	3 dl. plain yoghurt
½ teaspoon ground cardamom	½ teaspoon ground cardamom
1 teaspoon ground cumin	1 teaspoon ground cumin
1½ teaspoons turmeric	1½ teaspoons turmeric
3 lb. boneless leg of lamb, cut into 1-inch cubes	1⅓ kg. boneless leg of lamb, cut into 2½-cm. cubes
4–6 tablespoons olive oil	4–6 tablespoons olive oil
12 oz. Spanish onions, finely chopped	350 g. Spanish onions, finely chopped
2 cloves garlic, crushed	2 cloves garlic, crushed
1 teaspoon each ground ginger and dry mustard	1 teaspoon each ground ginger and dry mustard
½ teaspoon each freshly ground black pepper, cayenne pepper and ground cinnamon	½ teaspoon each freshly ground black pepper, cayenne pepper and ground cinnamon
pinch ground cloves	pinch ground cloves
1 tablespoon tomato paste	1 tablespoon tomato paste
4–6 tablespoons milk	4–6 tablespoons milk
salt	salt
2 teaspoons lemon juice	2 teaspoons lemon juice

1. In a bowl, mix yoghurt with cardamom, cumin and turmeric; add lamb and toss until thoroughly coated. Cover and marinate for 1 hour.

2. In a large pan, heat half the oil; add lamb and yoghurt marinade. Cook over a high heat, stirring, for 5 minutes. Remove from heat.

3. Sauté finely chopped onions and garlic in remaining oil until soft and golden. Add remaining spices and mix well. Cook, stirring, for 2 minutes longer to bring out flavours.

4. Add onion mixture to lamb, together with tomato paste, milk and a little salt, to taste. Bring to the boil over a low heat, stirring occasionally; cover and simmer very slowly for 30 minutes longer, or until lamb is very tender and sauce is thick. Stir occasionally to prevent lamb sticking.

5. Just before serving, add lemon juice and season to taste with a little more salt if necessary. If sauce seems too thin, simmer for another 2 to 3 minutes. Serve with usual curry accompaniments.

Serves 8

Chef's tip:
To add extra flavour to the dish, place ½ pint (3 dl.) milk with 2 tablespoons butter and 4 oz. (100 g.) desiccated coconut in a saucepan; bring slowly to the boil and simmer for 15 minutes. Strain through a sieve, pressing coconut, and use instead of milk in recipe.

Mediterranean Lamb and Vegetable Casserole

IMPERIAL	METRIC
4 large lamb chops or 8 lamb cutlets	4 large lamb chops or 8 lamb cutlets
salt and freshly ground black pepper	salt and freshly ground black pepper
1 tablespoon butter	1 tablespoon butter
1 tablespoon olive oil	1 tablespoon olive oil
8 button onions, peeled	8 button onions, peeled
1 green sweet pepper, cored, seeded and diced	1 green sweet pepper, cored, seeded and diced
½ pint chicken stock	3 dl. chicken stock
1 14-oz. can Italian peeled tomatoes, drained and chopped	1 396-g. can Italian peeled tomatoes, drained and chopped
bouquet garni	bouquet garni
4 large floury potatoes	4 large floury potatoes

1. Season lamb chops or cutlets with salt and freshly ground black pepper.

2. Heat butter and olive oil in a 3-pint (1¾-litre) flameproof casserole, and sauté button onions until golden. Add green pepper, and continue to sauté over a moderate heat for 3 or 4 minutes longer, until limp and golden. Remove button onions and pepper with a slotted spoon, and reserve.

3. In the remaining fat, brown lamb chops or cutlets thoroughly on both sides.

4. Return sautéed onions and pepper to the casserole; add stock and bring to the boil over a gentle heat, scraping casserole clean with a wooden spoon.

5. Add chopped tomatoes and bouquet garni and simmer gently, uncovered, for about 1 hour.

6. Meanwhile, peel potatoes and cut them lengthwise into thirds (or quarters if they are very large). Cover with cold salted water; bring to the boil and simmer for 4 to 5 minutes. Drain thoroughly.

7. When casserole has been simmering for an hour, submerge parboiled potatoes in cooking juices. Continue to simmer until meat is tender, and potatoes are soft and imbued with the flavour of the casserole.

8. Correct seasoning and serve very hot, straight from the casserole.

Serves 4

Chef's tip:
To peel onions, cut off top, then root with a sharp knife; peel off first and second skins. Do not break thin underskin—it is the oil released from here that makes you cry. Button onions are most readily peeled if you first place them in a bowl of boiling water for a minute, then drop into a bowl of cold water.

Greek Lamb and Runner Bean Stew

IMPERIAL	METRIC
1½–2 lb. fresh runner beans	675–900 g. fresh runner beans
salt	salt
3 tablespoons olive oil	3 tablespoons olive oil
1 Spanish onion, finely chopped	1 Spanish onion, finely chopped
1 clove garlic, finely chopped	1 clove garlic, finely chopped
8 lamb cutlets (best end chops)	8 lamb cutlets (best end chops)
freshly ground black pepper	freshly ground black pepper
1 14-oz. can Italian peeled tomatoes	1 396-g. can Italian peeled tomatoes
2 tablespoons finely chopped parsley	2 tablespoons finely chopped parsley

1. String runner beans—if they are *very* young and tender, they may only need topping and tailing—and cut into thin strips lengthwise.

2. Put beans in a colander set over a bowl. Sprinkle with 1 tablespoon salt, rubbing it into the beans with the palms of your hands. Put aside for at least ½ hour, or until beans are limp and some liquid has drained into bowl underneath.

3. In a large frying pan, heat 2 tablespoons olive oil and sauté onion and garlic over a moderate heat until soft and golden. Drain with a slotted spoon and transfer to a heavy, flameproof casserole.

4. Add remaining oil to frying pan and sauté chops until well browned on both sides. Season to taste with salt and freshly ground black pepper and transfer to casserole.

5. Lower heat under frying pan, pour in contents of can of tomatoes and cook over a moderate heat, scraping bottom and sides of pan clean with a wooden spoon. Pour over chops.

6. Rinse beans; shake them dry; add them to casserole and mix well. Cover tightly and simmer over a very low heat until beans are tender and the chops practically disintegrating, 45 minutes to 1 hour.

7. Correct seasoning; turn stew into a deep serving dish and sprinkle with finely chopped parsley. Serve very hot.

Serves 4

Chef's tip:
If at any time you inadvertently over-salt a stew, casserole or soup there are two remedies: add a peeled lump of raw potato to the dish then continue simmering and the potato will absorb some of the saltiness, or, add a little sugar to improve the flavour.

142

Baeckenhofe

IMPERIAL	METRIC
4 tablespoons lard	4 tablespoons lard
2 lb. onions, thinly sliced	900 g. onions, thinly sliced
salt and freshly ground black pepper	salt and freshly ground black pepper
1½ lb. pork shoulder	675 g. pork shoulder
1½ lb. lamb shoulder	675 g. lamb shoulder
1 lb. boned shin of veal	450 g. boned shin of veal
2 lb. potatoes, sliced	900 g. potatoes, sliced
½ teaspoon each dried rosemary and thyme	½ teaspoon each dried rosemary and thyme
bouquet garni	bouquet garni
¼ pint dry white wine	1½ dl. dry white wine
¼ pint rich stock	1½ dl. rich stock
flour and water paste	flour and water paste

1. Select a large, oval, flameproof casserole with a tight-fitting lid. Preheat oven to moderate (350°F., 180°C., Gas Mark 4).

2. Melt lard in a frying pan and sauté onions gently until golden. Season generously with salt and freshly ground black pepper. Remove onions from pan with a slotted spoon and reserve.

3. Cut meats into even-sized cubes; season to taste and sauté in remaining fat until golden.

4. Cover bottom of casserole with half the onions, followed by a layer of sliced potatoes, using a third of total quantity. Sprinkle with salt and freshly ground black pepper.

5. Season meats with dried rosemary and thyme and place on bed of potatoes. Cover with another layer of potatoes, then add remaining onions, and top with a final layer of potatoes. Sprinkle with salt and freshly ground black pepper, and place bouquet garni on top.

6. Mix white wine with stock and pour into casserole. Cover casserole and bring to the boil on top of the stove. Skim; replace cover and seal cover to casserole with a band of pastry made with flour and water.

7. Place casserole in the oven and continue to bake for about 1 hour, or until meat and vegetables are very tender.

Serves 8

Chef's tip:
Do make up your own bouquet garni rather than buying the sort that resemble teabags. A basic bouquet garni consists of parsley stalks, bay leaf and two sprigs of thyme, all tied up in a small piece of muslin. This can be varied according to the dish and your fancy.

Mustard Chicken

IMPERIAL	METRIC
1 3½-lb. roasting chicken	1 1½-kg. roasting chicken
2 tablespoons flour	2 tablespoons flour
salt and freshly ground black pepper	salt and freshly ground black pepper
2 tablespoons butter	2 tablespoons butter
2 tablespoons olive oil	2 tablespoons olive oil
4 oz. fat bacon, diced and blanched	100 g. fat bacon, diced and blanched
4 shallots, finely chopped	4 shallots, finely chopped
bouquet garni	bouquet garni
¼ pint dry white wine	1½ dl. dry white wine
¼ pint chicken stock	1½ dl. chicken stock
2 teaspoons Dijon mustard	2 teaspoons Dijon mustard
1 teaspoon English mustard	1 teaspoon English mustard
½ pint double cream	3 dl. double cream

1. Cut chicken into eight serving pieces, two from each breast and two from each leg. Dust with flour which you have seasoned with salt and freshly ground black pepper.

2. In a heavy casserole, heat butter and oil, and sauté chicken pieces and diced, blanched bacon until golden brown.

3. Add finely chopped shallots and bouquet garni; moisten with dry white wine and stock, and bring to the boil. Lower heat; cover and simmer gently for about 20 minutes, or until chicken is tender.

4. With a slotted spoon, transfer chicken pieces to a heated serving dish. Keep hot.

5. Skim fat from sauce. Blend mustards smoothly with cream and stir into sauce. Bring to the boil, stirring, and simmer gently until sauce has reduced by about one third. Correct seasoning, adding more mustard and/or salt and freshly ground black pepper if necessary.

6. Spoon sauce over chicken pieces and serve immediately.

Serves 4

Chef's tip:
It may seem odd to use two different mustards in one recipe. This is because the flavour of English mustard is simply hot. The addition of the milder, spicier flavoured French Dijon mustard tempers this hotness to give a more subtle mustard flavour without the hotness.

Pollo al Chilindrón

IMPERIAL	METRIC
half a 3-lb. chicken	half a 1⅓-kg. chicken
6–8 oz. pork fillet	175–225 g. pork fillet
salt and freshly ground black pepper	salt and freshly ground black pepper
1 tablespoon flour	1 tablespoon flour
1 tablespoon butter	1 tablespoon butter
1 tablespoon olive oil	1 tablespoon olive oil
4 oz. fat bacon, cut into strips	100 g. fat bacon, cut into strips
1 red or green sweet pepper	1 red or green sweet pepper
4 oz. white button mushrooms, trimmed	100 g. white button mushrooms, trimmed
8 oz. button onions, peeled	225 g. button onions, peeled
¾ pint chicken stock	4 dl. chicken stock
¼ pint dry white wine	1½ dl. dry white wine
2 tablespoons tomato paste	2 tablespoons tomato paste
2 teaspoons soy sauce	2 teaspoons soy sauce
1 plump clove garlic, finely chopped	1 plump clove garlic, finely chopped
generous pinch dried tarragon	generous pinch dried tarragon
1 bay leaf	1 bay leaf

1. Divide chicken into four pieces, two from the breast and two from the leg. Cut pork fillet into ½-inch (1-cm.) cubes. Season chicken and pork with salt and freshly ground black pepper, and dust with flour.

2. In a large frying pan, heat butter and oil and sauté chicken pieces until crisp and golden brown. Transfer chicken to a casserole with a slotted spoon.

3. Brown pork cubes in remaining fat and transfer to casserole.

4. Still in the same fat, sauté bacon strips until crisp. Add to casserole.

5. Core and seed pepper and cut it into thin strips. Sauté in the bacon fat, together with button mushrooms and onions, until onions are golden brown. Add vegetables to the casserole and toss thoroughly with meat.

6. Rinse out frying pan with some of the stock, scraping bottom and sides with a wooden spoon to dislodge all the browned morsels stuck there. Pour into the casserole and pour in remaining stock, together with wine, tomato paste, soy sauce, finely chopped garlic, a generous pinch of dried tarragon and a bay leaf. Mix well; season to taste with salt and freshly ground black pepper.

7. Bring to the boil over a gentle heat; cover casserole and simmer gently for 45 minutes; then remove lid and continue to simmer for a final 15 minutes, or until meats are tender.

Serves 4

143

Mediterranean Chicken Casserole

IMPERIAL	METRIC
1 3-lb. frying chicken	1 1⅓-kg. frying chicken
3 green sweet peppers	3 green sweet peppers
2–4 tablespoons olive oil	2–4 tablespoons olive oil
salt and freshly ground black pepper	salt and freshly ground black pepper
3 oz. cooked ham, diced	75 g. cooked ham, diced
2 shallots, finely chopped	2 shallots, finely chopped
1 medium-sized onion, finely chopped	1 medium-sized onion, finely chopped
6 tomatoes, peeled, seeded and finely chopped	6 tomatoes, peeled, seeded and finely chopped
bouquet garni	bouquet garni
1 clove garlic, crushed	1 clove garlic, crushed
finely chopped parsley	finely chopped parsley

1. Divide chicken into ten pieces, i.e., one from each wing, two from each leg and two from each side of breast.

2. Skin peppers, then halve them and remove seeds. Cut peppers into neat strips.

3. Heat olive oil in a large, deep frying pan. Season chicken pieces with salt and freshly ground black pepper, and sauté in oil until golden brown all over.

4. Add diced ham and finely chopped shallots, and continue to sauté until they are golden brown.

5. Remove chicken pieces, ham and shallots from pan with a slotted spoon; keep hot on a deep plate over hot water.

6. In the same oil, sauté pepper strips for 5 to 8 minutes until soft. Remove with the slotted spoon and keep hot with chicken pieces.

7. Add finely chopped onion to pan and, when it is soft and golden brown, stir in peeled, seeded and finely chopped tomatoes, bouquet garni and crushed garlic. Simmer for 10 minutes, uncovered, then return all the sautéed ingredients to pan, spooning tomato mixture over them. Cover pan with a lid and simmer for 45 minutes, or until chicken pieces are tender.

8. Just before serving, season to taste with salt and freshly ground black pepper. Arrange chicken pieces in a heated serving dish. Pour over sauce and vegetables; sprinkle with finely chopped parsley and serve hot.

Serves 4–6

Chef's tip:
To skin peppers, place them under a hot grill and turn them frequently until they are blackened and blistered all over. Hold peppers under cold running water and peel off skins. Another method is to dry-fry peppers until blackened and proceed as above.

Hawaiian Chicken

IMPERIAL	METRIC
1 3½-lb. roasting chicken	1 1½-kg. roasting chicken
salt and freshly ground black pepper	salt and freshly ground black pepper
3 tablespoons corn oil	3 tablespoons corn oil
2 oz. flaked blanched almonds	50 g. flaked blanched almonds
¾ pint fresh orange juice	4 dl. fresh orange juice
2 oz. seedless raisins	50 g. seedless raisins
1 7-oz. can diced pineapple	1 198-g. can diced pineapple
4 tablespoons juice from canned pineapple	4 tablespoons juice from canned pineapple
¼ teaspoon ground cloves	¼ teaspoon ground cloves
pinch cinnamon	pinch cinnamon
1–1½ tablespoons cornflour	1–1½ tablespoons cornflour
1–2 tablespoons finely grated orange rind	1–2 tablespoons finely grated orange rind

1. Divide chicken into eight serving pieces: two from each leg and two from each breast. Season to taste with salt and freshly ground black pepper.

2. Heat corn oil in a heavy pan or flameproof casserole and sauté flaked almonds until a rich golden colour. Remove with a slotted spoon and put aside.

3. In same oil, brown chicken pieces on all sides over a steady heat. Squeeze fresh oranges to give ¾ pint (4 dl.) juice (see Chef's tip).

4. Return sautéed almonds to the pan; add raisins, pineapple chunks, orange juice, 4 tablespoons juice drained off from pineapple and the spices. Mix well and cover tightly.

5. Simmer for 45 minutes, or until chicken is tender.

6. Remove chicken pieces with a slotted spoon, allowing juices to drain back into pan; arrange on a heated serving dish and keep hot while you finish sauce.

7. Blend cornflour smoothly with a little of the pan juices and stir back into pan in a thin stream. Bring to the boil and simmer, stirring, until sauce is thick and translucent. Correct seasoning if necessary.

8. Spoon some of the sauce and garnish over the chicken. Sprinkle with finely grated orange rind and serve immediately, accompanied by remaining sauce and garnish in a separate sauceboat or bowl.

Serves 4

Chef's tip:
Use fresh orange juice, as canned orange juice makes the dish taste metallic. The average orange yields 4 tablespoons of juice; for the purposes of this recipe you will need 4 or 6 large oranges to give ¾ pint juice.

Southern Baked Beans

IMPERIAL	METRIC
1 lb. dried haricot beans	450 g. dried haricot beans
2 cloves garlic, crushed	2 cloves garlic, crushed
1 Spanish onion, thinly sliced	1 Spanish onion, thinly sliced
1 small dried hot red pepper	1 small dried hot red pepper
1 bay leaf	1 bay leaf
3 tablespoons molasses or black treacle	3 tablespoons molasses or black treacle
3 tablespoons tomato ketchup	3 tablespoons tomato ketchup
1 teaspoon dry mustard	1 teaspoon dry mustard
$\frac{1}{2}$ teaspoon ground ginger	$\frac{1}{2}$ teaspoon ground ginger
1–1$\frac{1}{2}$ teaspoons Worcestershire sauce	1–1$\frac{1}{2}$ teaspoons Worcestershire sauce
$\frac{1}{2}$ teaspoon salt	$\frac{1}{2}$ teaspoon salt
12 oz. salt pork, thinly sliced	350 g. salt pork, thinly sliced
2 oz. dark brown sugar	50 g. dark brown sugar

1. Put beans in a large pan and cover with 3 pints (1$\frac{3}{4}$ litres) water. Bring to the boil and simmer for 2 minutes; then remove pan from heat, cover and leave beans to soak for 1 hour.

2. Add crushed garlic, sliced onion, hot red pepper and bay leaf to the beans. Return pan to the heat; bring to the boil and cook gently, covered, until beans are tender, 45 minutes to 1 hour, depending on their quality.

3. Preheat oven to moderately hot (400°F., 200°C., Gas Mark 6).

4. When beans are cooked, drain them thoroughly, reserving liquid. Measure out 1 pint (6 dl.) of liquid (or make it up to 1 pint with water if necessary) and stir in remaining ingredients, except salt pork slices and sugar.

5. Arrange beans in a 4-pint (2$\frac{1}{4}$-litre) baking dish and lay pork slices on top. Pour over liquid and sprinkle pork slices with sugar.

6. Bake for 1 to 1$\frac{1}{2}$ hours, or until pork and beans are tender, and have absorbed the savoury-sweet sauce. Serve very hot.

Serves 6

Chef's tip:
A succulent and filling dish for an informal party. Let the pot stand for a few minutes when it comes out of the oven to allow bubbling juices to subside and soak into the beans. Instead of salt pork you can use unsmoked fat bacon.

Mexican Beans

IMPERIAL	METRIC
1 lb. red kidney beans	450 g. red kidney beans
1 Spanish onion, finely chopped	1 Spanish onion, finely chopped
2 cloves garlic, finely chopped	2 cloves garlic, finely chopped
salt	salt
2 tablespoons butter	2 tablespoons butter
1 tablespoon flour	1 tablespoon flour
$\frac{1}{2}$ teaspoon powdered cumin	$\frac{1}{2}$ teaspoon powdered cumin
2 tablespoons Mexican chili powder	2 tablespoons Mexican chili powder
bouquet garni	bouquet garni
$\frac{1}{2}$ pint beef stock	3 dl. beef stock
freshly ground black pepper	freshly ground black pepper

1. Put beans in a large pan; cover with cold water and bring to the boil over a low heat. Remove pan from heat; cover and leave beans to soak for 1 hour.

2. Drain beans and transfer them to a large casserole. Stir in finely chopped onion and garlic, cover with fresh water and add salt, to taste. Bring to the boil again and simmer, covered, for 1 hour, or until beans are soft but still whole. Drain well and return to casserole.

3. Mash butter, flour, powdered cumin and chili powder to a stiff, smooth paste. Gradually add hot stock, stirring well to prevent lumps forming. Pour over beans. Add bouquet garni and season to taste with salt and freshly ground black pepper.

4. Bring to the boil again, stirring gently, and simmer, stirring occasionally, for about 45 minutes, or until sauce is smooth and rich. Remove bouquet garni just before serving.

Serves 6–8

Chef's tip:
These hot, spicy beans should be served on a bed of rice—allow about 1 lb. rice weighed raw, to the full recipe of beans above. Be sure not to confuse Mexican chili powder with powdered chillis, though, or your dish will be inedibly hot.

Cooking with Wine

It has been claimed that for a food loving Frenchman, a carafe of his favourite *vin ordinaire* is as important to a meal as a loaf of crisp French bread. We can't get the crisp French loaf, but for most of us today, a bottle of non-vintage plonk—whether it is Spanish, Yugoslav or French—is no longer beyond our means.

There has been a veritable revolution in the interest in wine in this country in the last few years. Before and just after the war, there was a general feeling that to serve wine with a meal was only for special occasions or 'just for the rich'. This is no longer true. It is no longer the hallmark of the connoisseur to have a bottle of wine on the table. And the British housewife is fast catching up with her Continental counterpart, who has known this little kitchen secret all along: to make an everday dish an event, just add a little wine.

Of course, for the novice imbiber, the way to choosing what wine to serve with what dish seems fraught with problems and dangers. But relax. The traditional rule laid down for serving 'red wine with red meat and white wine with white meat' is only a broad generalisation and should be accepted as such. You'll find that in practice a red beaujolais can accompany a roast chicken admirably and a dry white Burgundy is absolutely delicious served with slices of cold rare roast beef or a pâté of duck, pork and veal. Indeed, a great friend of mine, a French woman and the wife of one of France's best known wine growers, prefers to choose her wine according to what she feels like at the moment. If it's cold weather, she sticks to red and on a hot day, she prefers something dry and white—a white Burgundy, a light wine from the Loire, a Moselle, a Rhine, or a rosé. This relaxed attitude is the right one. So don't be foxed by tradition, choose the wine that you like and the wine you can afford. And when planning your meal, think of the sauce you are serving with your dish. For example, if the sauce is a lusty tomato-based creation from southern France, a simple red wine from the lower slopes of Burgundy or a Provençal red is best whether the sauce is served on chicken, veal, pork or a rare grilled steak. One of my favourite fish dishes, for instance, is turbot poached in a sparkling red wine called Bouzy and then served with an excitingly new 'red butter' made with fresh butter beaten into a reduction of finely chopped shallots and red wine. Delicious.

Wine in this country is sufficiently cheap to be used generously in cooking. Try it for stewing, basting or grilling; use it adventurously as a substitute for other liquids or as an agent to blend flavours in a ragoût or a casserole. Add red wine to a marinade for beef, lamb, pork or game. Use wine—both white and red—to strengthen soups and sauces. (And I don't mean adding a splash of indifferent sherry to a mixture of tinned soups.)

Don't be afraid to experiment. Think of wine in cooking as just another of the necessary good ingredients like butter, olive oil, onions and herbs. It will round out and add savour to the general flavour of your cooking. And a note to teetotallers: wine loses its alcohol content in cooking and its taste actually changes.

Use wine to tenderise as well as flavour all manner of casseroles—superb slow-cooking daubes and ragoûts of meat and poultry and game, seared in a little butter or olive oil, enhanced with the flavour of aromatic herbs, and then simmered gently for an hour or two in a sauce enriched with good stock and fine wine. This is the sort of cooking which made French cooks famous the world over.

You'll find that you, too, will gain a wonderful reputation if you keep those 'ends of bottles' (the bit left over from your table wine) to add flavour and savour to your cooking. Just a few tablespoons of red wine, or dry sherry, port or Marsala, can add enormously to the flavour of a gravy or a casserole. And when there are no wines left over, use an inexpensive wine. You'll find that a dry white wine will improve almost every way of cooking fish. Use it, too, for chicken dishes or veal Marengo, and for giving a wonderful golden glaze to roast veal or chicken after the fat has been taken off. Two of my favourite red wine dishes are *boeuf sauté à la bourguignonne* and chicken in red wine, tender pieces of chicken or beef sautéed in butter and olive oil with a few bits of diced fat salt bacon until golden, then simmered with tiny white onions and button mushrooms until tender (see pages 151 and 153). These are truly great dishes. And although time-consuming, they are well worth the trouble.

Poached Salmon with Sauce Verte

IMPERIAL	METRIC
4 salmon steaks, 1 inch thick	4 salmon steaks, 2½ cm. thick
Court-bouillon:	*Court-bouillon:*
½ pint dry white wine	3 dl. dry white wine
1 tablespoon olive oil	1 tablespoon olive oil
bouquet garni	bouquet garni
½ teaspoon salt	½ teaspoon salt
Sauce verte:	*Sauce verte:*
½ pint thick home-made mayonnaise	3 dl. thick home-made mayonnaise
1 oz. fresh parsley sprigs	25 g. fresh parsley sprigs
1 oz. fresh watercress leaves	25 g. fresh watercress leaves
salt	salt
2 tablespoons finely chopped parsley	2 tablespoons finely chopped parsley
1 tablespoon finely chopped watercress	1 tablespoon finely chopped watercress
1 tablespoon finely chopped fresh tarragon	1 tablespoon finely chopped fresh tarragon
freshly ground black pepper	freshly ground black pepper
lemon juice	lemon juice

1. Wrap each salmon steak tightly in butter muslin and tie with string so steaks maintain a neat, compact shape during poaching.

2. Place all ingredients for court-bouillon plus ¼ pint (1½ dl.) water together in a large, shallow casserole. Place steaks in poaching liquor and bring to boil over a moderate heat.

3. As soon as liquid boils, turn steaks over, cover casserole with a well-fitting lid and remove from heat. Leave salmon steaks to cool in liquor without removing lid. When cool enough, transfer casserole to the refrigerator.

4. Make sauce verte by preparing a mayonnaise with a flavouring of French mustard and lemon juice or wine vinegar.

5. Wash parsley sprigs and watercress thoroughly.

6. Bring a pint of salted water to the boil. Plunge in parsley and watercress and boil for 6 minutes. Drain thoroughly and press as dry as possible between the folds of a cloth.

7. Pound blanched greens to a paste in a mortar. Rub through a fine sieve to make a smooth purée.

8. Beat purée into mayonnaise, together with fresh herbs, and if necessary, correct seasoning with more salt and freshly ground black pepper and a little lemon juice.

9. Chill for a few hours before serving to allow flavour of herbs to develop. Drain salmon steaks and serve with the sauce.

Serves 4

Oven-poached Sole with Bercy Sauce

IMPERIAL	METRIC
4 sole, about 12 oz. each	4 sole, about 350 g. each
1 lemon	1 lemon
3 tablespoons finely chopped parsley	3 tablespoons finely chopped parsley
butter	butter
8 oz. button mushrooms, sliced	225 g. button mushrooms, sliced
½ pint dry white wine	3 dl. dry white wine
Bercy sauce:	*Bercy sauce:*
4 oz. beef marrow, diced	100 g. beef marrow, diced
4 shallots, finely chopped	4 shallots, finely chopped
½ pint dry white wine	3 dl. dry white wine
8 oz. softened butter	225 g. softened butter
2 tablespoons finely chopped parsley	2 tablespoons finely chopped parsley
2 tablespoons lemon juice	2 tablespoons lemon juice
salt and freshly ground black pepper	salt and freshly ground black pepper

1. Make sauce by poaching diced marrow in boiling water. Drain and cool.

2. In a double saucepan, simmer finely chopped shallots in white wine over direct heat until liquid is reduced to a third of its original quantity.

3. Remove from heat and whisk until slightly cooled, then gradually whisk in diced, softened butter over hot water until sauce thickens.

4. Stir in diced beef marrow, parsley and lemon juice; season to taste with salt and freshly ground black pepper. Keep hot.

5. Remove black skin only from sole and lay them, skinned side up, on a board.

6. Halve lemon; squeeze one half, slice other half thinly.

7. Preheat oven to moderate (375°F., 190°C., Gas Mark 5).

8. Make an incision in each sole down length of backbone on skinned side and slide a thin knife blade under each side. Sprinkle 'pockets' with half the finely chopped parsley, a few drops of lemon juice, and salt and freshly ground black pepper.

9. Butter an ovenproof dish, large enough to take fish in one layer. Sprinkle with sliced mushrooms and remaining parsley; place fish on top.

10. Add white wine and just enough water to cover fish. Cover with buttered paper. Bring to simmering point on top of stove. Transfer to oven.

11. Bake for 20 minutes. Transfer to a heated serving dish. Serve with a little of the sauce spooned over sole and remainder served separately. Garnish with parsley.

Serves 4

Filets de Sole au Vermouth

IMPERIAL	METRIC
2 sole, weighing about 1½ lb. each, filleted	2 sole, weighing about 675 g. each, filleted
salt and freshly ground black pepper	salt and freshly ground black pepper
6 tablespoons dry vermouth	6 tablespoons dry vermouth
butter	butter
1 teaspoon tomato paste	1 teaspoon tomato paste
20 small button mushrooms	20 small button mushrooms
lemon juice	lemon juice
6 tablespoons double cream	6 tablespoons double cream
2 egg yolks	2 egg yolks
chopped parsley and thin lemon slices, to garnish	chopped parsley and thin lemon slices, to garnish

1. Place seasoned sole fillets in a flameproof, shallow casserole or large frying pan.

2. Mix vermouth, 6 tablespoons melted butter and tomato paste and pour over fish. Bring to the boil and reduce heat to a simmer for 5 minutes or until fish is just cooked.

3. Whilst fish is cooking, sauté mushrooms in 1 tablespoon melted butter and a little lemon juice over a low heat for 10 minutes.

4. Drain sole fillets and place on a heated serving dish. Cover and keep hot.

5. Add drained mushrooms to sauce remaining in pan.

6. Beat cream and egg yolks together; add to contents of pan. Reheat gently, stirring constantly, until sauce has thickened slightly. Do not allow sauce to reach boiling point or it may curdle. Season to taste with salt and freshly ground black pepper.

7. Pour sauce over sole fillets; sprinkle with finely chopped parsley and serve hot, garnished with parsley and lemon slices.

Serves 4

Chef's tip:
To fillet a fish use a sharp, flexible knife. Cut straight down back of fish following bone line; insert knife under flesh; remove with long, clean strokes. Take first fillet from left side of fish, working from head to tail; then turn fish around and work from tail to head; repeat on other side of fish.

Coquilles au Sauce Vin Blanc

IMPERIAL	METRIC
1 lb. frozen scallops	450 g. frozen scallops
6–8 fl. oz. dry white wine	1¾–2¼ dl. dry white wine
1 small onion, quartered	1 small onion, quartered
bouquet garni	bouquet garni
salt and freshly ground black pepper	salt and freshly ground black pepper
2 tablespoons butter	2 tablespoons butter
1 small onion, finely chopped	1 small onion, finely chopped
12 button mushrooms, thinly sliced	12 button mushrooms, thinly sliced
2 tablespoons finely chopped parsley	2 tablespoons finely chopped parsley
¼ pint double cream	1½ dl. double cream
2 egg yolks	2 egg yolks

1. Place scallops in a saucepan with white wine, onion, bouquet garni, a little salt and freshly ground black pepper, and just enough water to cover.

2. Bring slowly to the boil, then simmer gently for 5 minutes or until scallops are just tender.

3. Drain scallops, reserving poaching liquor. Slice and place in a serving dish. Cover and keep warm.

4. Strain poaching liquor back into saucepan and boil briskly until reduced to ¼ pint (1½ dl.). Remove from heat.

5. In a frying pan, heat butter until frothy. Sauté onion and mushrooms over a moderate heat until softened but not coloured, about 10 minutes.

6. Stir in parsley and spread mixture over scallops; cover and keep warm.

7. Beat cream and egg yolks together in a bowl. Pour on hot reduced poaching liquor in a thin stream, stirring briskly as you do so. Return sauce to frying pan.

8. Heat sauce very gently, stirring constantly. Do not allow it to boil or it may curdle. Continue to heat gently until sauce has thickened and reduced slightly to a coating consistency. Taste and season with salt and freshly ground black pepper.

9. Pour sauce over scallops and serve immediately.

Serves 4

Chef's tip:
Unless you are very sure of what you are doing when heating an egg-based sauce over direct heat, I recommend that you use an asbestos mat to put between the pan and the source of heat. Be extremely careful not to overcook the scallops.

Beef Steak and Kidney Pie

IMPERIAL	METRIC
2 lb. buttock steak	900 g. buttock steak
12 oz. ox kidney	350 g. ox kidney
seasoned flour	seasoned flour
3 tablespoons butter	3 tablespoons butter
3 tablespoons olive oil	3 tablespoons olive oil
1 large onion, finely chopped	1 large onion, finely chopped
½ pint beef stock	3 dl. beef stock
bouquet garni	bouquet garni
2 teaspoons Worcestershire sauce	2 teaspoons Worcestershire sauce
4 oz. button mushrooms, sliced	100 g. button mushrooms, sliced
1 tablespoon chopped parsley	1 tablespoon chopped parsley
3–4 tablespoons port	3–4 tablespoons port
8 oz. rough puff pastry	225 g. rough puff pastry
beaten egg, to glaze	beaten egg, to glaze

1. Trim excess fat from meat and cut into 1-inch (2½-cm.) cubes. Remove fat and cores from kidney and cut into ¼-inch (½-cm.) slices. Toss meat cubes and kidney slices in seasoned flour.

2. Heat butter and oil in a heavy saucepan or casserole. Sauté meat, a little at a time, over a high heat until thoroughly browned. Drain and remove meat. Reserve.

3. Fry onion in fat remaining in pan for about 10 minutes or until softened.

4. Return meat to pan, along with stock, bouquet garni and Worcestershire sauce.

5. Bring to the boil; cover and simmer for 1 hour. Then uncover and cook for another 15 minutes.

6. Add sliced mushrooms and parsley and simmer gently, uncovered, for a further 15 minutes. Remove from heat and stir in port. Cover and leave until cold.

7. Make pastry and refrigerate until ready to use.

8. Preheat oven to fairly hot (425°F., 220°C., Gas Mark 7).

9. Place meat mixture in a 1¾-pint (1-litre) pie dish.

10. Roll out pastry to ⅛ inch (3 mm.) thick. Dampen edge of pie dish with water and lay a rim of pastry around it. Brush the rim with water and cover pie with a pastry lid. Pinch edges of pastry together to seal them well. Make an air vent in the centre and decorate with 'leaves' made from pastry trimmings.

11. Glaze with beaten egg. Place pie on baking sheet and bake for 30 to 35 minutes or until pie is golden brown.

Serves 4–6

Braised Steak in Red Wine

IMPERIAL	METRIC
2 lb. tender steak, rump or sirloin	900 g. tender steak, rump or sirloin
1 clove garlic	1 clove garlic
seasoned flour	seasoned flour
3–4 tablespoons lard	3–4 tablespoons lard
salt and freshly ground black pepper	salt and freshly ground black pepper
2 medium-sized onions, finely chopped	2 medium-sized onions, finely chopped
1 8-oz. can peeled tomatoes	1 226-g. can peeled tomatoes
generous pinch oregano	generous pinch oregano
generous pinch rosemary	generous pinch rosemary
8 tablespoons red wine	8 tablespoons red wine
12 small white onions	12 small white onions

1. Preheat oven to cool (225°F., 110°C., Gas Mark ¼).

2. Cut steak into serving pieces. Rub them all over with a cut clove of garlic; dust with seasoned flour, and pound with a meat mallet to flatten them.

3. In a frying pan, brown steaks on both sides in lard over a high heat. Season to taste with salt and freshly ground black pepper, and transfer to a flameproof casserole.

4. To fat remaining in the pan, add finely chopped onions and sauté until soft and golden brown. Season lightly with salt; add tomatoes, herbs and red wine, and stir over a low heat until well blended. Then simmer, uncovered, until sauce has reduced by one third.

5. Pour sauce over meat; cover casserole and bake in the oven for about 1¾ to 2 hours, or until meat is tender.

6. Half an hour before the end of cooking time, add the small white onions. Serve hot.

Serves 4–6

Chef's tip:
Although this is best made with good steak, you can substitute a more economical cut of beef if you like and adjust the cooking time accordingly; and you can exchange the red wine in the recipe for lager if you prefer.

Boeuf Sauté à la Bourguignonne

IMPERIAL	METRIC
2½ lb. topside of beef	1¼ kg. topside of beef
8 oz. fat streaky bacon, sliced and diced	225 g. fat streaky bacon, sliced and diced
18 button onions	18 button onions
18 baby carrots	18 baby carrots
2 tablespoons flour	2 tablespoons flour
bouquet garni	bouquet garni
¼ pint beef stock	1½ dl. beef stock
2 garlic cloves, crushed	2 garlic cloves, crushed
18 button mushrooms	18 button mushrooms
2 teaspoons redcurrant jelly	2 teaspoons redcurrant jelly
1 teaspoon tomato paste	1 teaspoon tomato paste
salt and freshly ground black pepper	salt and freshly ground black pepper
finely chopped parsley, to garnish	finely chopped parsley, to garnish
Marinade:	*Marinade:*
1 pint red wine	6 dl. red wine
2 carrots, cut into chunks	2 carrots, cut into chunks
1 medium-sized onion, quartered	1 medium-sized onion, quartered
¼ teaspoon dried thyme	¼ teaspoon dried thyme
2 bay leaves	2 bay leaves

1. Cut beef into 1-inch (2½-cm.) cubes and place in a bowl with marinade ingredients. Cover and leave overnight.

2. In a large, heavy saucepan or casserole, sauté diced bacon until it begins to crisp; remove with a slotted spoon and reserve.

3. Fry button onions and carrots in remaining fat until lightly coloured, drain and reserve together with bacon.

4. Drain beef well. Reserve marinade, discarding carrots and onions.

5. Sauté drained beef, a small batch at a time, in remaining fat, until brown.

6. Sprinkle with flour and continue cooking until flour browns, then add reserved marinade (including bay leaves), bouquet garni, stock, ½ pint (3 dl.) water and garlic, and finally return carrots, onions and bacon to pan. Stir, bring to the boil and reduce to a gentle simmer.

7. Simmer gently for 1¾ hours, uncovered. Add mushrooms. Continue cooking for a further 30 minutes or until meat is tender and sauce is reduced by half. Discard bouquet garni and bay leaves. Stir in redcurrant jelly and tomato paste. Season to taste with salt and freshly ground black pepper, if necessary. Sprinkle with finely chopped parsley and serve very hot.

Serves 5–6

Oxtail Ragoût

IMPERIAL	METRIC
1 2½-lb. oxtail, cut into sections	1 1¼-kg. oxtail, cut into sections
seasoned flour	seasoned flour
4 oz. fat bacon slices, diced	100 g. fat bacon slices, diced
12–16 button onions	12–16 button onions
8 baby carrots	8 baby carrots
butter	butter
1 tablespoon olive oil	1 tablespoon olive oil
½ pint dry red wine	3 dl. dry red wine
½ pint beef stock	3 dl. beef stock
½ pint tomato juice	3 dl. tomato juice
1 clove garlic, crushed	1 clove garlic, crushed
bouquet garni	bouquet garni
12 button mushrooms	12 button mushrooms
1 teaspoon flour	1 teaspoon flour
salt and freshly ground black pepper	salt and freshly ground black pepper
chopped parsley, to garnish	chopped parsley, to garnish

1. Toss oxtail in seasoned flour.

2. Sauté bacon in a large, heavy casserole until fat runs and bacon begins to crisp. Remove with a slotted spoon and reserve.

3. Sauté onions and carrots in remaining fat until lightly coloured; drain and reserve with bacon.

4. Add 1 tablespoon butter and oil to casserole and heat until butter froths. Sauté pieces of oxtail over a fairly high heat until browned. Pour off any remaining fat.

5. Return bacon and sautéed vegetables to casserole. Add wine, stock, tomato juice, garlic and bouquet garni.

6. Bring to the boil, cover and simmer gently for 2 hours. Uncover and simmer for a further 1½ to 2 hours or until meat falls from the bone. Thirty minutes before end of cooking time, add button mushrooms.

7. Strain sauce from casserole and skim fat from surface.

8. Mash 1 teaspoon butter with the flour; add in small pieces to strained, skimmed sauce. Bring slowly to the boil, stirring. Simmer for 2 minutes and season to taste with salt and freshly ground black pepper, if necessary.

9. Pour sauce over oxtail and vegetables. Reheat, sprinkle with chopped parsley and serve.

Serves 4

Calves' Liver in Red Wine

IMPERIAL	METRIC
12 large thin slices calves' liver	12 large thin slices calves' liver
2–4 tablespoons seasoned flour	2–4 tablespoons seasoned flour
2–3 large Spanish onions, thinly sliced	2–3 large Spanish onions, thinly sliced
4 tablespoons butter	4 tablespoons butter
pinch tarragon	pinch tarragon
$\frac{1}{2}$ pint light red or rosé wine	3 dl. light red or rosé wine
salt and freshly ground black pepper	salt and freshly ground black pepper
1 tablespoon French mustard	1 tablespoon French mustard

1. Dust slices of liver with seasoned flour.

2. Sauté thinly sliced onions in a frying pan in half the butter until golden; cover pan and simmer onions until very soft and melting, about 10 to 15 minutes, taking care not to let them brown. Remove onions from pan with a slotted spoon and keep hot.

3. Melt remaining butter in the same frying pan, adding a pinch of tarragon. When butter is foaming, add liver slices and sear quickly; this will not take more than 2 or 3 minutes on each side. Remove liver slices to a heated serving dish and keep hot while you finish the sauce.

4. Pour wine into the frying pan and bring to the boil over a high heat, scraping bottom and sides of pan clean with a wooden spoon. Correct seasoning, adding salt and freshly ground black pepper if necessary. Lower heat and add mustard, stirring until sauce is smooth. Simmer for 1 minute; then add onions, mix well and check seasoning once more.

5. Pour onion mixture over liver. Sprinkle entire dish with chopped parsley and serve immediately.

Serves 6

Chef's tip:
Insist on even, thin slices of liver no more than $\frac{1}{4}$ inch ($\frac{1}{2}$ cm.) thick. Cook very quickly as excessive heat and cooking both toughen liver; like kidneys the liver should remain slightly pink inside. Do not crowd the frying pan—use two if necessary.

Kidneys in Red Wine Sauce

IMPERIAL	METRIC
1 lb. lambs' kidneys	450 g. lambs' kidneys
2 tablespoons butter	2 tablespoons butter
1 tablespoon olive oil	1 tablespoon olive oil
1 clove garlic, crushed	1 clove garlic, crushed
1 small onion, finely chopped	1 small onion, finely chopped
$2\frac{1}{2}$ tablespoons flour	$2\frac{1}{2}$ tablespoons flour
4 oz. button mushrooms, thinly sliced	100 g. button mushrooms, thinly sliced
generous pinch each thyme and basil	generous pinch each thyme and basil
1 bay leaf	1 bay leaf
salt and freshly ground black pepper	salt and freshly ground black pepper
$\frac{1}{4}$ pint dry red wine	$1\frac{1}{2}$ dl. dry red wine
$\frac{1}{4}$ pint beef stock	$1\frac{1}{2}$ dl. beef stock
triangles of bread, to make croûtons	triangles of bread, to make croûtons
1 teaspoon tomato paste	1 teaspoon tomato paste
3 large tomatoes, skinned, seeded and diced	3 large tomatoes, skinned, seeded and diced
$\frac{1}{2}$ teaspoon soy sauce	$\frac{1}{2}$ teaspoon soy sauce
$\frac{1}{2}$ teaspoon Worcestershire sauce	$\frac{1}{2}$ teaspoon Worcestershire sauce
1 teaspoon finely chopped parsley	1 teaspoon finely chopped parsley

1. Skin kidneys. Snip out cores, using a pair of scissors. Cut each kidney across into fairly thick slices.

2. In a large frying pan, heat butter and oil until butter froths. Sauté garlic and onion for about 4 minutes or until golden.

3. Add kidneys, stirring for 4 to 5 minutes.

4. Remove pan from heat. Drain kidney slices and remove from pan and reserve in a warm place. Sprinkle flour into pan and stir. Add mushrooms and herbs and season with salt and freshly ground black pepper, before gradually stirring in wine and stock.

5. Return pan to heat and bring to the boil, stirring. Simmer gently, uncovered, for 10 minutes.

6. Meanwhile, either shallow- or deep-fry croûtons until golden. Drain on kitchen paper and keep warm.

7. Add tomato paste, diced tomato, soy sauce and Worcestershire sauce and the kidneys. Stir and heat for a further 2 to 3 minutes.

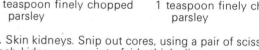

8. Pour kidney mixture into a warmed serving dish. Arrange croûtons around edge of dish. Sprinkle all over with finely chopped parsley and serve very hot.

Serves 4

Sweetbreads in Cream Wine Sauce

IMPERIAL	METRIC
1 lb. lambs' sweetbreads	450 g. lambs' sweetbreads
lemon juice	lemon juice
$\frac{1}{4}$ pint dry white wine	$1\frac{1}{2}$ dl. dry white wine
$\frac{1}{4}$ pint chicken stock	$1\frac{1}{2}$ dl. chicken stock
4 oz. button mushrooms, thinly sliced	100 g. button mushrooms, thinly sliced
1 tablespoon butter	1 tablespoon butter
2 egg yolks	2 egg yolks
4 tablespoons double cream	4 tablespoons double cream
salt and freshly ground black pepper	salt and freshly ground black pepper
6 stuffed olives, chopped	6 stuffed olives, chopped

1. Preheat oven to moderate (375°F., 190°C., Gas Mark 5).

2. Remove membranes from sweetbreads. Soak in a bowl of cold water for 1 to 2 hours, changing water frequently.

3. Drain sweetbreads and place in a saucepan; cover with cold water. Add 1 teaspoon lemon juice and bring to the boil. Simmer for 1 to 2 minutes. Remove sweetbreads from heat and plunge into cold water.

4. Drain sweetbreads and break into small pieces; arrange in a serving dish.

5. Mix wine and stock and pour over sweetbreads.

6. Sauté sliced mushrooms in butter and $\frac{1}{2}$ teaspoon lemon juice over a moderate heat for 5 minutes.

7. Drain mushrooms and arrange on top of sweetbreads. Cover dish with a buttered paper.

8. Bake in preheated oven for 15 minutes.

9. Drain off juices from sweetbreads into top of a double saucepan; replace buttered paper and keep warm.

10. Boil juices briskly to reduce liquid by half.

11. Mix egg yolks and cream in a basin; pour reduced liquid onto cream mixture in a thin stream, stirring constantly.

12. Return saucepan to heat over base pan of simmering water. Stir frequently until sauce thickens (about 10 minutes). Season to taste with salt and freshly ground black pepper and pour over sweetbreads.

13. Sprinkle with chopped, stuffed olives and leave to stand for 5 minutes before serving.

Serves 3–4

Chef's tip:
If sweetbreads are not to be cooked within 24 hours, they should be soaked and blanched (as above) which will help preserve them.

Chicken in Red Wine

IMPERIAL	METRIC
$\frac{1}{2}$ pint robust red wine	3 dl. robust red wine
1 tablespoon olive oil	1 tablespoon olive oil
2 tablespoons butter	2 tablespoons butter
4 slices streaky bacon, diced	4 slices streaky bacon, diced
1 3- to 3$\frac{1}{2}$-lb. roasting chicken, cut into 8	1 1$\frac{1}{3}$- to 1$\frac{1}{2}$-kg. roasting chicken, cut into 8
4 tablespoons brandy	4 tablespoons brandy
$\frac{1}{4}$ pint well-flavoured chicken stock	1$\frac{1}{2}$ dl. well-flavoured chicken stock
12 small button onions, peeled	12 small button onions, peeled
1 bay leaf	1 bay leaf
2 cloves	2 cloves
$\frac{1}{4}$ teaspoon thyme	$\frac{1}{4}$ teaspoon thyme
salt and freshly ground black pepper	salt and freshly ground black pepper
12 button mushrooms	12 button mushrooms
4 tablespoons finely chopped parsley	4 tablespoons finely chopped parsley
1 tablespoon flour	1 tablespoon flour

1. Pour wine into a small pan; boil to reduce to $\frac{1}{4}$ pint (1$\frac{1}{2}$ dl.).

2. In a large casserole, heat oil with 1 tablespoon butter; add diced bacon and sauté gently for 5 minutes.

3. Add chicken pieces; fry gently for a further 15 minutes, turning frequently to brown evenly.

4. When chicken is well coloured, heat brandy in a large metal ladle or a small pan. Ignite and pour over chicken.

5. Allow flames to subside; then pour in reduced red wine and chicken stock; add button onions, herbs, and salt and freshly ground black pepper to taste. Bring to the boil over a moderate heat; lower heat until liquid just bubbles, cover casserole tightly and simmer very gently for 20 minutes.

6. Add button mushrooms and chopped parsley to casserole; replace lid and simmer for a further 15 minutes, or until chicken and vegetables are tender.

7. In a small cup, mash flour and remaining butter.

8. Drain chicken and vegetables and transfer to a heated dish; keep hot while you finish sauce.

9. Skim pan juices of fat if necessary and thicken with butter and flour paste, adding it in tiny pieces and stirring until dissolved. Bring sauce to the boil, stirring, and simmer for a minute or two longer. Discard bay leaf and season to taste with more salt and freshly ground pepper if necessary.

10. Return chicken and vegetables to casserole. Simmer for 2 or 3 minutes longer before serving.

Serves 4

Poulet Chasseur

IMPERIAL	METRIC
1 4-lb. chicken, jointed	1 1¾-kg. chicken, jointed
seasoned flour	seasoned flour
2 tablespoons butter	2 tablespoons butter
2 tablespoons olive oil	2 tablespoons olive oil
1 medium-sized onion, chopped	1 medium-sized onion, chopped
1 clove garlic, crushed	1 clove garlic, crushed
½ pint dry white wine	3 dl. dry white wine
1–2 tablespoons tomato paste	1–2 tablespoons tomato paste
¼ pint chicken stock	1½ dl. chicken stock
4 oz. button mushrooms, sliced	100 g. button mushrooms, sliced
½ bay leaf	½ bay leaf
generous pinch dried thyme	generous pinch dried thyme
pinch dried tarragon	pinch dried tarragon
salt and freshly ground black pepper	salt and freshly ground black pepper
8 oz. tomatoes, peeled, seeded and chopped	225 g. tomatoes, peeled, seeded and chopped
1 tablespoon brandy	1 tablespoon brandy

1. Toss chicken joints in seasoned flour.

2. Heat butter and oil together in a medium-sized heavy casserole until butter froths.

3. Fry chicken joints, turning frequently until evenly browned all over. Drain and remove from casserole; place on a plate.

4. Sauté chopped onion and garlic over a moderate heat in remaining fat for 5 minutes.

5. Add wine and boil briskly until reduced by half. Stir in tomato paste, stock, sliced mushrooms, herbs and a little seasoning. Return chicken joints to casserole.

6. Cover and simmer very gently for 1 hour or until chicken is tender.

7. Drain and remove chicken joints. Place in a warmed serving dish; cover and keep hot.

8. Skim fat from juices remaining in casserole. Add chopped tomatoes and brandy; bring slowly to the boil. Taste, and season if necessary. Pour sauce over chicken joints.

Serves 4

Chef's tip:
When buying frozen chicken watch for brownish areas called 'freezer burn', which indicate dehydration or long and improper storage. The ideal accompaniment to the above dish is home-made green noodles.

Chicken with Cucumber

IMPERIAL	METRIC
1 3½- to 4-lb. roasting chicken, jointed	1 1½- to 1¾-kg. roasting chicken, jointed
seasoned flour	seasoned flour
1 tablespoon olive oil	1 tablespoon olive oil
2 tablespoons butter	2 tablespoons butter
3 tablespoons brandy	3 tablespoons brandy
¼ pint double cream	1½ dl. double cream
2 large cucumbers, halved, deseeded and cut into 1-inch strips	2 large cucumbers, halved, deseeded and cut into 2½-cm. strips
salt and freshly ground black pepper	salt and freshly ground black pepper
3–4 tablespoons dry white wine	3–4 tablespoons dry white wine
¼ teaspoon lemon juice	¼ teaspoon lemon juice
1 tablespoon flour	1 tablespoon flour
chopped parsley, to garnish	chopped parsley, to garnish

1. Toss chicken joints in seasoned flour.

2. In a heavy casserole, heat olive oil and 1 tablespoon butter until butter froths.

3. Fry chicken joints in hot fat, turning frequently until golden brown all over.

4. Heat brandy in a small saucepan; ignite and pour over chicken joints.

5. When flames have subsided, add cream, cucumber, and a little salt and freshly ground black pepper to taste.

6. Cover casserole and simmer very gently for 30 minutes, then uncover and cook for a further 30 minutes or until chicken is tender.

7. Drain and remove chicken joints and cucumber; place in a warmed serving dish. Cover and keep hot.

8. Add wine and lemon juice to sauce remaining in casserole.

9. Mix 1 tablespoon each flour and butter to make a smooth paste; add to sauce in small pieces. Bring sauce to the boil, stirring. Boil gently for 2 minutes.

10. Season to taste with salt and freshly ground black pepper, if necessary. Pour sauce over chicken and cucumber. Serve immediately, garnished with chopped parsley.

Serves 4

Chef's tip:
Do not be concerned about the seeming lack of liquid in the casserole, before covering it to simmer for 30 minutes—you will be surprised just how much moisture the cucumbers will give out. It is not necessary to peel the cucumbers.

Caneton à la Bigarade

IMPERIAL	METRIC
4 tablespoons butter	4 tablespoons butter
1 oven-ready duck, 3–4 lb.	1 oven-ready duck, 1⅓–1¾ kg.
salt and freshly ground black pepper	salt and freshly ground black pepper
2 lemons	2 lemons
4 medium-sized, thin-skinned oranges	4 medium-sized, thin-skinned oranges
1 tablespoon sugar	1 tablespoon sugar
1 tablespoon wine vinegar	1 tablespoon wine vinegar
¼ pint dry white vermouth	1½ dl. dry white vermouth
1½ teaspoons cornflour	1½ teaspoons cornflour
2 tablespoons Curaçao	2 tablespoons Curaçao
2 tablespoons redcurrant jelly	2 tablespoons redcurrant jelly
1 tablespoon orange marmalade	1 tablespoon orange marmalade
2 fresh oranges, thinly sliced, to garnish	2 fresh oranges, thinly sliced, to garnish

1. Preheat oven to moderate (350°F., 180°C., Gas Mark 4).

2. Melt butter in roasting tin on top of stove; sauté duck until crisp and golden all over. Season with salt and freshly ground black pepper.

3. Transfer roasting tin to oven; roast duck for 50 to 60 minutes or until tender, basting occasionally.

4. While duck is roasting, squeeze lemons and 2 oranges. Remove zest from remaining oranges and cut it into thin strips; then peel and segment oranges.

5. Melt sugar in wine vinegar over a low heat; simmer, stirring, until it turns a deep, golden caramel. Stir in lemon and orange juice and vermouth; mix well, season to taste. Add orange segments and simmer gently for 5 minutes. Drain segments and remove. Keep segments and syrup warm separately.

6. When duck is cooked, transfer to a heated serving dish. Surround with poached orange segments and return to the oven, leaving door ajar, to keep hot while you finish sauce.

7. Mix cornflour to a smooth paste with Curaçao. Drain almost all the fat from the roasting tin. Stir in orange poaching syrup and cornflour paste and cook over a moderate heat until sauce is smooth and thickened. Stir in redcurrant jelly, marmalade and strips of orange zest; stir until melted and season to taste with salt and black pepper.

8. Remove duck from the oven and decorate dish with thin slices of fresh orange. Spoon some of the sauce over the duck to glaze it and serve remainder separately in a heated sauceboat.

Serves 3–4

Cheese Fondue

IMPERIAL	METRIC
1 lb. Gruyère cheese, coarsely grated (or 8 oz. Gruyère and 8 oz. Emmenthal cheese)	450 g. Gruyère cheese, coarsely grated (or 225 g. Gruyère and 225 g. Emmenthal cheese)
1 teaspoon cornflour	1 teaspoon cornflour
½ clove garlic	½ clove garlic
½ pint dry white wine	3 dl. dry white wine
2–4 tablespoons Kirsch	2–4 tablespoons Kirsch
freshly grated nutmeg	freshly grated nutmeg
salt and freshly ground black pepper	salt and freshly ground black pepper
paprika	paprika
crusty French bread, to serve	crusty French bread, to serve

1. Toss grated cheese with cornflour.

2. Rub inside of an earthenware casserole or fondue cooker with cut surface of garlic. Pour in dry white wine and cook over a low heat until wine starts to bubble.

3. Add cheese gradually and blend, stirring continuously, until smooth.

4. Add Kirsch, freshly grated nutmeg, and salt and freshly ground black pepper and a pinch of paprika to taste. Serve with chunks of crusty French bread.

Serves 4–6

Chef's tip:
Measure all ingredients and have them ready to add with one hand—your other hand will be busy stirring the mixture with a wooden spoon. Although Kirsch is the traditional ingredient, you can use slivovitz or cognac; whatever the wine is, it *must* be dry.

English Strawberry Trifle

IMPERIAL	METRIC
8 oz. fresh strawberries	225 g. fresh strawberries
2–4 tablespoons dry sherry	2–4 tablespoons dry sherry
2 tablespoons icing sugar	2 tablespoons icing sugar
3 tablespoons cornflour	3 tablespoons cornflour
4 tablespoons castor sugar	4 tablespoons castor sugar
$\frac{1}{2}$ pint milk	3 dl. milk
$\frac{1}{2}$ pint single cream	3 dl. single cream
3 eggs	3 eggs
1 teaspoon vanilla essence	1 teaspoon vanilla essence
1 tablespoon butter	1 tablespoon butter
1 swiss roll, cut into 8 slices	1 swiss roll, cut into 8 slices
$\frac{1}{2}$ pint double cream	3 dl. double cream
1 oz. blanched almonds, toasted and slivered	25 g. blanched almonds, toasted and slivered

1. Reserve nine strawberries for decoration. Hull and slice remainder and place in a bowl. Sprinkle with dry sherry and icing sugar. Leave to macerate for at least 1 hour.

2. Mix cornflour and sugar in a bowl; blend in a little of measured milk to give a smooth paste.

3. Heat remaining milk and single cream in the top of a double saucepan, over direct heat.

4. When milk reaches boiling point, pour onto cornflour paste in bowl, stirring vigorously.

5. Return custard to top of double saucepan and bring to the boil over direct heat, stirring constantly until sauce boils and thickens. Boil gently for a further 2 minutes. Remove from heat.

6. Separate eggs and place whites of two of the eggs in a separate bowl. Stir egg yolks quickly into custard.

7. Return custard to heat over base saucepan of simmering water. Cook for 10 minutes, stirring frequently.

8. Strain sauce into a bowl. Stir in vanilla essence and butter. Leave until just warm, stirring frequently to prevent a skin forming on the top.

9. Line base of a 4-pint (2$\frac{1}{4}$-litre) glass bowl with slices of swiss roll. Pile strawberries including their juices on top.

10. Beat the two egg whites until stiff but not dry. Fold gently into custard and pour over strawberries, levelling off top with a knife. Chill until firm.

11. Pipe swirls of whipped double cream around edge of dish. Top swirls with reserved strawberries and slivered almonds. Chill until ready to serve.

Serves 6–8

Peaches and Raspberries in White Wine

IMPERIAL	METRIC
1 lb. sugar	450 g. sugar
2 cloves	2 cloves
3 sticks cinnamon	3 sticks cinnamon
2–3 strips thinly pared orange and lemon rind	2–3 strips thinly pared orange and lemon rind
4–6 large peaches, or 8–12 small ones	4–6 large peaches, or 8–12 small ones
$\frac{1}{2}$ pint white wine	3 dl. white wine
1–2 punnets fresh raspberries	100–225 g. fresh raspberries
whipped cream, to serve	whipped cream, to serve

1. In a large, wide saucepan, dissolve sugar in $\frac{1}{2}$ pint (3 dl.) water over a very low heat; add cloves, cinnamon sticks and orange and lemon rind (pared off with a potato peeler). Then carefully drop peaches into syrup and simmer, uncovered, for 10 minutes.

2. Add wine and continue to simmer for a further 10 minutes, or until peaches are cooked. Remove pan from heat.

3. Take peaches from syrup with a slotted spoon, one by one. Hold peach gently in a towel so you do not burn your hand, and carefully peel skin off with your fingers. You will find the skin comes off quite easily. Repeat with other peaches, arranging them with raspberries in a serving dish.

4. Simmer cooking juices until reduced to the consistency of a light syrup. Cool syrup and spoon over fruit.

5. Chill fruit in refrigerator until ready to serve. Serve very cold with whipped cream.

Serves 4–6

Chef's tip:
Take care not to allow peaches to become overcooked and mushy when poaching in the syrup. This dish can also be done with red wine if you prefer but you will probably need to add additional red food colouring to it before serving.

Arance alla Marsala

IMPERIAL	METRIC
8 oz. sugar	225 g. sugar
¼ pint Marsala	1½ dl. Marsala
juice of 1 lemon	juice of 1 lemon
8 juicy, thin-skinned oranges	8 juicy, thin-skinned oranges

1. In a heavy pan, combine sugar with Marsala, lemon juice and ¼ pint (1½ dl.) water. Bring to the boil over a low heat, stirring occasionally.

2. Meanwhile, pare zest (the coloured part of the peel) from oranges thinly, using a potato peeler, and cut into thin strips.

3. Remove remaining peel from oranges, making sure that you take off every scrap of the bitter white pith.

4. Stir strips of zest into syrup and simmer until syrup is reduced by about one third, stirring occasionally. Remove pan from heat and allow syrup to cool.

5. Slice each orange horizontally with a sharp knife over a shallow plate to catch juices. Remove pips, and put each orange together again, sticking a long cocktail stick through it vertically to hold the slices together.

6. Arrange oranges in a deep glass bowl. Stir the orange juice that escaped into the syrup and spoon over oranges, decorating each one with a little bundle of caramelised zest. Chill until ready to serve.

Serves 8

Chef's tip:
A very quick and easy dish, similar to the one above, is to remove all peel and white pith from oranges; then slice oranges into rounds and arrange in a flat heatproof dish. Caramelise 8 oz. (225 g.) sugar; immediately pour over sliced oranges. Sprinkle w th Grand Marnier; chill until caramel is liquid and serve.

Fruit Salad with Champagne

IMPERIAL	METRIC
3 navel oranges	3 navel oranges
1 medium-sized ripe pineapple	1 medium-sized ripe pineapple
2–3 tablespoons lemon juice	2–3 tablespoons lemon juice
4 ripe pears, peeled, cored and sliced	4 ripe pears, peeled, cored and sliced
4 crisp dessert apples, peeled, cored and sliced	4 crisp dessert apples, peeled, cored and sliced
4 bananas, peeled and sliced	4 bananas, peeled and sliced
4 oz. black grapes, halved and seeded	100 g. black grapes, halved and seeded
4 oz. green grapes, halved and seeded	100 g. green grapes, halved and seeded
4 fresh peaches, peeled, stoned and sliced	4 fresh peaches, peeled, stoned and sliced
1 small, ripe honeydew melon, halved, seeded, flesh cut into ½-inch cubes	1 small, ripe honeydew melon, halved, seeded, flesh cut into 1-cm. cubes
icing sugar	icing sugar
2–3 tablespoons brandy	2–3 tablespoons brandy
½ pint champagne	3 dl. champagne

1. Segment oranges and place in bowl together with reserved juices.

2. Peel pineapple and slice in half down length of fruit; slice each piece into half again to give four long quarters. Remove cores from each section; slice fruit into bite-size chunks.

3. Add lemon juice to orange segments and reserved juices in bowl.

4. Toss sliced pears, apples and bananas in the juice as you prepare them; then add pineapple, grapes, peaches and melon.

5. Dust with icing sugar to taste and sprinkle with brandy. Cover and chill, gently tossing fruit occasionally so each piece has a chance to macerate in the juices.

6. Just before serving, transfer all fruit and juices to a serving bowl; pour over champagne and serve immediately.

Serves 8–10

Chef's tip:
Just like most casseroles and stews this fruit salad benefits if the flavours are given plenty of time to develop and blend with one another. Do not cut the fruits into too small pieces, the individual fruits should be large enough to be identified in the spoon.

Index